THE STRAIN

THE FALL

VOLUME 3

STORY BY **GUILLERMO DEL TORO** AND **CHUCK HOGAN**

SCRIPT BY **DAVID LAPHAM**

ART BY **MIKE HUDDLESTON**

COLORS BY **DAN JACKSON**

THE SILVER ANGEL

SCRIPT AND ART BY **DAVID LAPHAM**

COLORS BY **LEE LOUGHRIDGE**

LETTERS BY **CLEM ROBINS**

COVER ART BY **E. M. GIST**

DARK HORSE BOOKS

PRESIDENT & PUBLISHER MIKE RICHARDSON   EDITOR SIERRA HAHN   ASSISTANT EDITOR JIM GIBBONS   DESIGNER TINA ALESSI

SPECIAL THANKS TO GARY UNGAR AND IAN GIBSON

EXECUTIVE VICE PRESIDENT NEIL HANKERSON CHIEF FINANCIAL OFFICER TOM WEDDLE VICE PRESIDENT OF PUBLISHING RANDY STRADLEY VICE PRESIDENT OF BOOK TRADE SALES MICHAEL MARTENS VICE PRESIDENT OF BUSINESS AFFAIRS ANITA NELSON EDITOR IN CHIEF SCOTT ALLIE VICE PRESIDENT OF MARKETING MATT PARKINSON VICE PRESIDENT OF PRODUCT DEVELOPMENT DAVID SCROGGY VICE PRESIDENT OF INFORMATION TECHNOLOGY DALE LaFOUNTAIN SENIOR DIRECTOR OF PRINT, DESIGN, AND PRODUCTION DARLENE VOGEL GENERAL COUNSEL KEN LIZZI EDITORIAL DIRECTOR DAVEY ESTRADA SENIOR BOOKS EDITOR CHRIS WARNER EXECUTIVE EDITOR DIANA SCHUTZ DIRECTOR OF PRINT AND DEVELOPMENT CARY GRAZZINI ART DIRECTOR LIA RIBACCHI DIRECTOR OF SCHEDULING CARA NIECE DIRECTOR OF INTERNATIONAL LICENSING TIM WIESCH DIRECTOR OF DIGITAL PUBLISHING MARK BERNARDI

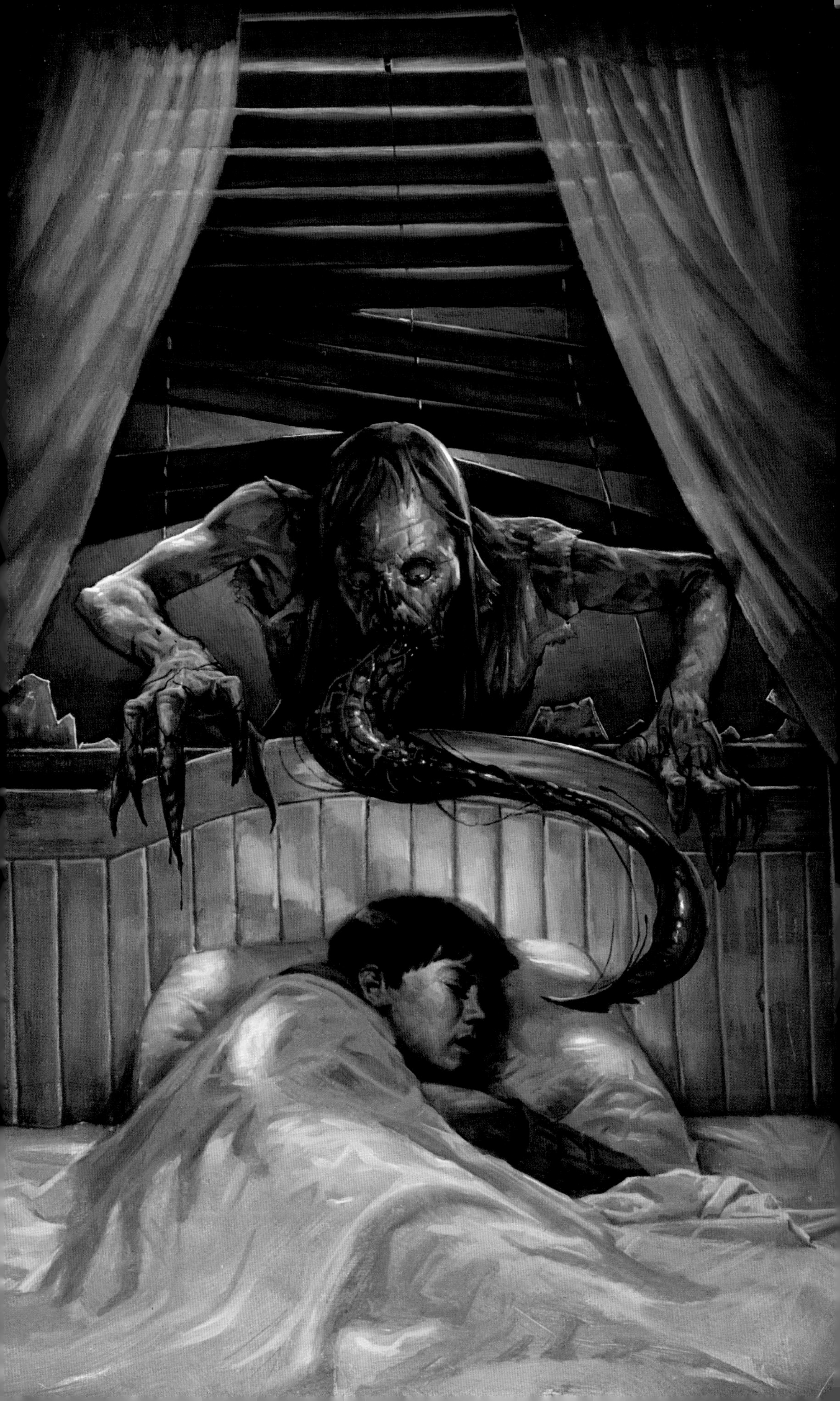

They have always been here.

VAMPIRES.

In secret and in darkness.

WAITING.

Now their time has come.

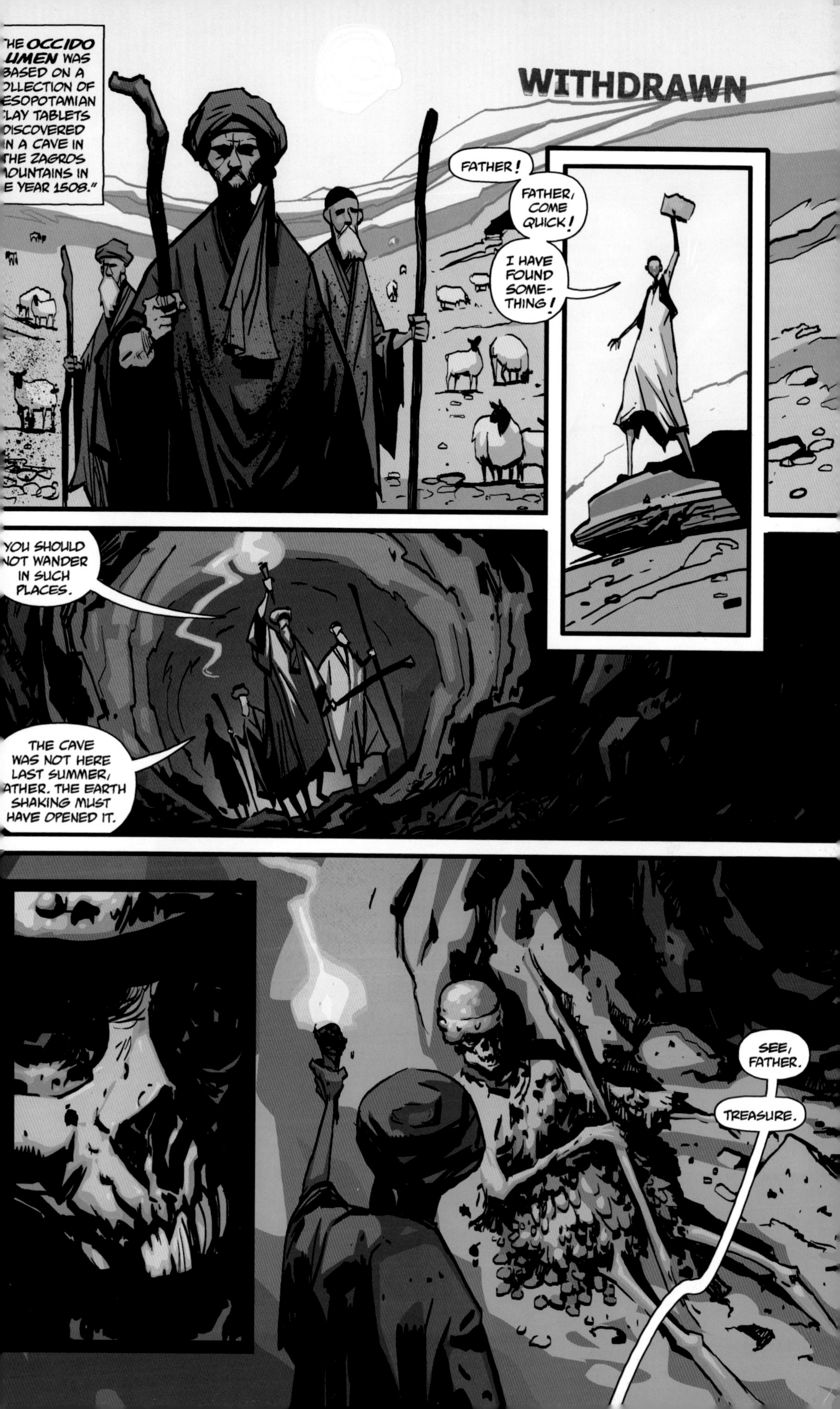

HE OCCIDO UMEN WAS BASED ON A OLLECTION OF ESOPOTAMIAN LAY TABLETS DISCOVERED IN A CAVE IN THE ZAGROS OUNTAINS IN E YEAR 1508."
WITHDRAWN
FATHER!
FATHER, COME QUICK!
I HAVE FOUND SOME-THING!
YOU SHOULD NOT WANDER IN SUCH PLACES.
THE CAVE WAS NOT HERE LAST SUMMER, ATHER. THE EARTH SHAKING MUST HAVE OPENED IT.
SEE, FATHER.
TREASURE.

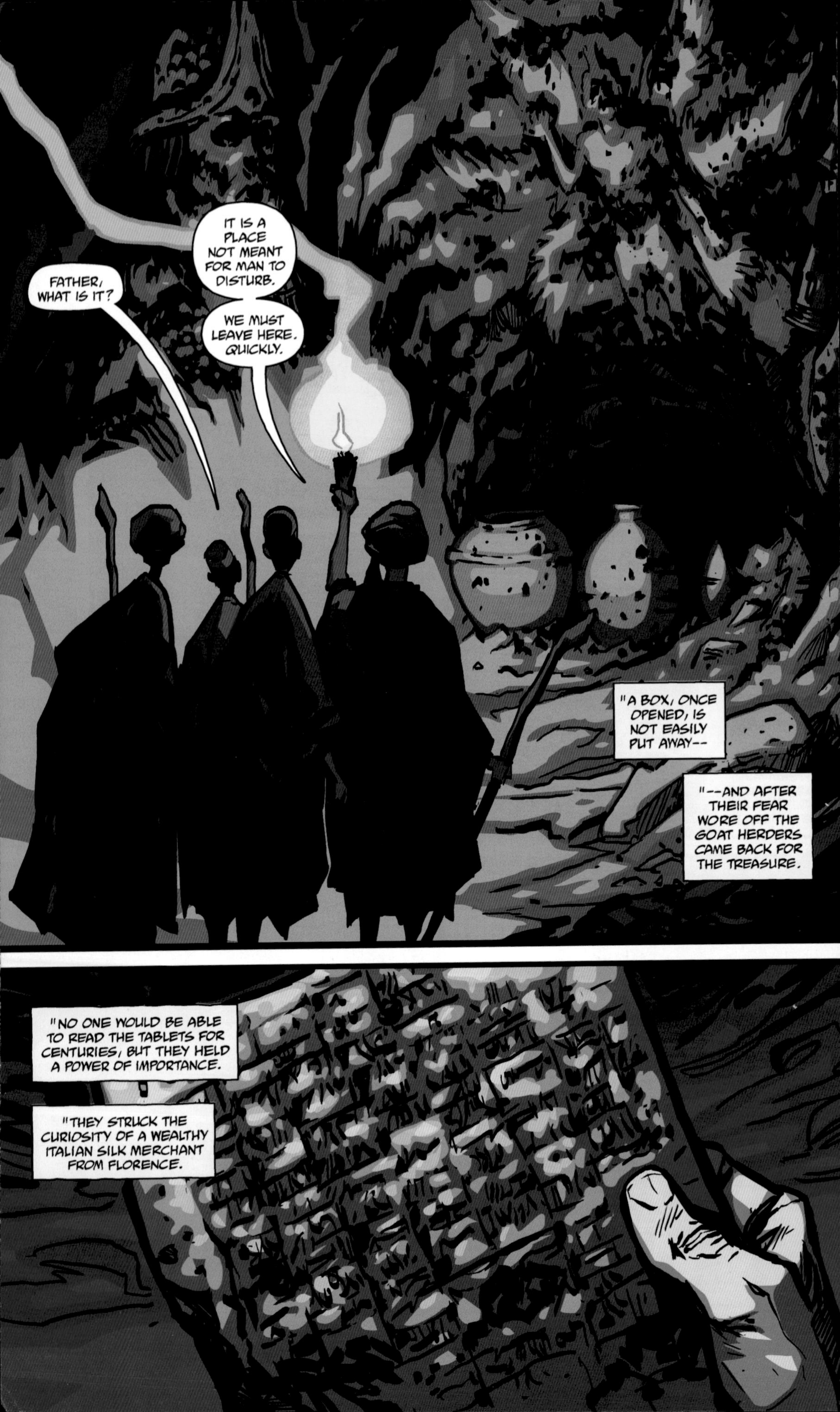
FATHER, WHAT IS IT?
IT IS A PLACE NOT MEANT FOR MAN TO DISTURB.
WE MUST LEAVE HERE. QUICKLY.
"A BOX, ONCE OPENED, IS NOT EASILY PUT AWAY--
"--AND AFTER THEIR FEAR WORE OFF THE GOAT HERDERS CAME BACK FOR THE TREASURE.
"NO ONE WOULD BE ABLE TO READ THE TABLETS FOR CENTURIES, BUT THEY HELD A POWER OF IMPORTANCE.
"THEY STRUCK THE CURIOSITY OF A WEALTHY ITALIAN SILK MERCHANT FROM FLORENCE.

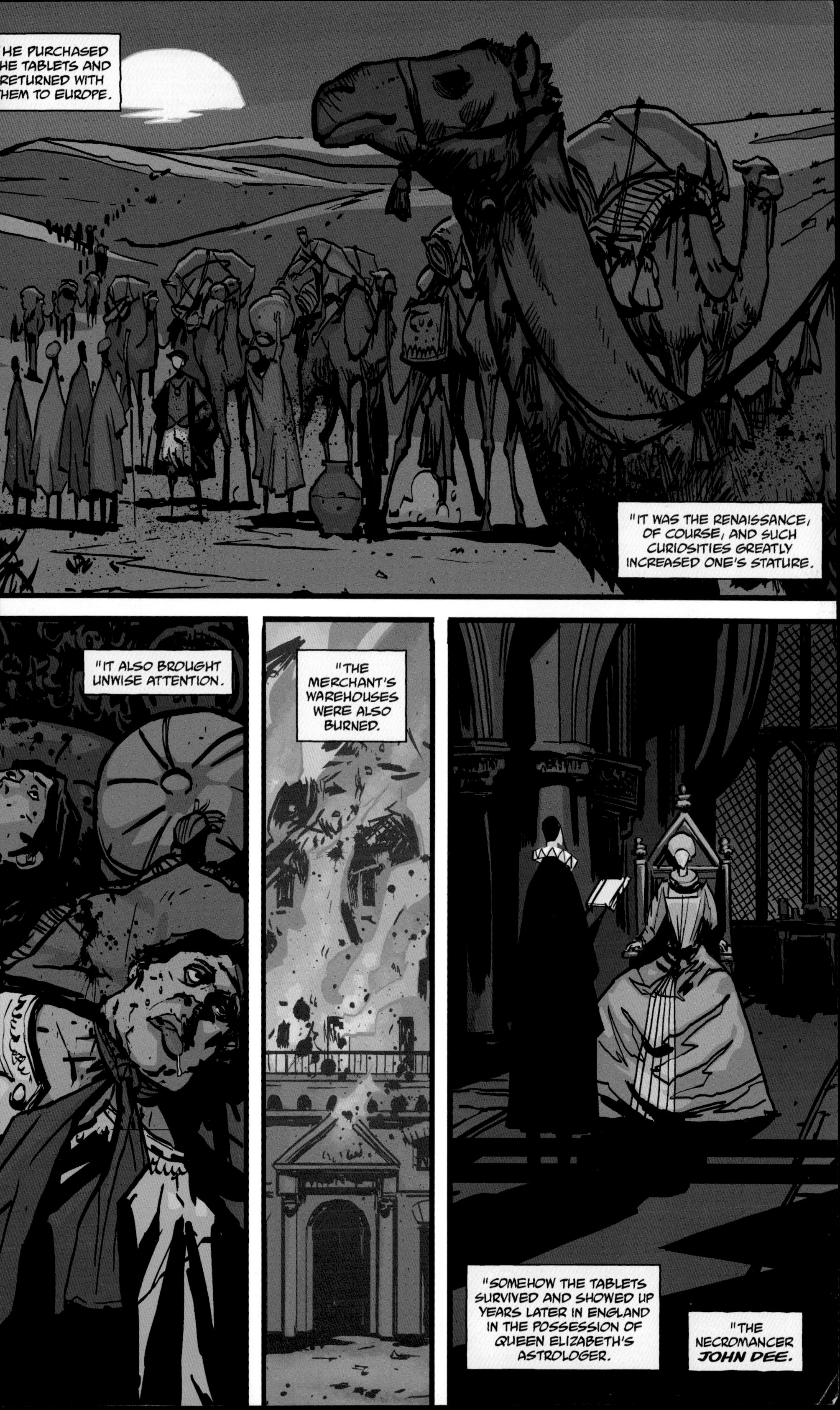
HE PURCHASED HE TABLETS AND RETURNED WITH HEM TO EUROPE.
"IT WAS THE RENAISSANCE, OF COURSE, AND SUCH CURIOSITIES GREATLY INCREASED ONE'S STATURE.
"IT ALSO BROUGHT UNWISE ATTENTION.
"THE MERCHANT'S WAREHOUSES WERE ALSO BURNED.
"SOMEHOW THE TABLETS SURVIVED AND SHOWED UP YEARS LATER IN ENGLAND IN THE POSSESSION OF QUEEN ELIZABETH'S ASTROLOGER.
"THE NECROMANCER **JOHN DEE.**

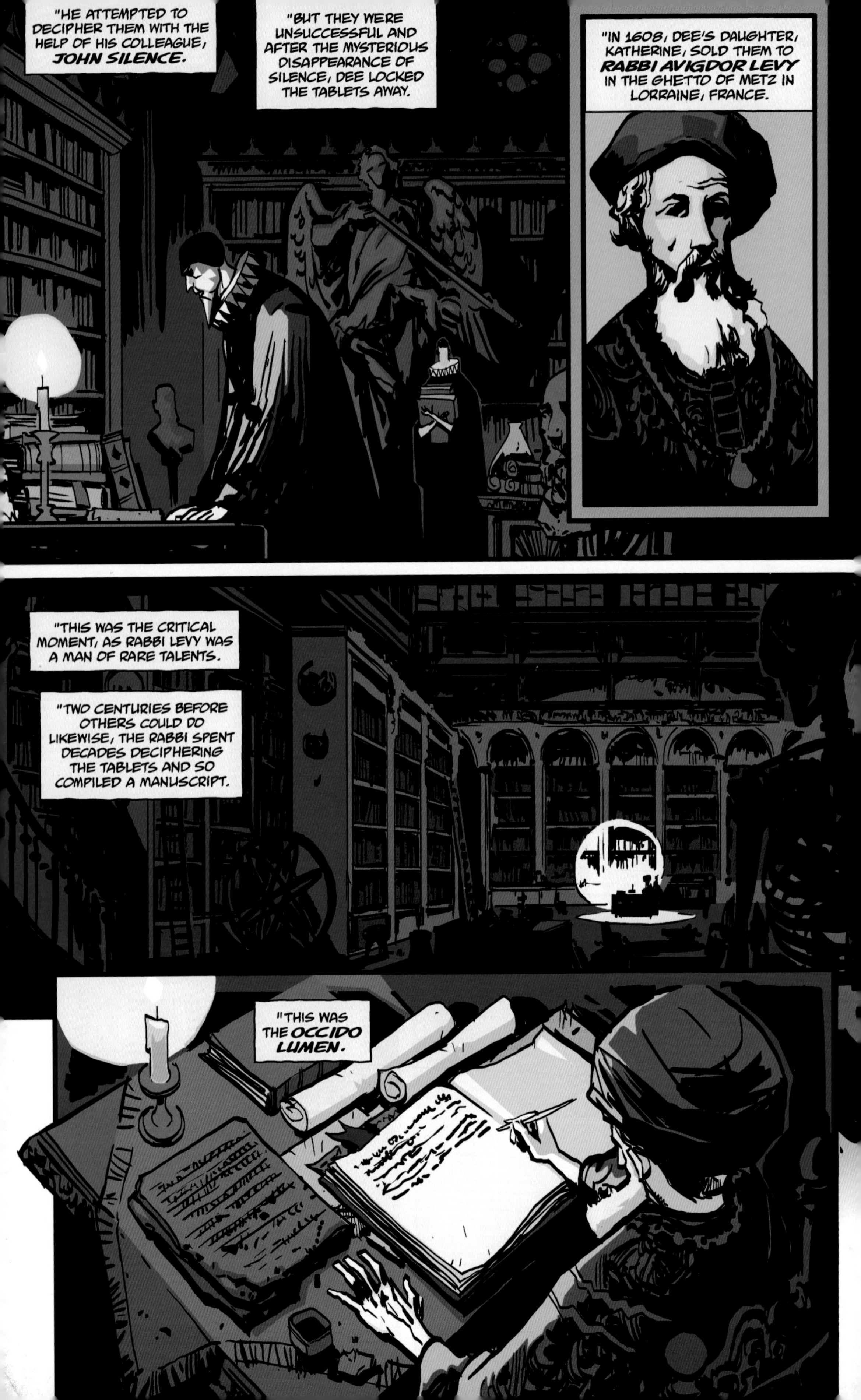
"HE ATTEMPTED TO DECIPHER THEM WITH THE HELP OF HIS COLLEAGUE, JOHN SILENCE.
"BUT THEY WERE UNSUCCESSFUL AND AFTER THE MYSTERIOUS DISAPPEARANCE OF SILENCE, DEE LOCKED THE TABLETS AWAY.
"IN 1608, DEE'S DAUGHTER, KATHERINE, SOLD THEM TO RABBI AVIGDOR LEVY IN THE GHETTO OF METZ IN LORRAINE, FRANCE.
"THIS WAS THE CRITICAL MOMENT, AS RABBI LEVY WAS A MAN OF RARE TALENTS.
"TWO CENTURIES BEFORE OTHERS COULD DO LIKEWISE, THE RABBI SPENT DECADES DECIPHERING THE TABLETS AND SO COMPILED A MANUSCRIPT.
"THIS WAS THE OCCIDO LUMEN.

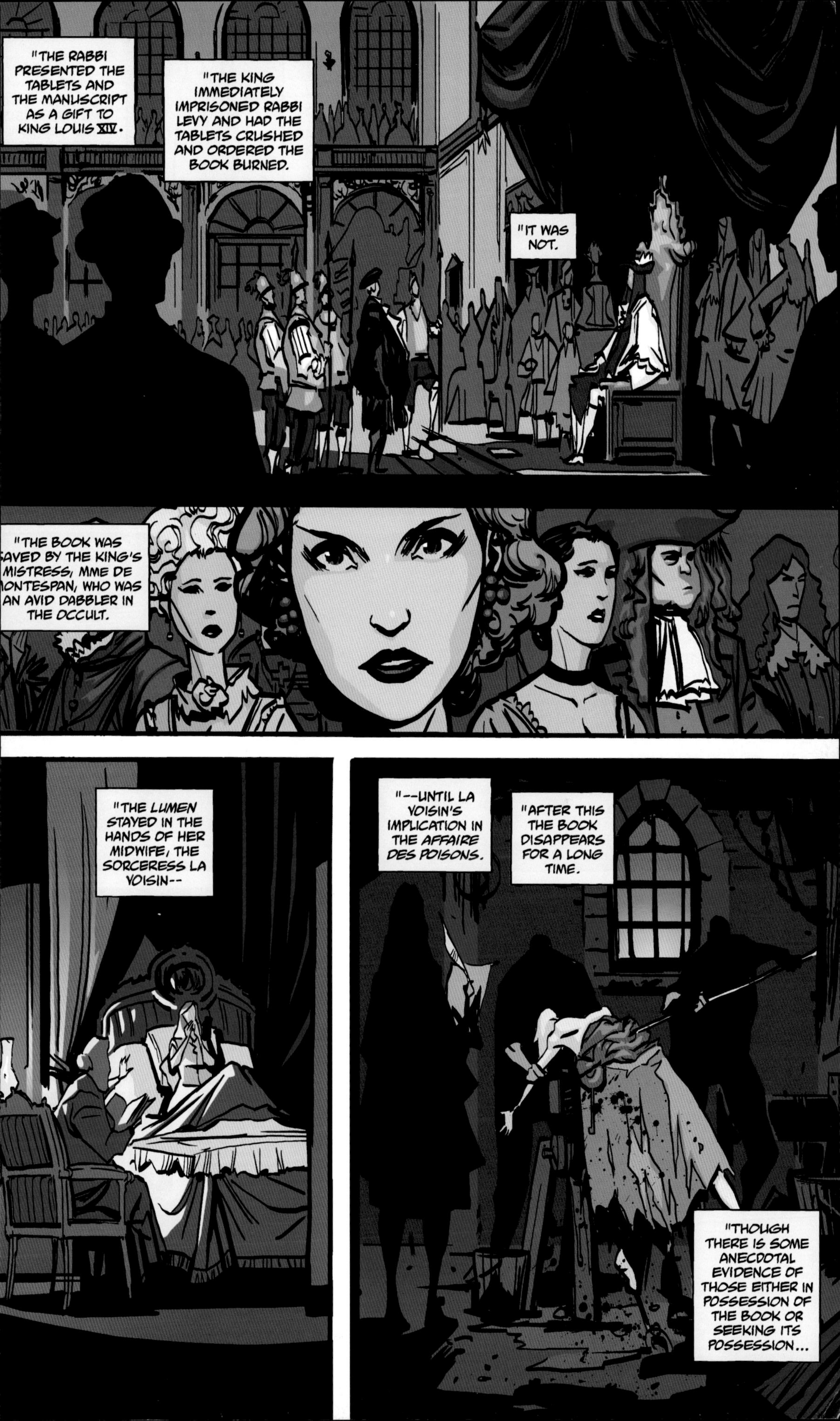
"THE RABBI PRESENTED THE TABLETS AND THE MANUSCRIPT AS A GIFT TO KING LOUIS XIV.
"THE KING IMMEDIATELY IMPRISONED RABBI LEVY AND HAD THE TABLETS CRUSHED AND ORDERED THE BOOK BURNED.
"IT WAS NOT.
"THE BOOK WAS SAVED BY THE KING'S MISTRESS, MME DE MONTESPAN, WHO WAS AN AVID DABBLER IN THE OCCULT.
"THE *LUMEN* STAYED IN THE HANDS OF HER MIDWIFE, THE SORCERESS LA VOISIN--
"--UNTIL LA VOISIN'S IMPLICATION IN THE *AFFAIRE DES POISONS*.
"AFTER THIS THE BOOK DISAPPEARS FOR A LONG TIME.
"THOUGH THERE IS SOME ANECDOTAL EVIDENCE OF THOSE EITHER IN POSSESSION OF THE BOOK OR SEEKING ITS POSSESSION...

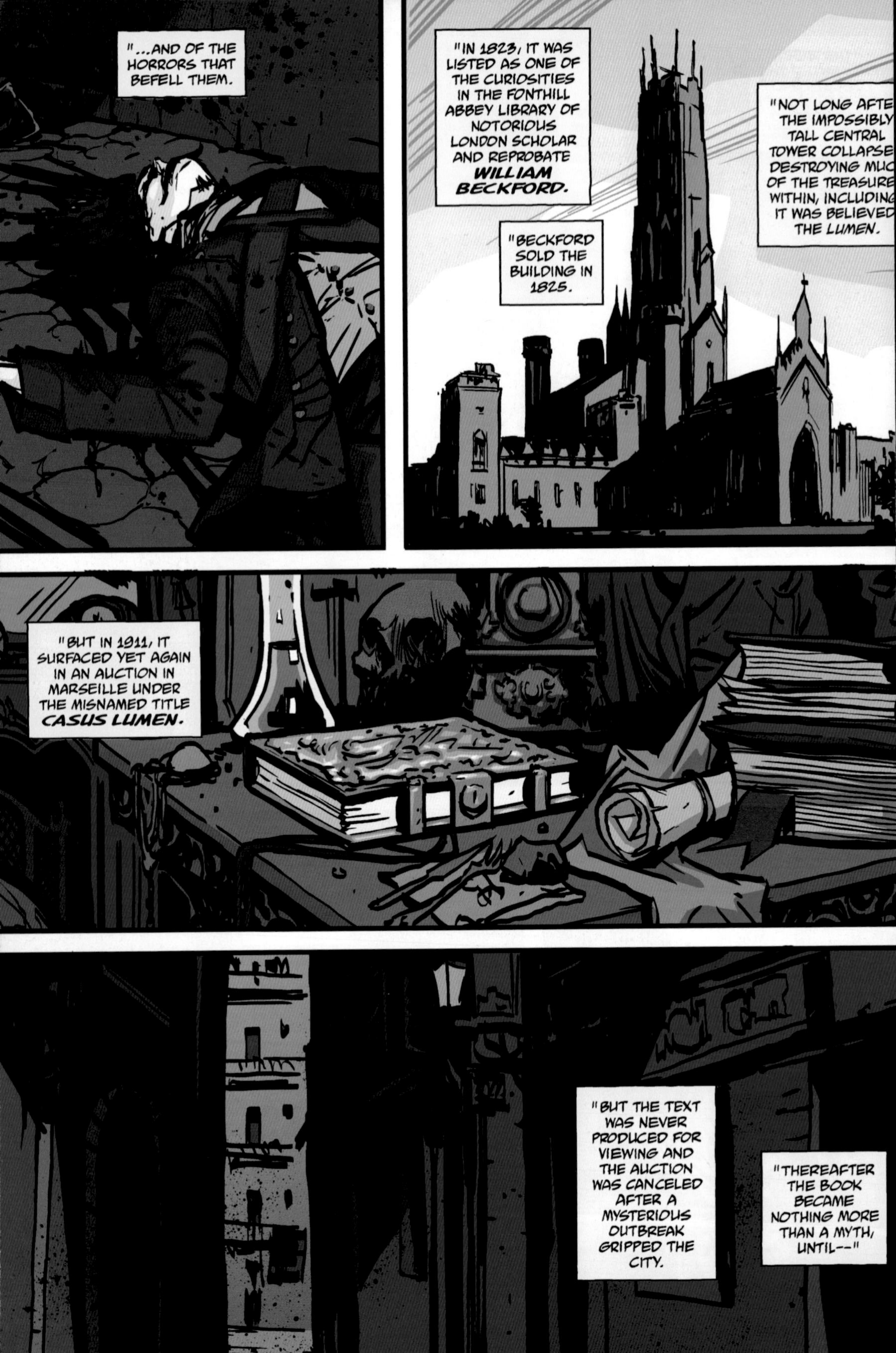
"...AND OF THE HORRORS THAT BEFELL THEM.
"IN 1823, IT WAS LISTED AS ONE OF THE CURIOSITIES IN THE FONTHILL ABBEY LIBRARY OF NOTORIOUS LONDON SCHOLAR AND REPROBATE WILLIAM BECKFORD.
"BECKFORD SOLD THE BUILDING IN 1825.
"NOT LONG AFTE THE IMPOSSIBLY TALL CENTRAL TOWER COLLAPSE DESTROYING MUC OF THE TREASURE WITHIN, INCLUDING IT WAS BELIEVED THE LUMEN.
"BUT IN 1911, IT SURFACED YET AGAIN IN AN AUCTION IN MARSEILLE UNDER THE MISNAMED TITLE CASUS LUMEN.
"BUT THE TEXT WAS NEVER PRODUCED FOR VIEWING AND THE AUCTION WAS CANCELED AFTER A MYSTERIOUS OUTBREAK GRIPPED THE CITY.
"THEREAFTER THE BOOK BECAME NOTHING MORE THAN A MYTH, UNTIL--"

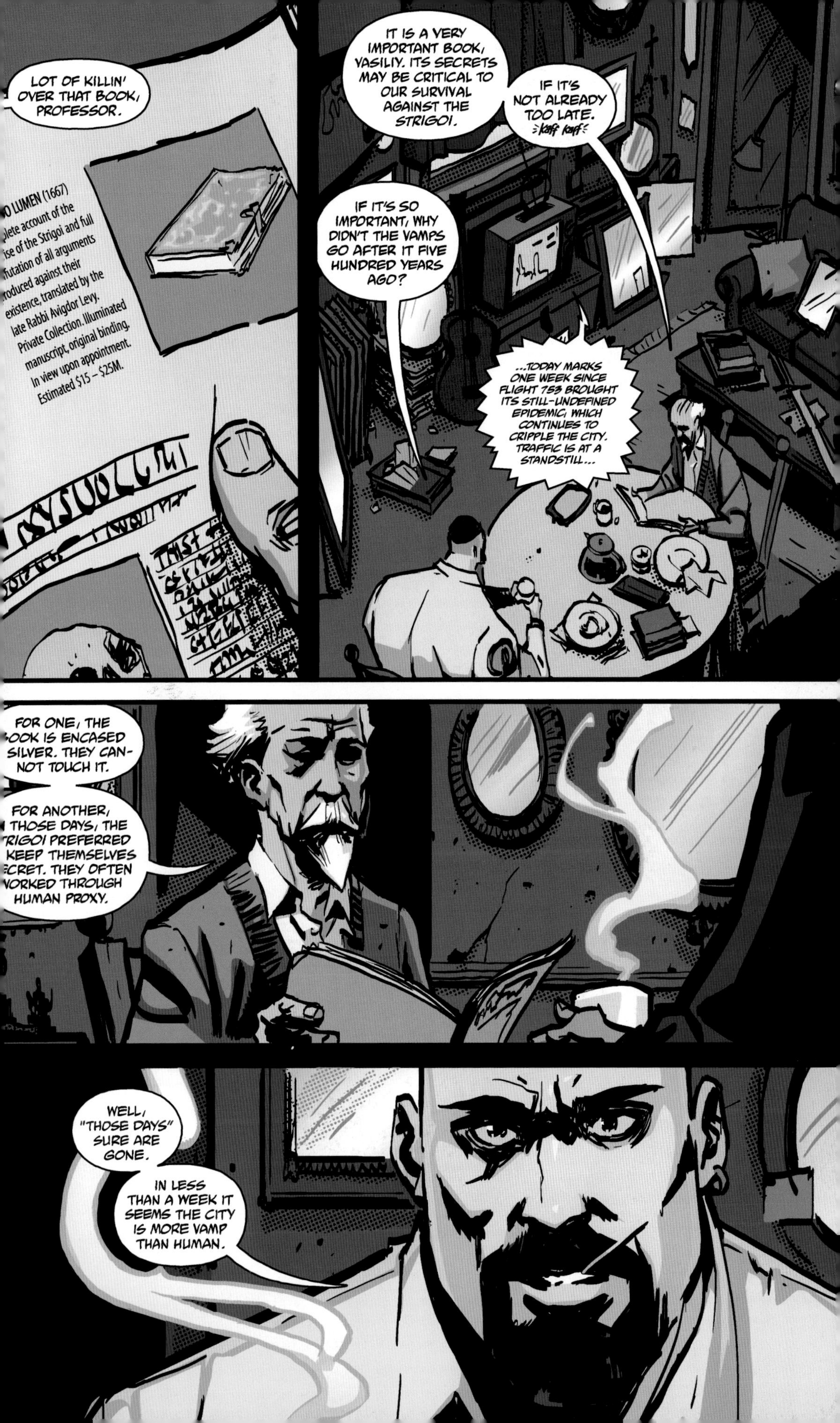
LOT OF KILLIN' OVER THAT BOOK, PROFESSOR.
O LUMEN (1667)
plete account of the
ise of the Strigoi and full
futation of all arguments
roduced against their
existence, translated by the
late Rabbi Avigdor Levy.
Private Collection. Illuminated
manuscript, original binding.
In view upon appointment.
Estimated $15 – $25M.
IT IS A VERY IMPORTANT BOOK, VASILIY. ITS SECRETS MAY BE CRITICAL TO OUR SURVIVAL AGAINST THE STRIGOI.
IF IT'S NOT ALREADY TOO LATE.
KAFF KAFF
IF IT'S SO IMPORTANT, WHY DIDN'T THE VAMPS GO AFTER IT FIVE HUNDRED YEARS AGO?
...TODAY MARKS ONE WEEK SINCE FLIGHT 753 BROUGHT ITS STILL-UNDEFINED EPIDEMIC, WHICH CONTINUES TO CRIPPLE THE CITY. TRAFFIC IS AT A STANDSTILL...
FOR ONE, THE OOK IS ENCASED SILVER. THEY CAN-NOT TOUCH IT.
FOR ANOTHER, THOSE DAYS, THE TRIGOI PREFERRED KEEP THEMSELVES ECRET. THEY OFTEN VORKED THROUGH HUMAN PROXY.
WELL, "THOSE DAYS" SURE ARE GONE.
IN LESS THAN A WEEK IT SEEMS THE CITY IS MORE VAMP THAN HUMAN.

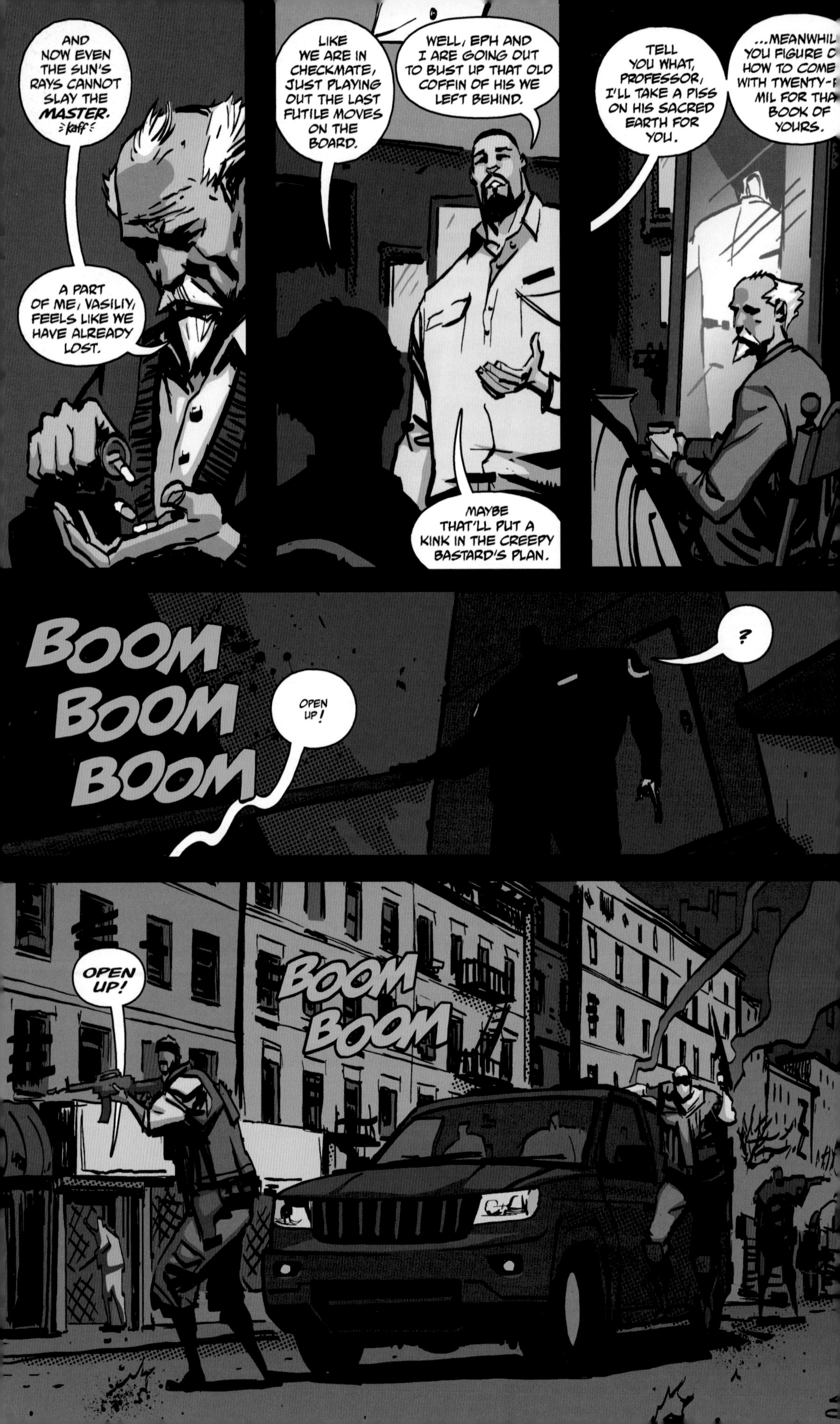
AND NOW EVEN THE SUN'S RAYS CANNOT SLAY THE MASTER. kaff
A PART OF ME, VASILIY, FEELS LIKE WE HAVE ALREADY LOST.
LIKE WE ARE IN CHECKMATE, JUST PLAYING OUT THE LAST FUTILE MOVES ON THE BOARD.
WELL, EPH AND I ARE GOING OUT TO BUST UP THAT OLD COFFIN OF HIS WE LEFT BEHIND.
MAYBE THAT'LL PUT A KINK IN THE CREEPY BASTARD'S PLAN.
TELL YOU WHAT, PROFESSOR, I'LL TAKE A PISS ON HIS SACRED EARTH FOR YOU.
...MEANWHIL YOU FIGURE C HOW TO COME WITH TWENTY- MIL FOR THA BOOK OF YOURS.
BOOM BOOM BOOM
OPEN UP!
?
OPEN UP!
BOOM BOOM

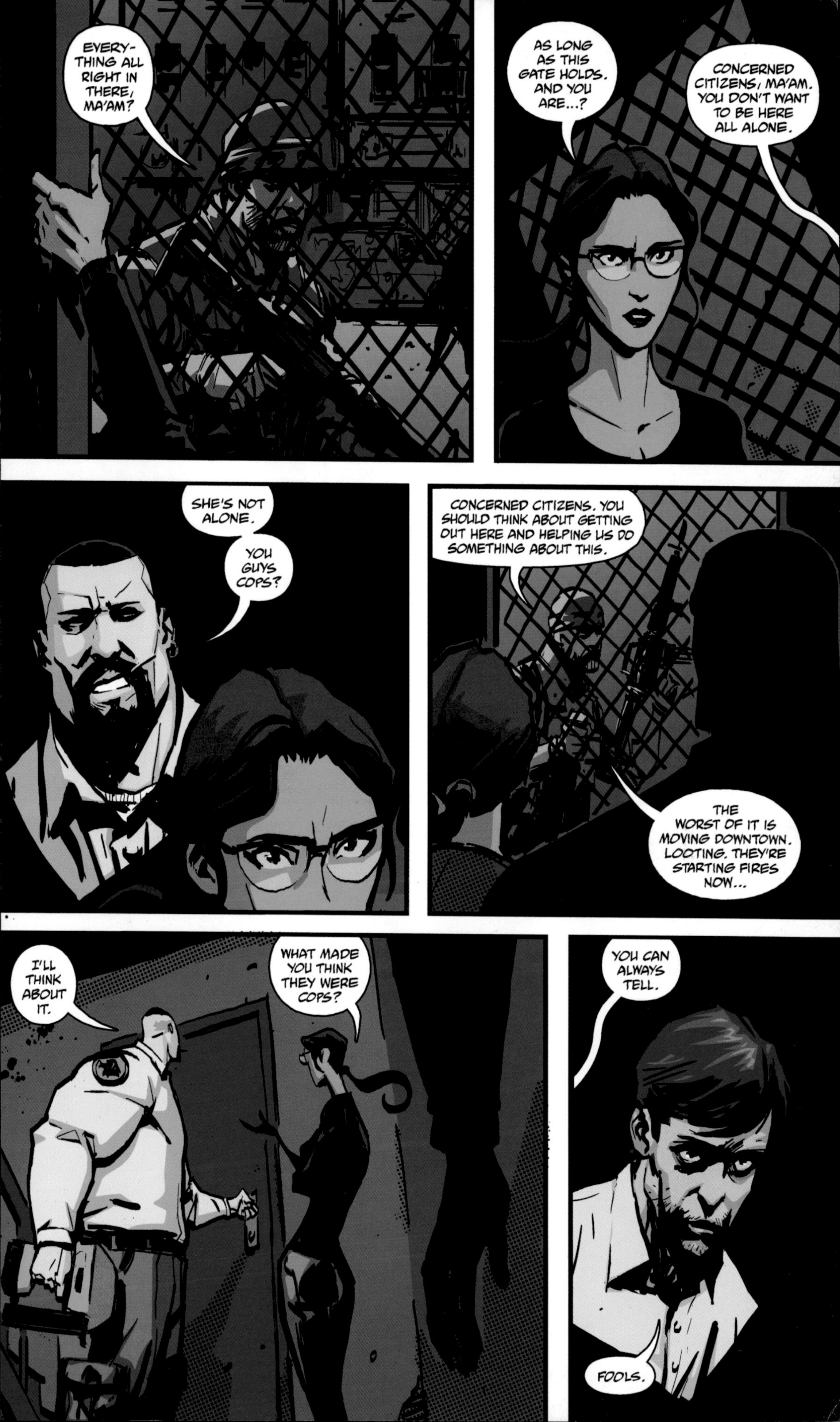
EVERY-THING ALL RIGHT IN THERE, MA'AM?
AS LONG AS THIS GATE HOLDS. AND YOU ARE...?
CONCERNED CITIZENS, MA'AM. YOU DON'T WANT TO BE HERE ALL ALONE.
SHE'S NOT ALONE.
YOU GUYS COPS?
CONCERNED CITIZENS. YOU SHOULD THINK ABOUT GETTING OUT HERE AND HELPING US DO SOMETHING ABOUT THIS.
THE WORST OF IT IS MOVING DOWNTOWN. LOOTING. THEY'RE STARTING FIRES NOW...
I'LL THINK ABOUT IT.
WHAT MADE YOU THINK THEY WERE COPS?
YOU CAN ALWAYS TELL.
FOOLS.

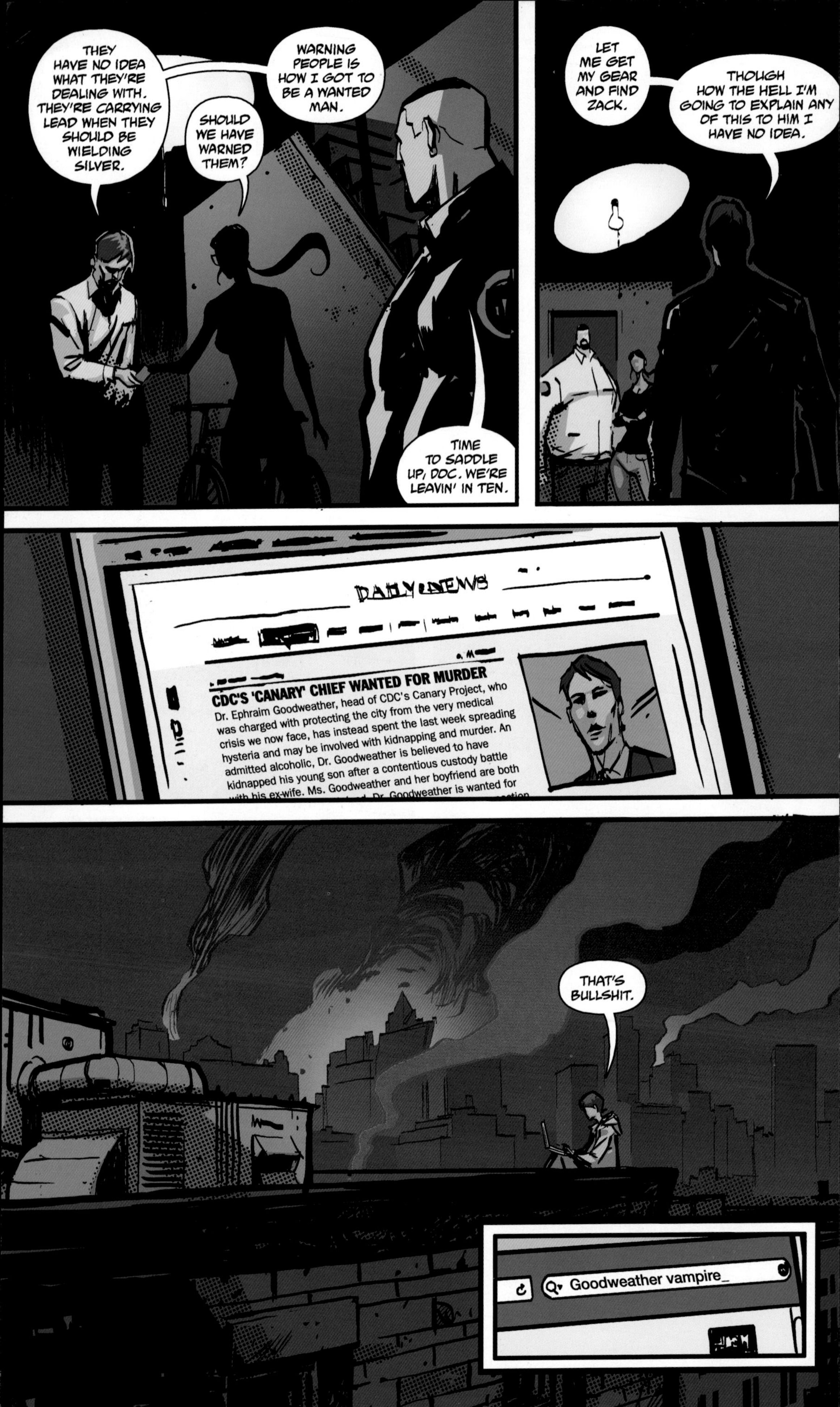

THEY HAVE NO IDEA WHAT THEY'RE DEALING WITH. THEY'RE CARRYING LEAD WHEN THEY SHOULD BE WIELDING SILVER.
SHOULD WE HAVE WARNED THEM?
WARNING PEOPLE IS HOW I GOT TO BE A WANTED MAN.
TIME TO SADDLE UP, DOC. WE'RE LEAVIN' IN TEN.
LET ME GET MY GEAR AND FIND ZACK.
THOUGH HOW THE HELL I'M GOING TO EXPLAIN ANY OF THIS TO HIM I HAVE NO IDEA.
CDC'S 'CANARY' CHIEF WANTED FOR MURDER
Dr. Ephraim Goodweather, head of CDC's Canary Project, who
was charged with protecting the city from the very medical
crisis we now face, has instead spent the last week spreading
hysteria and may be involved with kidnapping and murder. An
admitted alcoholic, Dr. Goodweather is believed to have
kidnapped his young son after a contentious custody battle
THAT'S BULLSHIT.
Goodweather vampire_

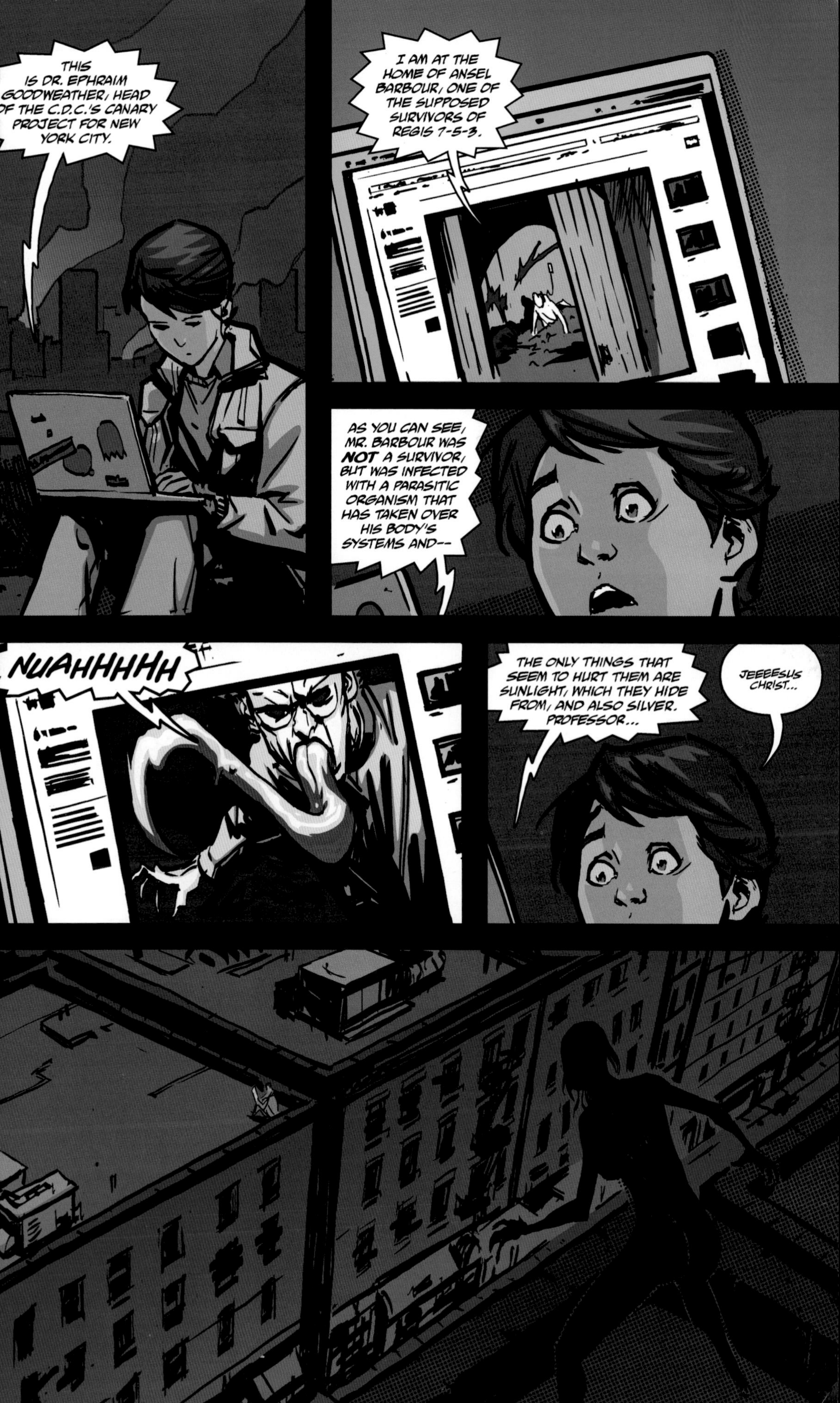
THIS IS DR. EPHRAIM GOODWEATHER, HEAD OF THE C.D.C.'S CANARY PROJECT FOR NEW YORK CITY.
I AM AT THE HOME OF ANSEL BARBOUR, ONE OF THE SUPPOSED SURVIVORS OF REGIS 7-5-3.
AS YOU CAN SEE, MR. BARBOUR WAS NOT A SURVIVOR, BUT WAS INFECTED WITH A PARASITIC ORGANISM THAT HAS TAKEN OVER HIS BODY'S SYSTEMS AND--
NUAHHHHH
THE ONLY THINGS THAT SEEM TO HURT THEM ARE SUNLIGHT, WHICH THEY HIDE FROM, AND ALSO SILVER. PROFESSOR...
JEEEESUS CHRIST...

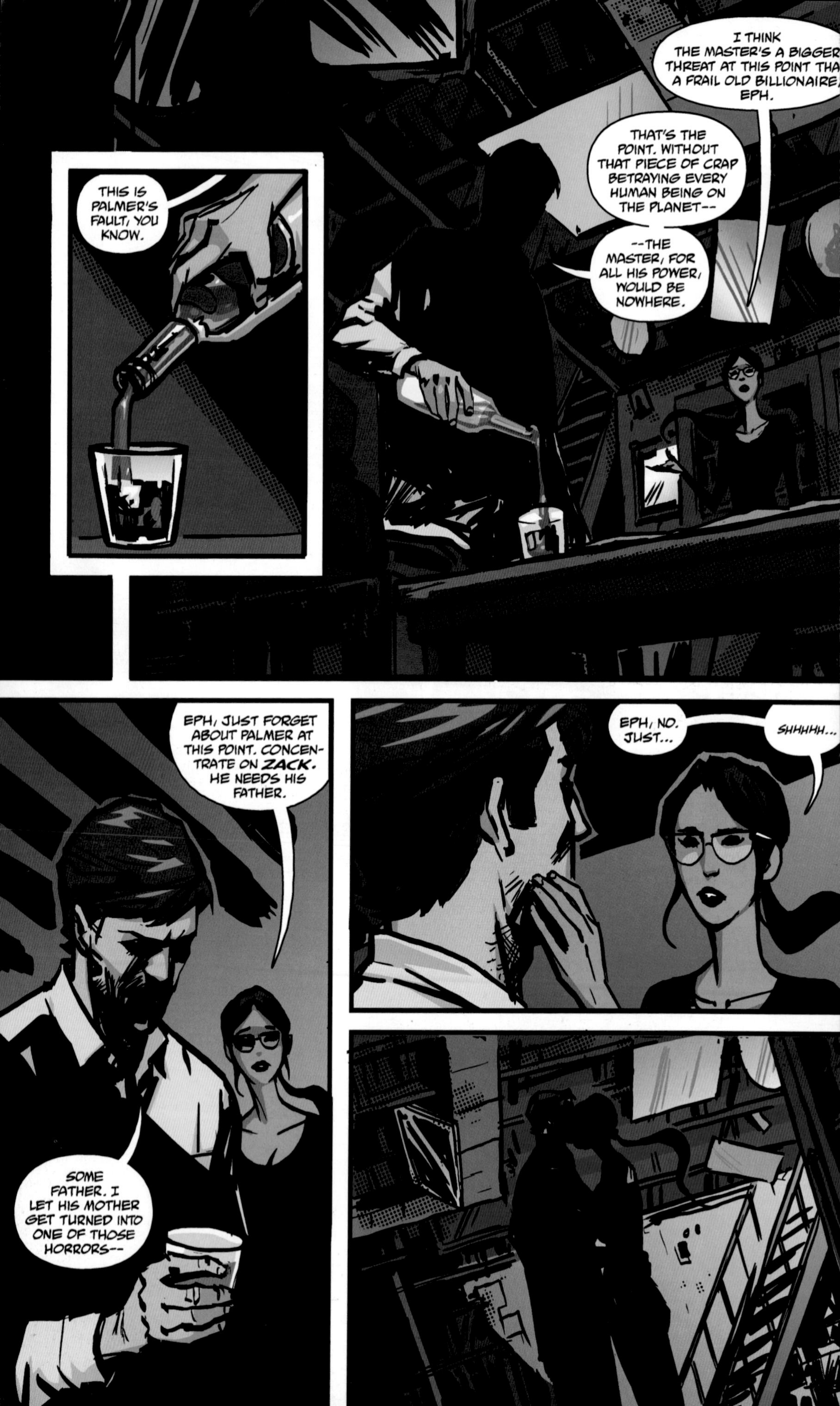

I THINK THE MASTER'S A BIGGER THREAT AT THIS POINT THAN A FRAIL OLD BILLIONAIRE, EPH.
THIS IS PALMER'S FAULT, YOU KNOW.
THAT'S THE POINT. WITHOUT THAT PIECE OF CRAP BETRAYING EVERY HUMAN BEING ON THE PLANET--
--THE MASTER, FOR ALL HIS POWER, WOULD BE NOWHERE.
EPH, JUST FORGET ABOUT PALMER AT THIS POINT. CONCENTRATE ON ZACK. HE NEEDS HIS FATHER.
SOME FATHER. I LET HIS MOTHER GET TURNED INTO ONE OF THOSE HORRORS--
EPH, NO. JUST...
SHHHHH...

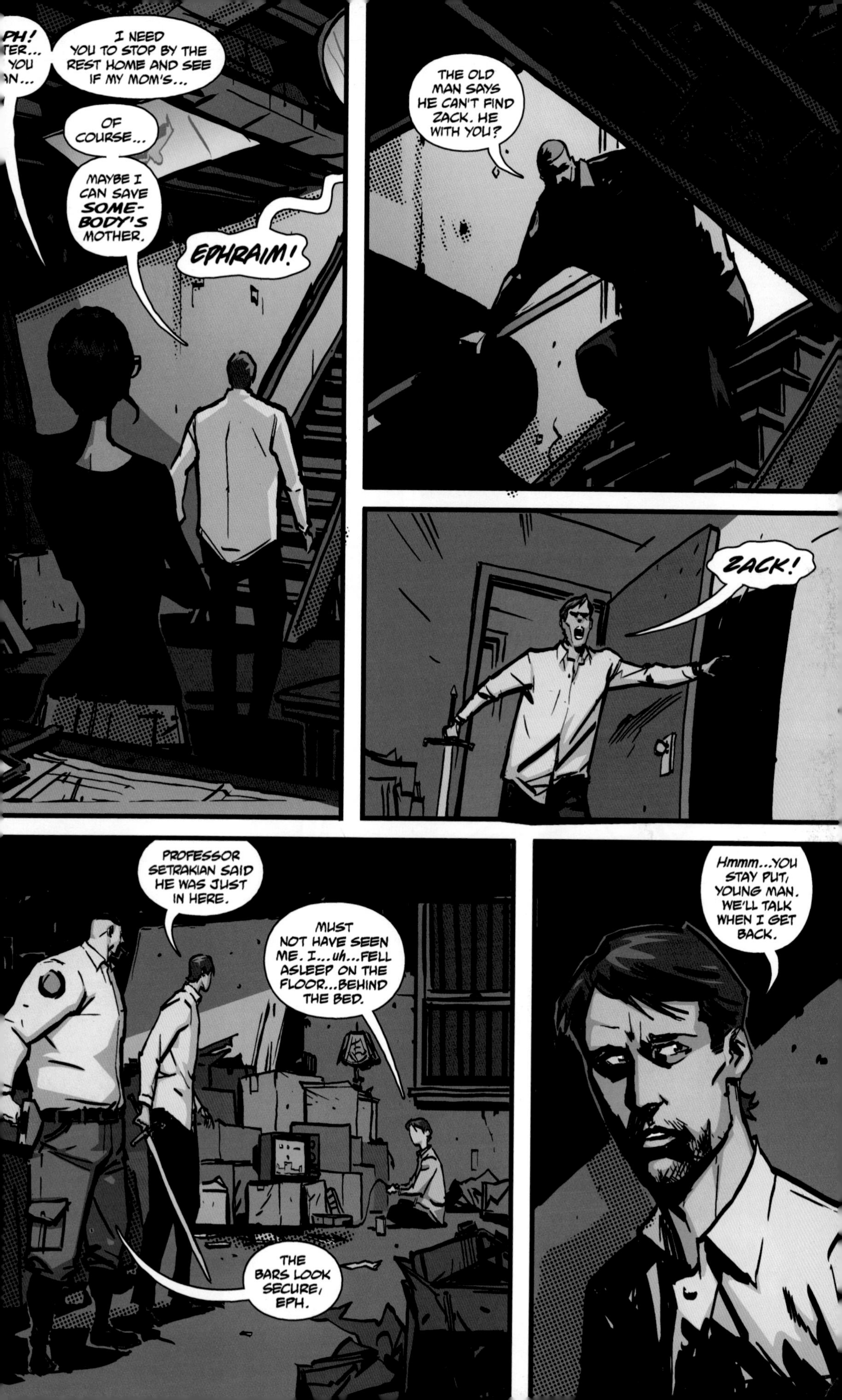

PH! TER... YOU AN...
I NEED YOU TO STOP BY THE REST HOME AND SEE IF MY MOM'S...
OF COURSE...
MAYBE I CAN SAVE SOMEBODY'S MOTHER.
EPHRAIM!
THE OLD MAN SAYS HE CAN'T FIND ZACK. HE WITH YOU?
ZACK!
PROFESSOR SETRAKIAN SAID HE WAS JUST IN HERE.
MUST NOT HAVE SEEN ME. I...uh...FELL ASLEEP ON THE FLOOR...BEHIND THE BED.
THE BARS LOOK SECURE, EPH.
Hmmm...YOU STAY PUT, YOUNG MAN. WE'LL TALK WHEN I GET BACK.

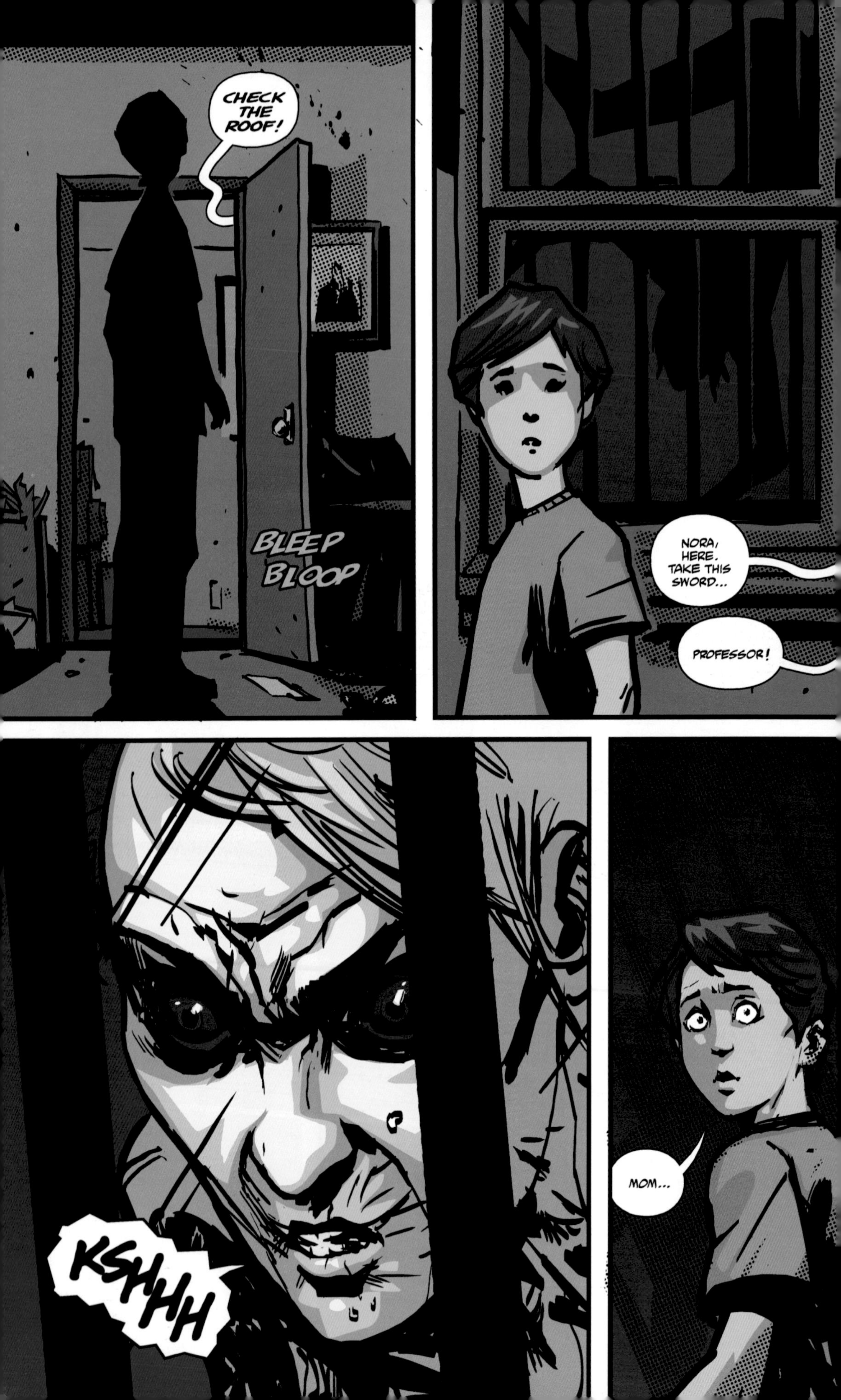
CHECK THE ROOF!
BLEEP BLOOP
NORA, HERE. TAKE THIS SWORD...
PROFESSOR!
KSHHH
MOM...

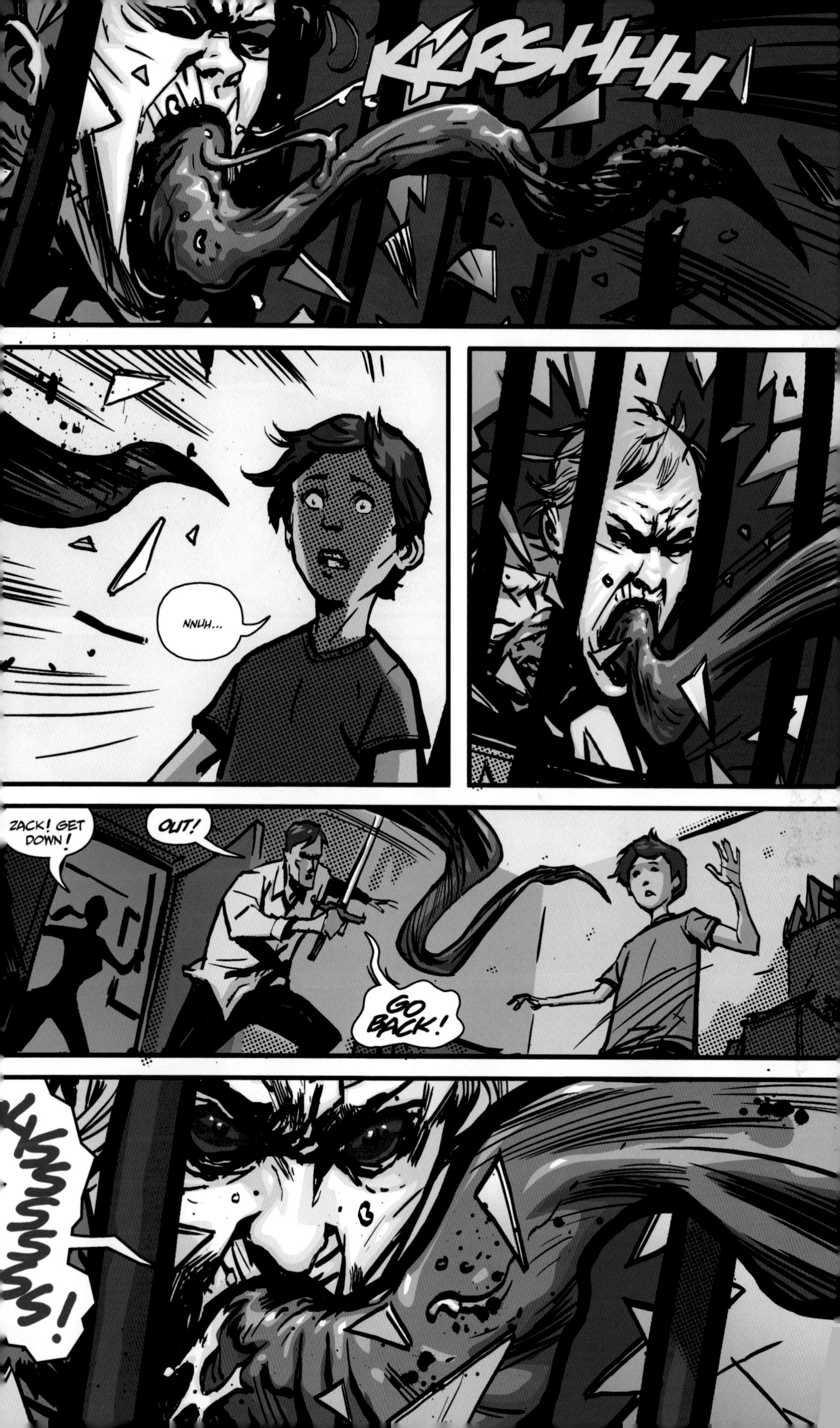
KKRSHHH
NNUH...
ZACK! GET DOWN!
OUT!
GO BACK!
KKSSSSSS!

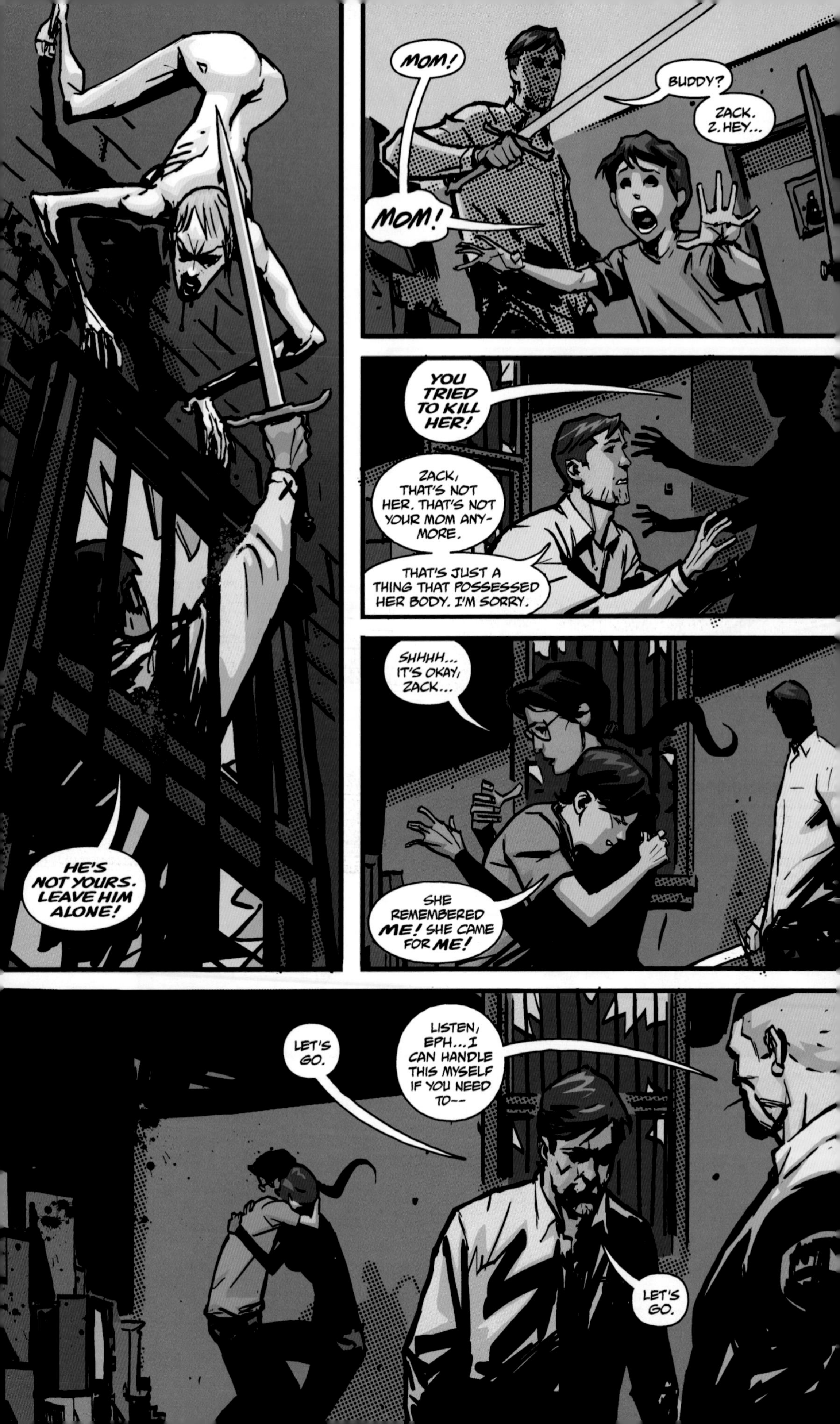
HE'S NOT YOURS. LEAVE HIM ALONE!
MOM!
MOM!
BUDDY?
ZACK. Z. HEY...
YOU TRIED TO KILL HER!
ZACK, THAT'S NOT HER. THAT'S NOT YOUR MOM ANY-MORE.
THAT'S JUST A THING THAT POSSESSED HER BODY. I'M SORRY.
SHHHH... IT'S OKAY, ZACK...
SHE REMEMBERED ME! SHE CAME FOR ME!
LET'S GO.
LISTEN, EPH... I CAN HANDLE THIS MYSELF IF YOU NEED TO--
LET'S GO.

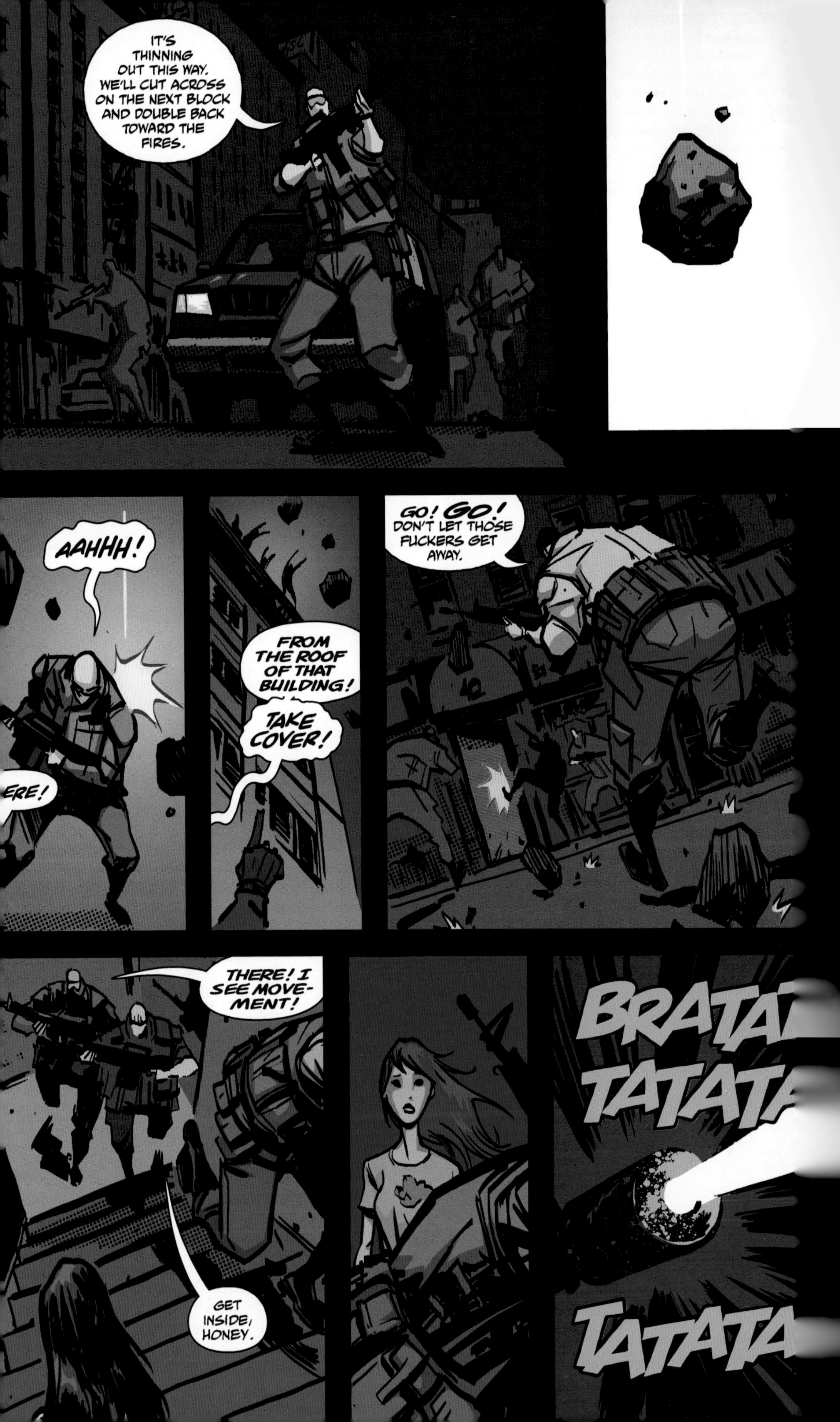
IT'S THINNING OUT THIS WAY. WE'LL CUT ACROSS ON THE NEXT BLOCK AND DOUBLE BACK TOWARD THE FIRES.
AAHHH!
ERE!
FROM THE ROOF OF THAT BUILDING!
TAKE COVER!
GO! GO! DON'T LET THOSE FUCKERS GET AWAY.
THERE! I SEE MOVE-MENT!
GET INSIDE, HONEY.
BRATA
TATATA
TATATA

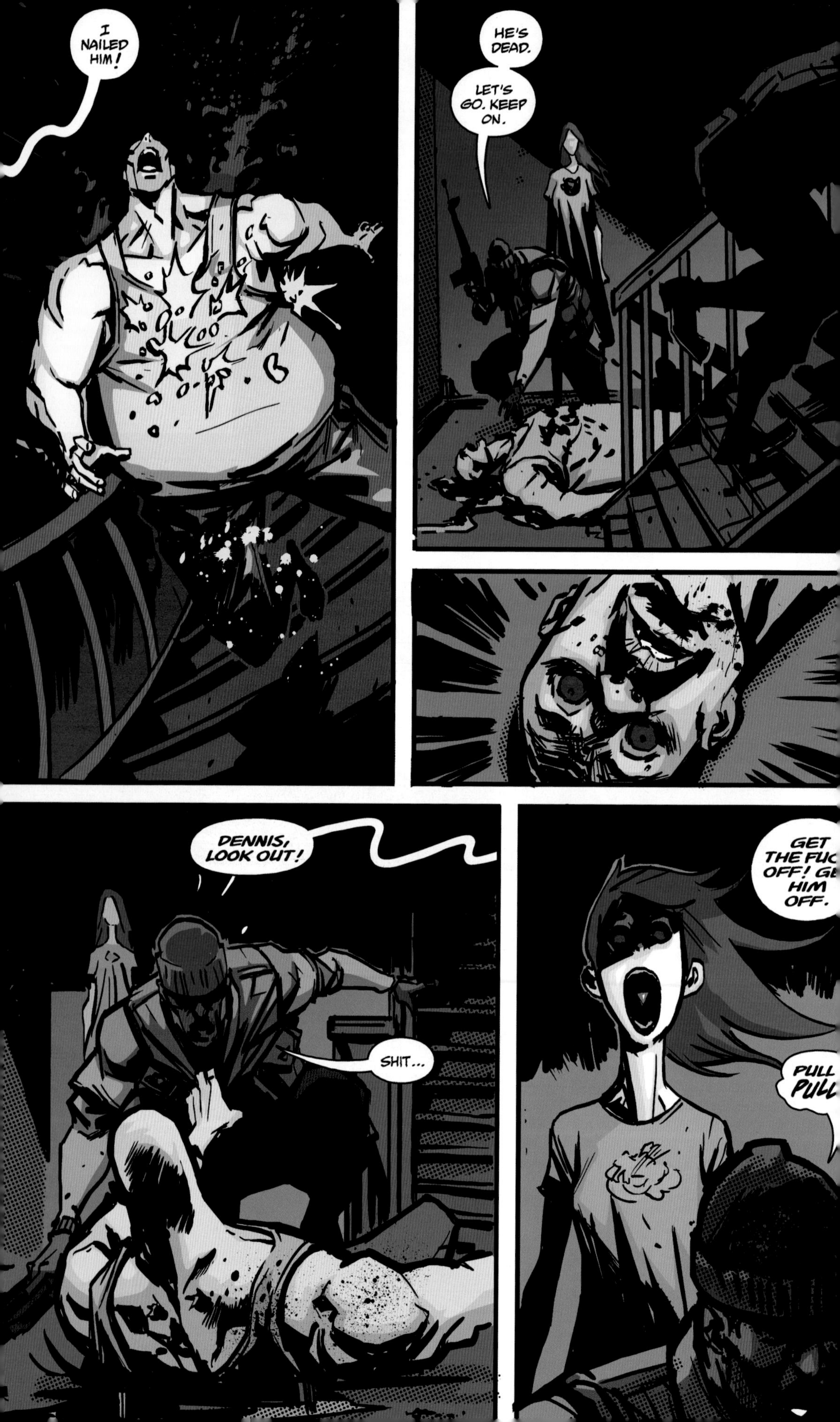
I NAILED HIM!
HE'S DEAD.
LET'S GO. KEEP ON.
DENNIS, LOOK OUT!
SHIT...
GET THE FU
OFF! GE
HIM OFF.
PULL
PULL

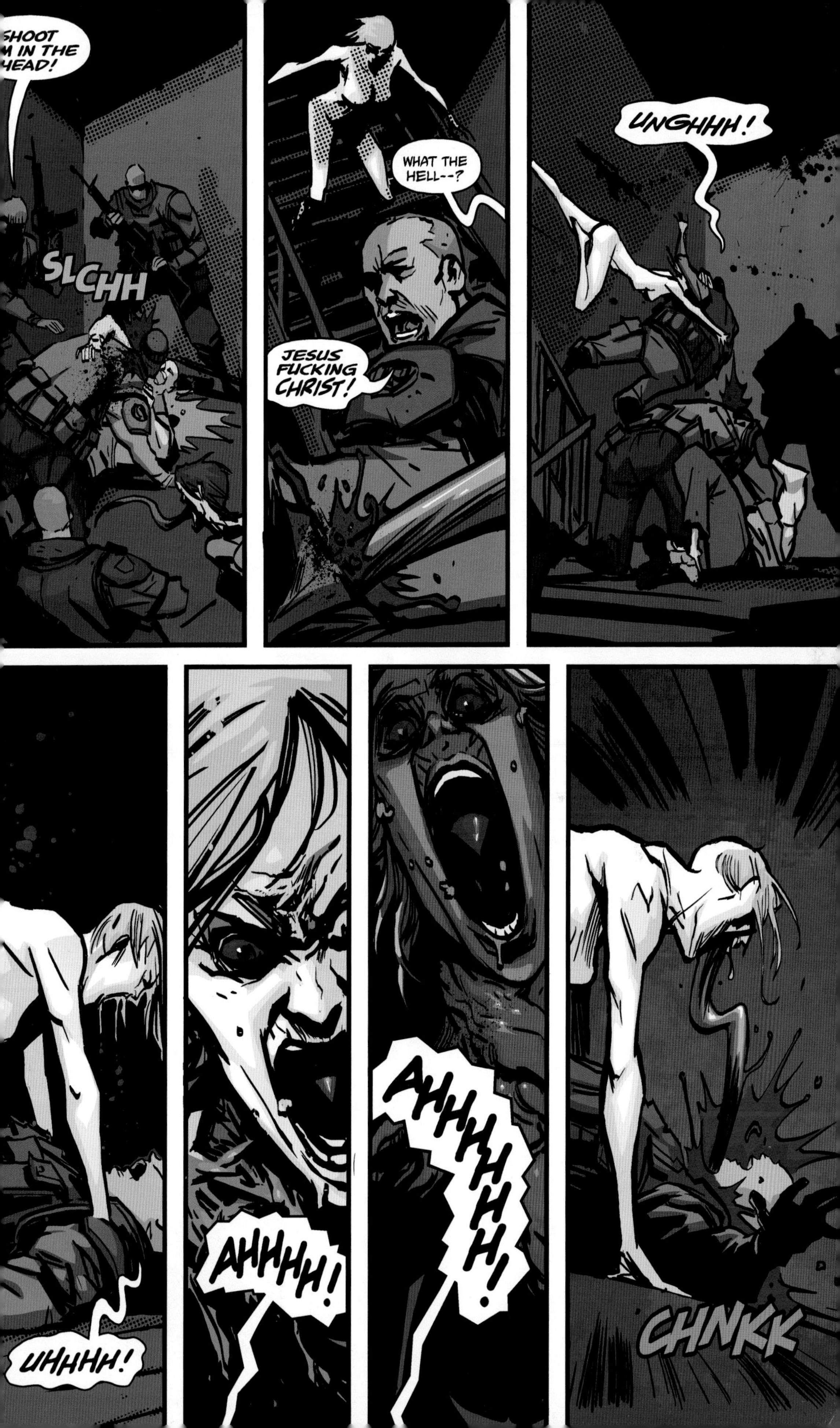
SHOOT
M IN THE
HEAD!
SLCHH
WHAT THE HELL--?
JESUS FUCKING CHRIST!
UNGHHH!
UHHHH!
AHHHH!
AHHHHHHH!
CHNKK

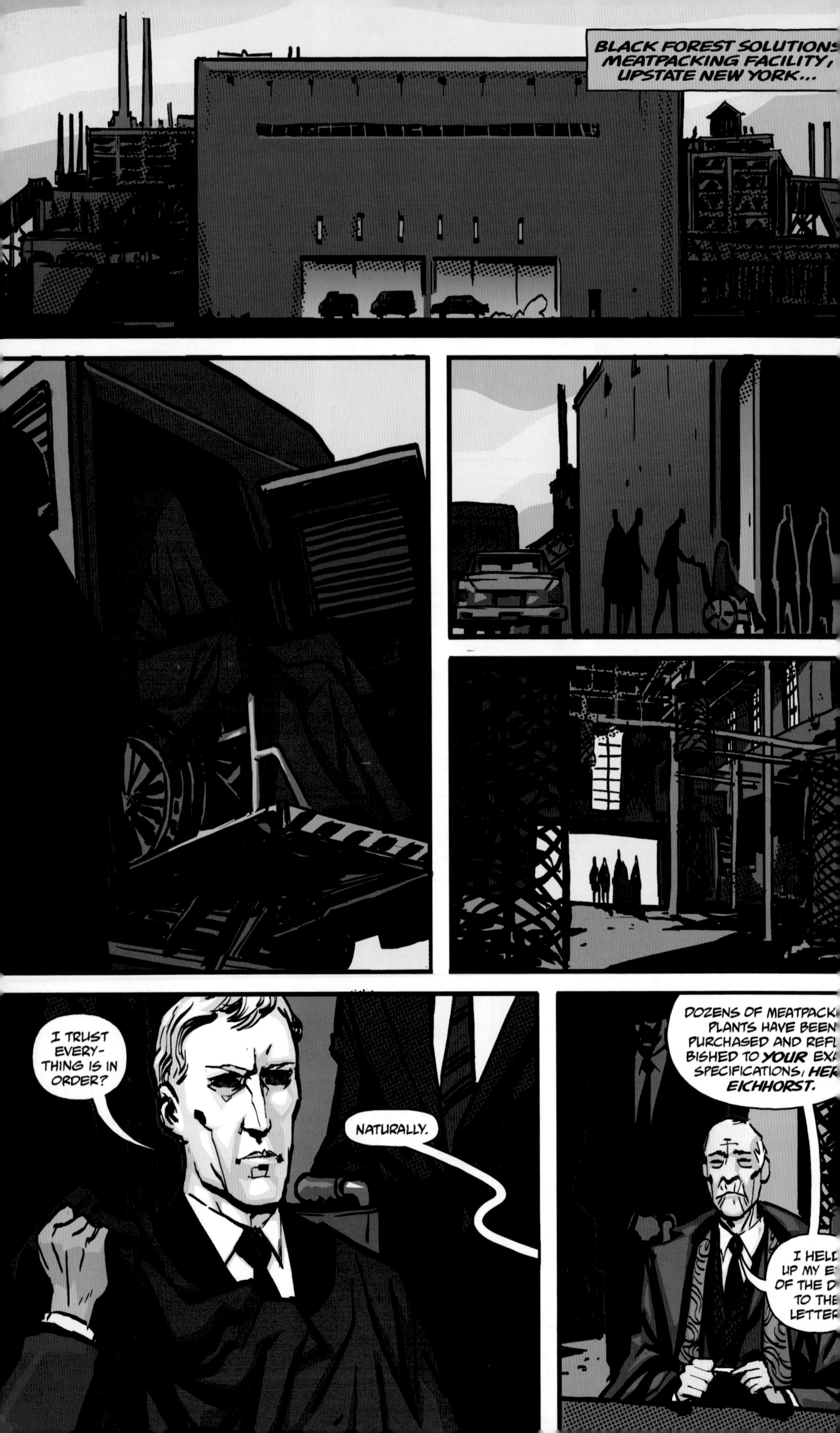
BLACK FOREST SOLUTIONS MEATPACKING FACILITY, UPSTATE NEW YORK...
I TRUST EVERY-THING IS IN ORDER?
NATURALLY.
DOZENS OF MEATPACK PLANTS HAVE BEEN PURCHASED AND REFU BISHED TO YOUR EXA SPECIFICATIONS, HER EICHHORST.
I HELD UP MY E OF THE D TO THE LETTER

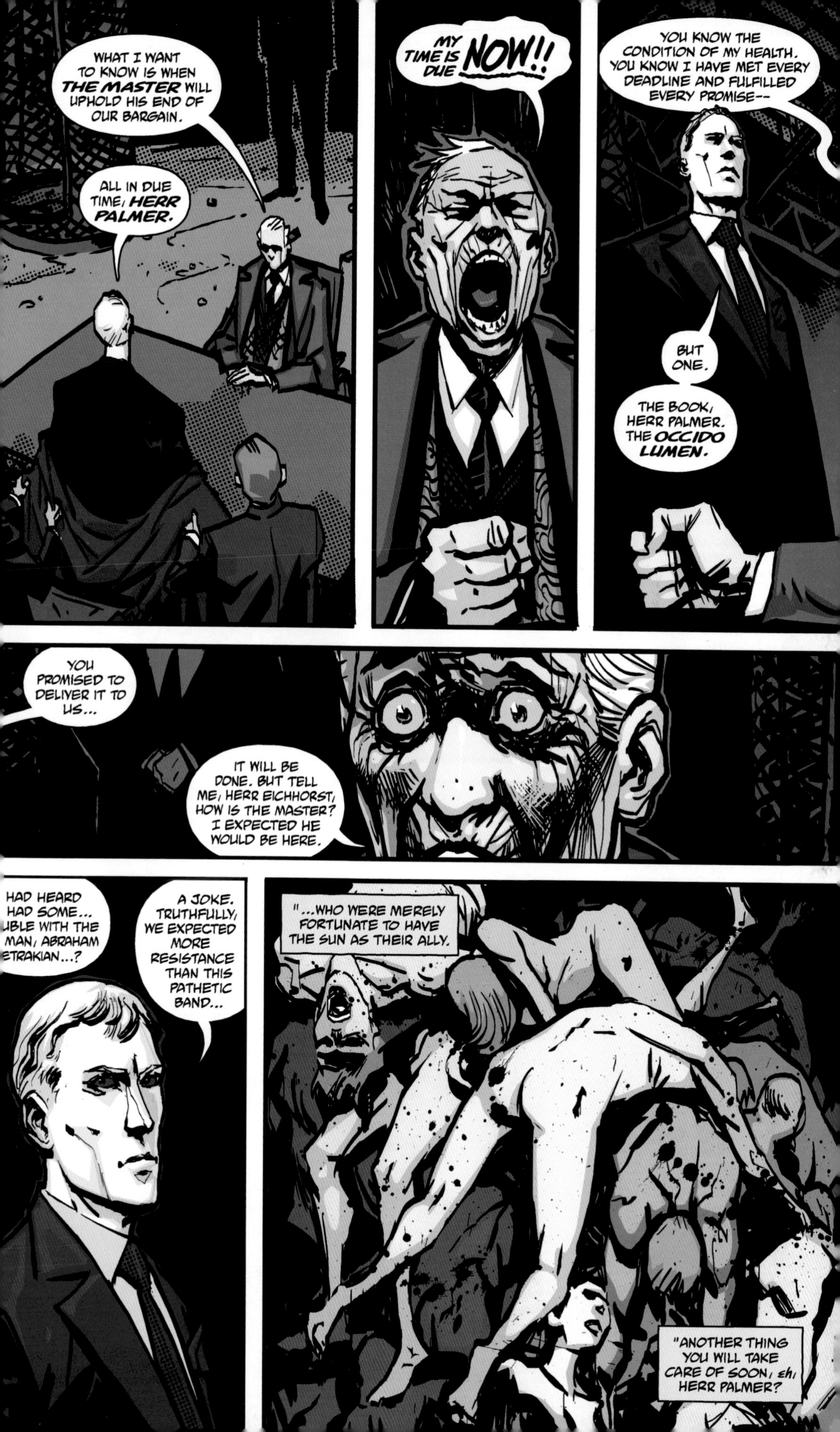
WHAT I WANT TO KNOW IS WHEN THE MASTER WILL UPHOLD HIS END OF OUR BARGAIN.
ALL IN DUE TIME, HERR PALMER.
MY TIME IS DUE NOW!!
YOU KNOW THE CONDITION OF MY HEALTH. YOU KNOW I HAVE MET EVERY DEADLINE AND FULFILLED EVERY PROMISE--
BUT ONE.
THE BOOK, HERR PALMER. THE OCCIDO LUMEN.
YOU PROMISED TO DELIVER IT TO US...
IT WILL BE DONE. BUT TELL ME, HERR EICHHORST, HOW IS THE MASTER? I EXPECTED HE WOULD BE HERE.
HAD HEARD HAD SOME... UBLE WITH THE MAN, ABRAHAM ETRAKIAN...?
A JOKE. TRUTHFULLY, WE EXPECTED MORE RESISTANCE THAN THIS PATHETIC BAND...
"...WHO WERE MERELY FORTUNATE TO HAVE THE SUN AS THEIR ALLY.
"ANOTHER THING YOU WILL TAKE CARE OF SOON, EH, HERR PALMER?

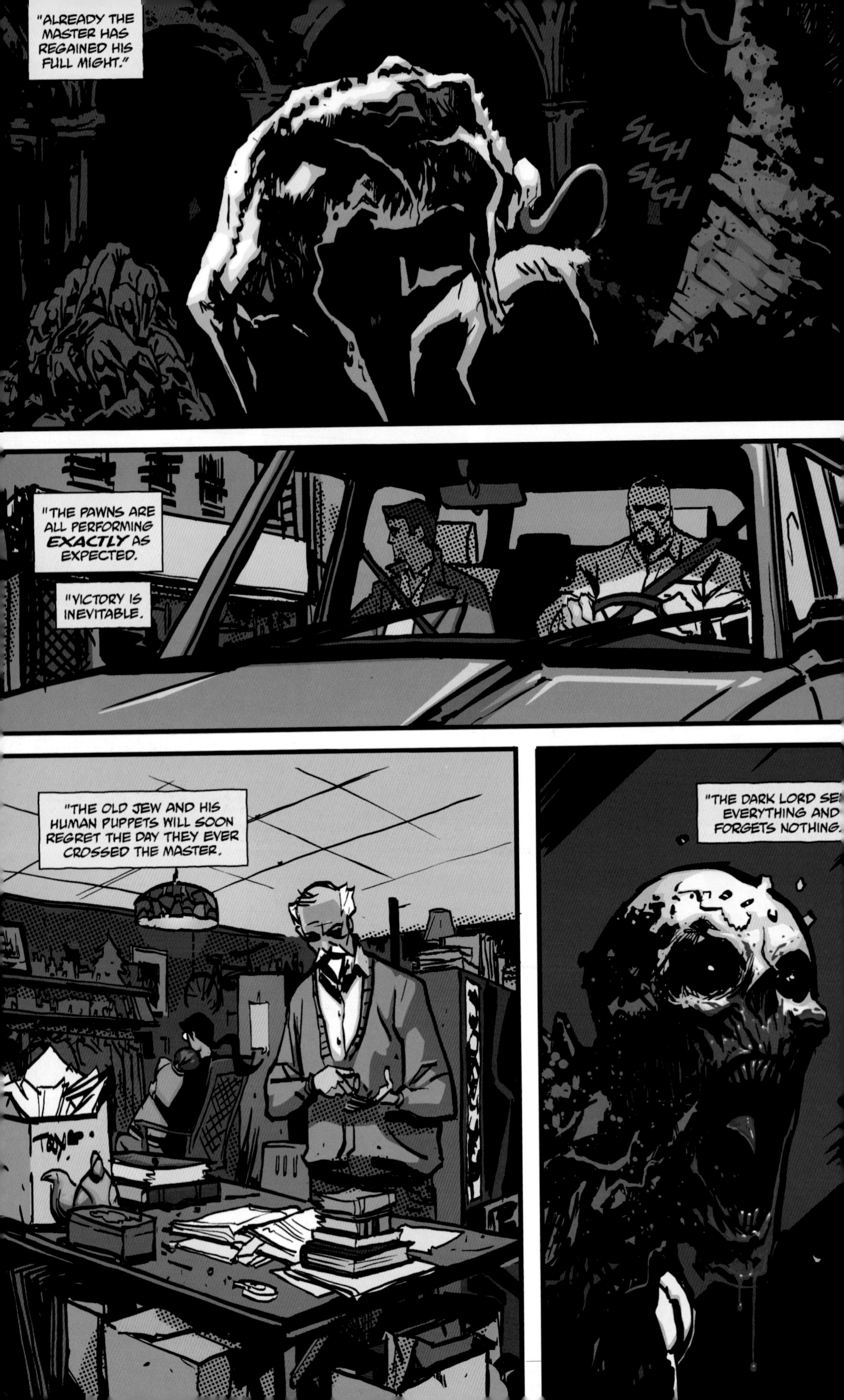
"ALREADY THE MASTER HAS REGAINED HIS FULL MIGHT."
SLCH
SLCH
"THE PAWNS ARE ALL PERFORMING **EXACTLY** AS EXPECTED.
"VICTORY IS INEVITABLE.
"THE OLD JEW AND HIS HUMAN PUPPETS WILL SOON REGRET THE DAY THEY EVER CROSSED THE MASTER.
"THE DARK LORD SE
EVERYTHING AND
FORGETS NOTHING.

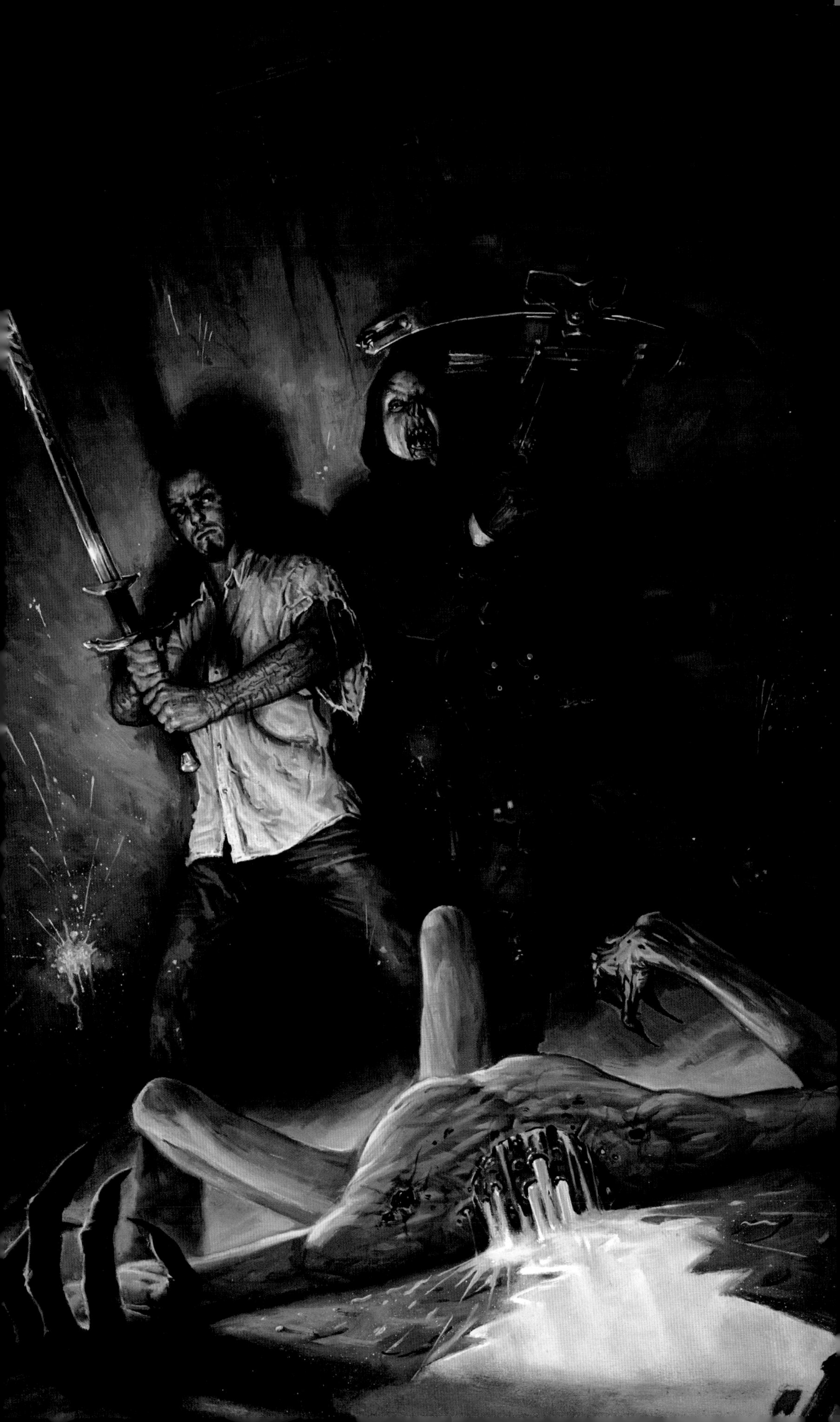

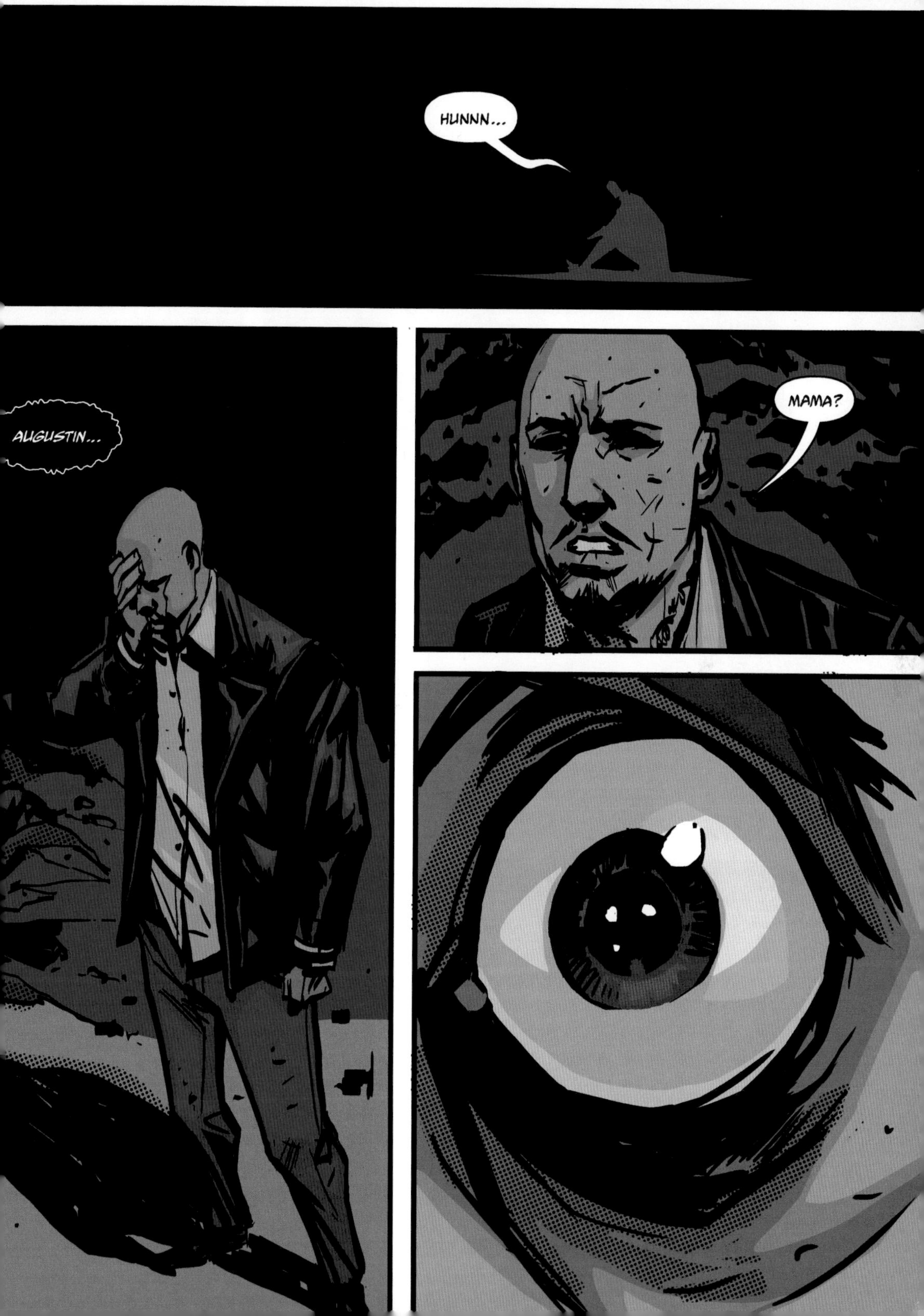
HUNNN...
AUGUSTIN...
MAMA?

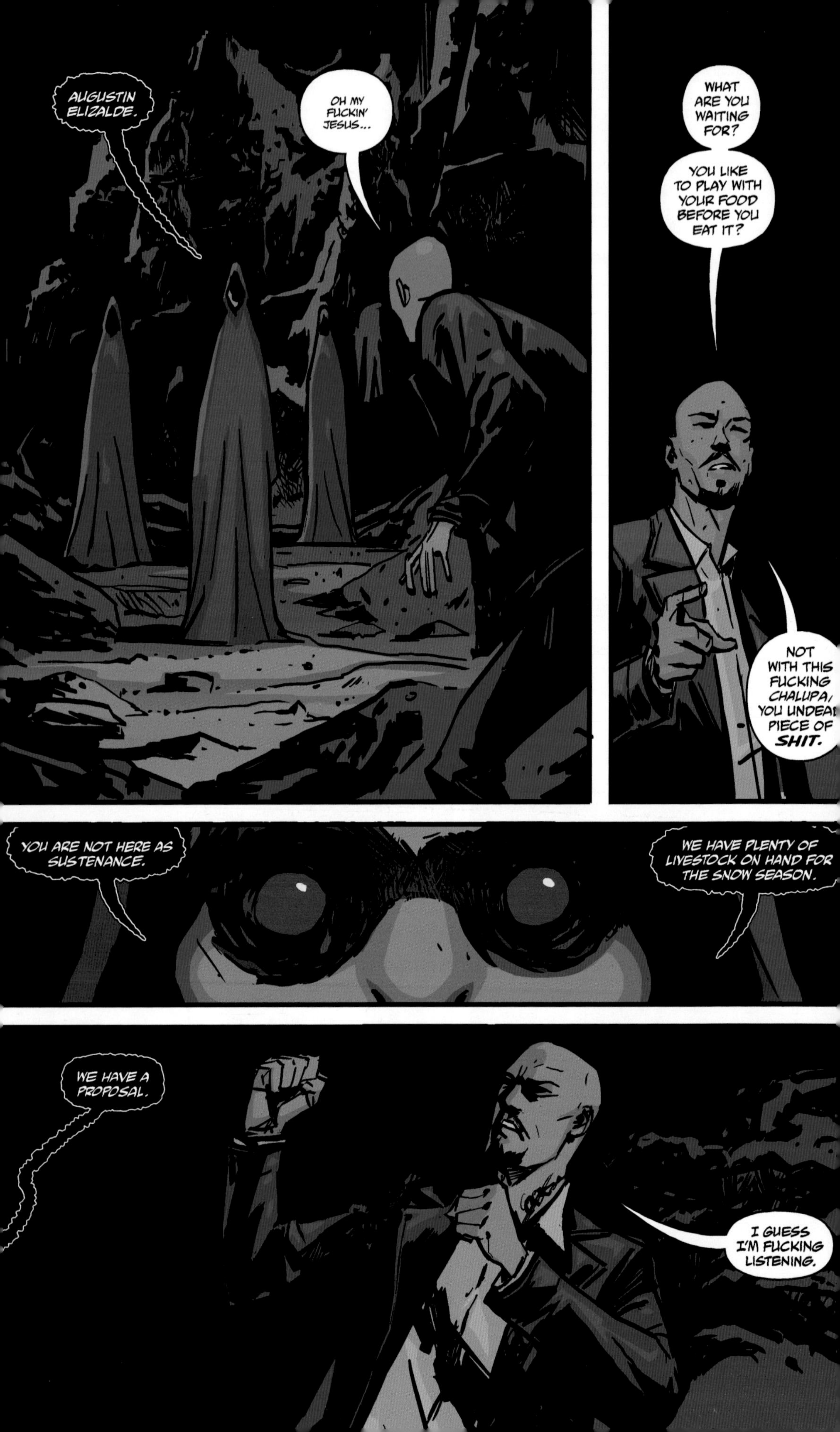
AUGUSTIN ELIZALDE.
OH MY FUCKIN' JESUS...
WHAT ARE YOU WAITING FOR?
YOU LIKE TO PLAY WITH YOUR FOOD BEFORE YOU EAT IT?
NOT WITH THIS FUCKING CHALUPA, YOU UNDEAD PIECE OF SHIT.
YOU ARE NOT HERE AS SUSTENANCE.
WE HAVE PLENTY OF LIVESTOCK ON HAND FOR THE SNOW SEASON.
WE HAVE A PROPOSAL.
I GUESS I'M FUCKING LISTENING.

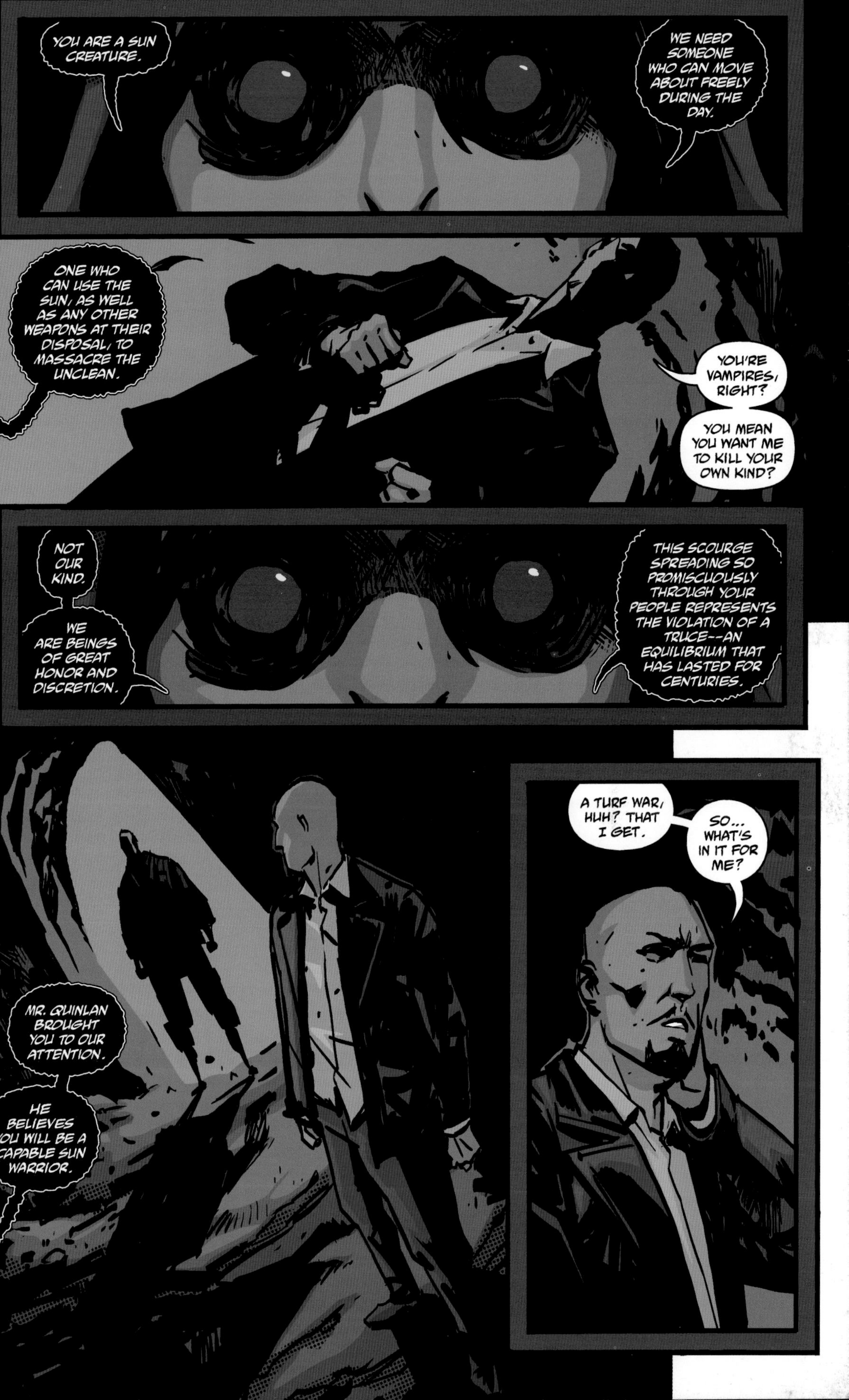
YOU ARE A SUN CREATURE.
WE NEED SOMEONE WHO CAN MOVE ABOUT FREELY DURING THE DAY.
ONE WHO CAN USE THE SUN, AS WELL AS ANY OTHER WEAPONS AT THEIR DISPOSAL, TO MASSACRE THE UNCLEAN.
YOU'RE VAMPIRES, RIGHT?
YOU MEAN YOU WANT ME TO KILL YOUR OWN KIND?
NOT OUR KIND.
WE ARE BEINGS OF GREAT HONOR AND DISCRETION.
THIS SCOURGE SPREADING SO PROMISCUOUSLY THROUGH YOUR PEOPLE REPRESENTS THE VIOLATION OF A TRUCE--AN EQUILIBRIUM THAT HAS LASTED FOR CENTURIES.
MR. QUINLAN BROUGHT YOU TO OUR ATTENTION.
HE BELIEVES YOU WILL BE A CAPABLE SUN WARRIOR.
A TURF WAR, HUH? THAT I GET.
SO... WHAT'S IN IT FOR ME?

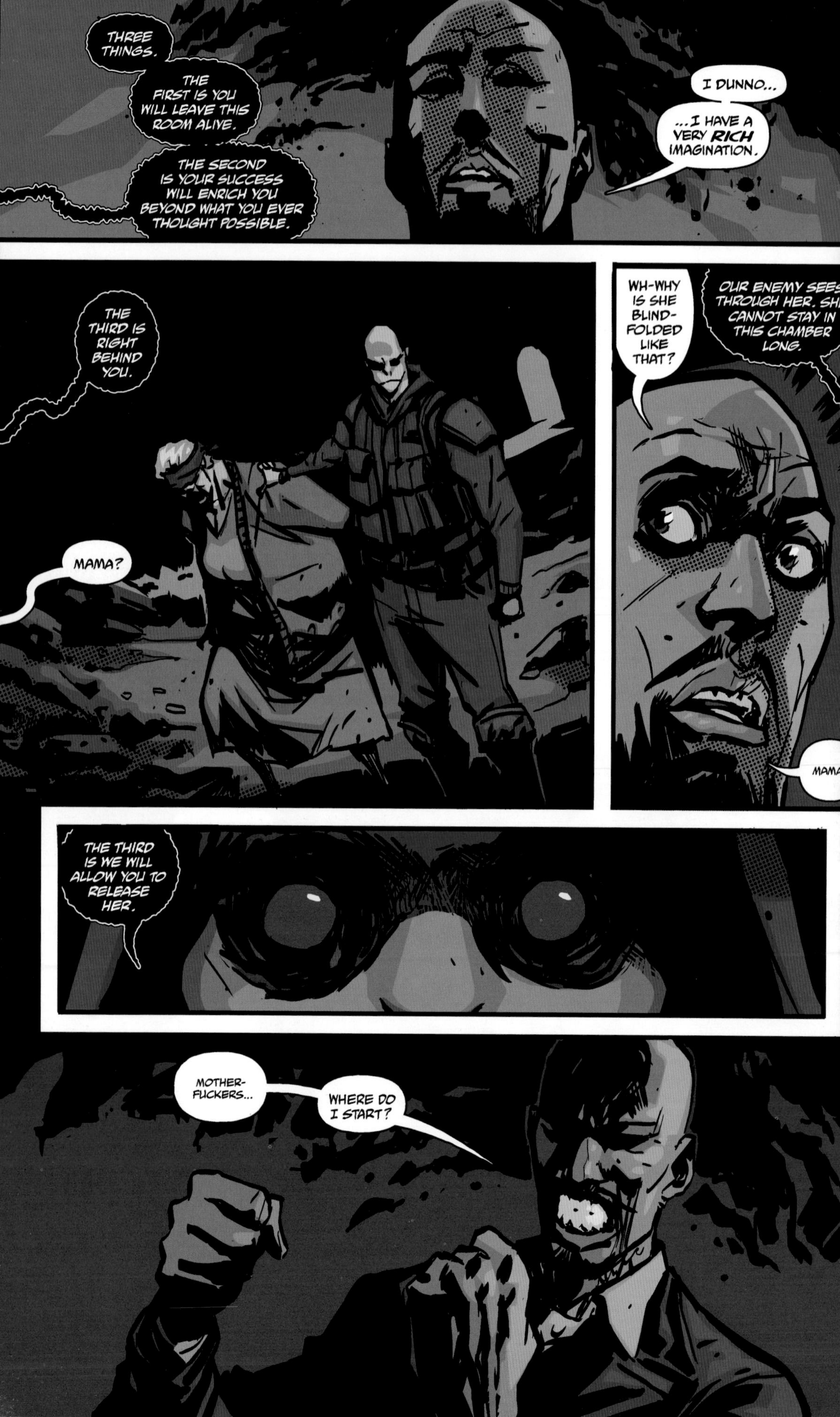
THREE THINGS.
THE FIRST IS YOU WILL LEAVE THIS ROOM ALIVE.
THE SECOND IS YOUR SUCCESS WILL ENRICH YOU BEYOND WHAT YOU EVER THOUGHT POSSIBLE.
I DUNNO...
...I HAVE A VERY RICH IMAGINATION.
THE THIRD IS RIGHT BEHIND YOU.
MAMA?
WH-WHY IS SHE BLIND-FOLDED LIKE THAT?
OUR ENEMY SEES THROUGH HER. SHE CANNOT STAY IN THIS CHAMBER LONG.
MAMA
THE THIRD IS WE WILL ALLOW YOU TO RELEASE HER.
MOTHER-FUCKERS...
WHERE DO I START?

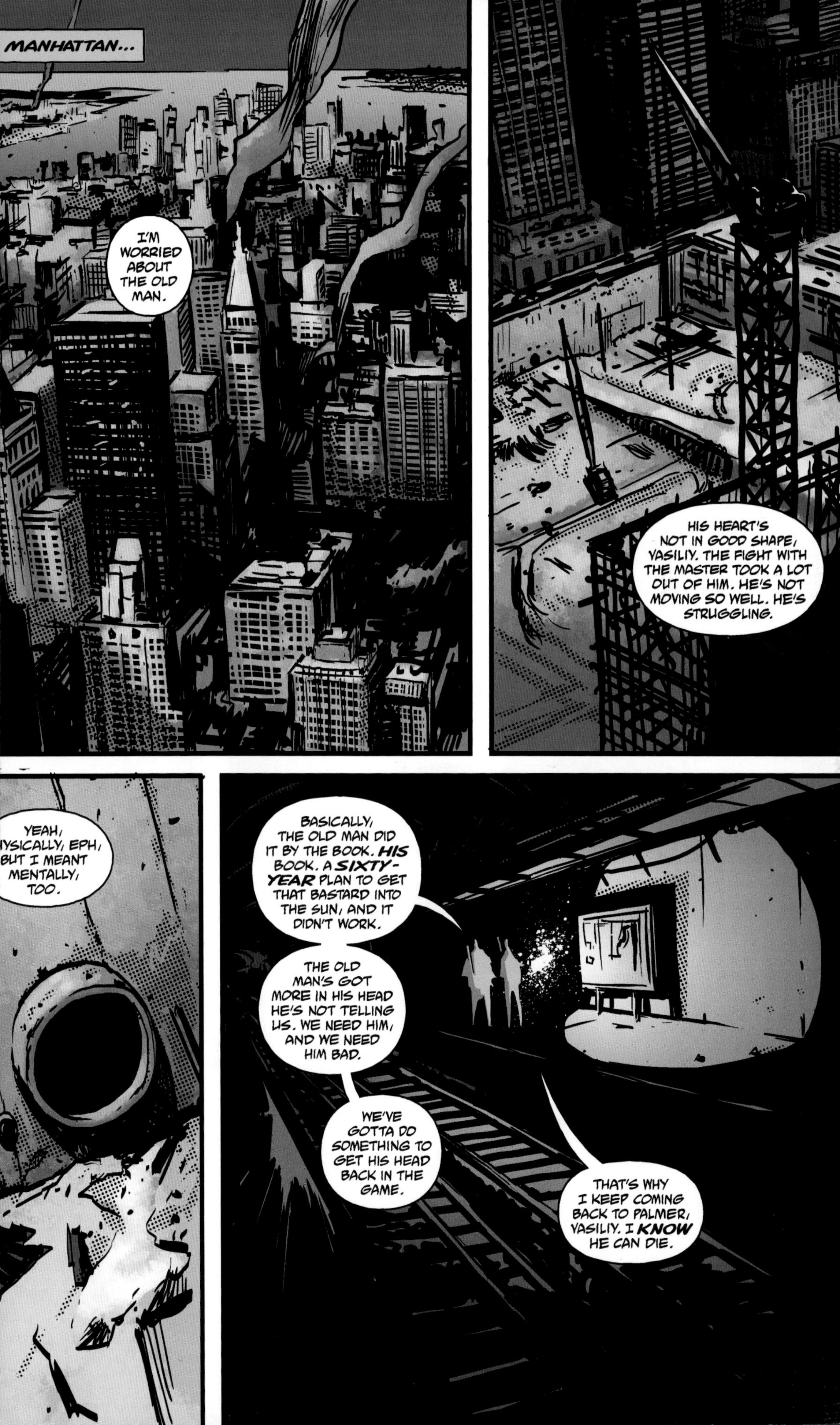
MANHATTAN...
I'M WORRIED ABOUT THE OLD MAN.
HIS HEART'S NOT IN GOOD SHAPE, VASILIY. THE FIGHT WITH THE MASTER TOOK A LOT OUT OF HIM. HE'S NOT MOVING SO WELL. HE'S STRUGGLING.
YEAH, YSICALLY, EPH, BUT I MEANT MENTALLY, TOO.
BASICALLY, THE OLD MAN DID IT BY THE BOOK. **HIS** BOOK. A ***SIXTY-YEAR*** PLAN TO GET THAT BASTARD INTO THE SUN, AND IT DIDN'T WORK.
THE OLD MAN'S GOT MORE IN HIS HEAD HE'S NOT TELLING US. WE NEED HIM, AND WE NEED HIM BAD.
WE'VE GOTTA DO SOMETHING TO GET HIS HEAD BACK IN THE GAME.
THAT'S WHY I KEEP COMING BACK TO PALMER, VASILIY. I ***KNOW*** HE CAN DIE.

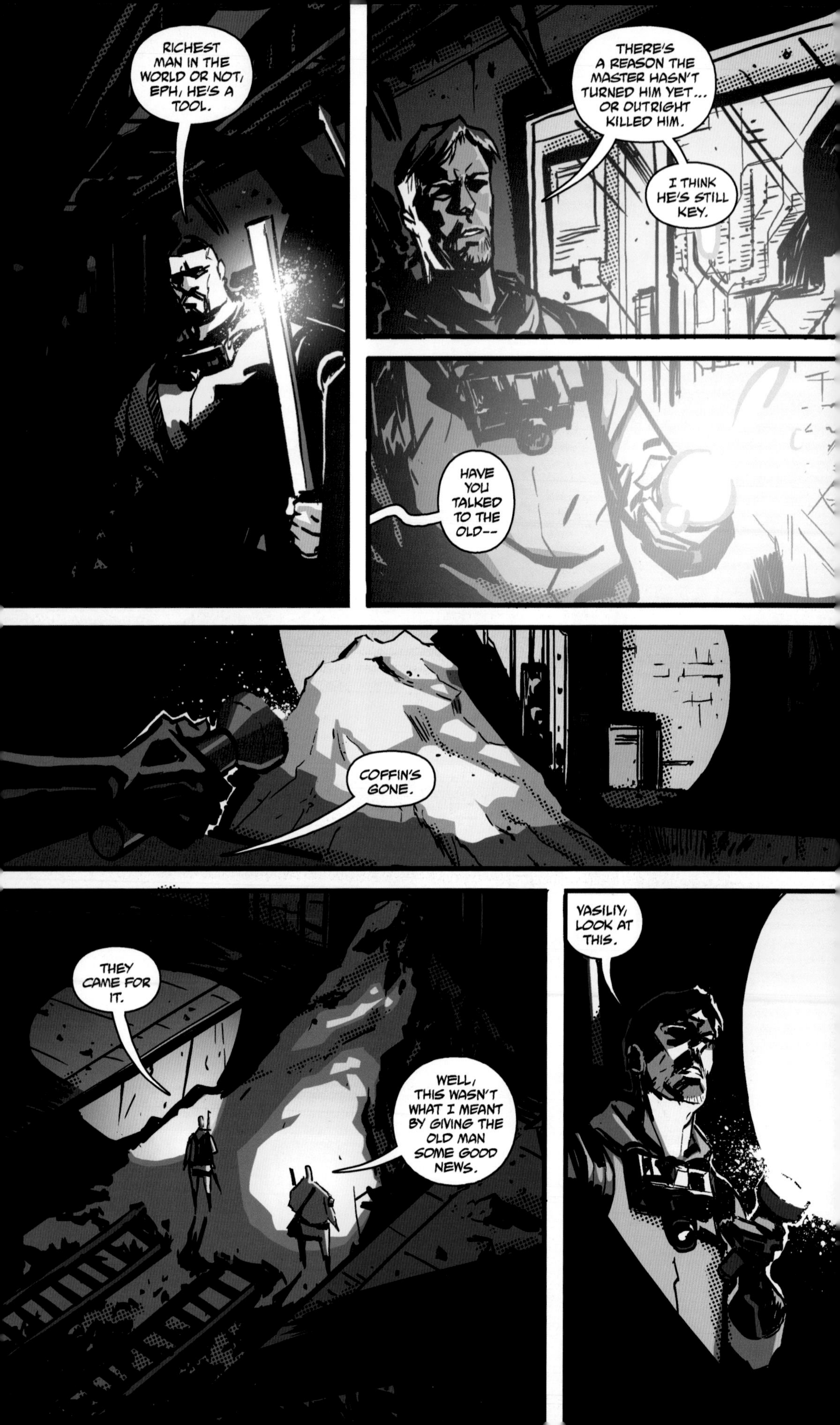
RICHEST MAN IN THE WORLD OR NOT, EPH, HE'S A TOOL.
THERE'S A REASON THE MASTER HASN'T TURNED HIM YET... OR OUTRIGHT KILLED HIM.
I THINK HE'S STILL KEY.
HAVE YOU TALKED TO THE OLD--
COFFIN'S GONE.
THEY CAME FOR IT.
WELL, THIS WASN'T WHAT I MEANT BY GIVING THE OLD MAN SOME GOOD NEWS.
VASILIY, LOOK AT THIS.

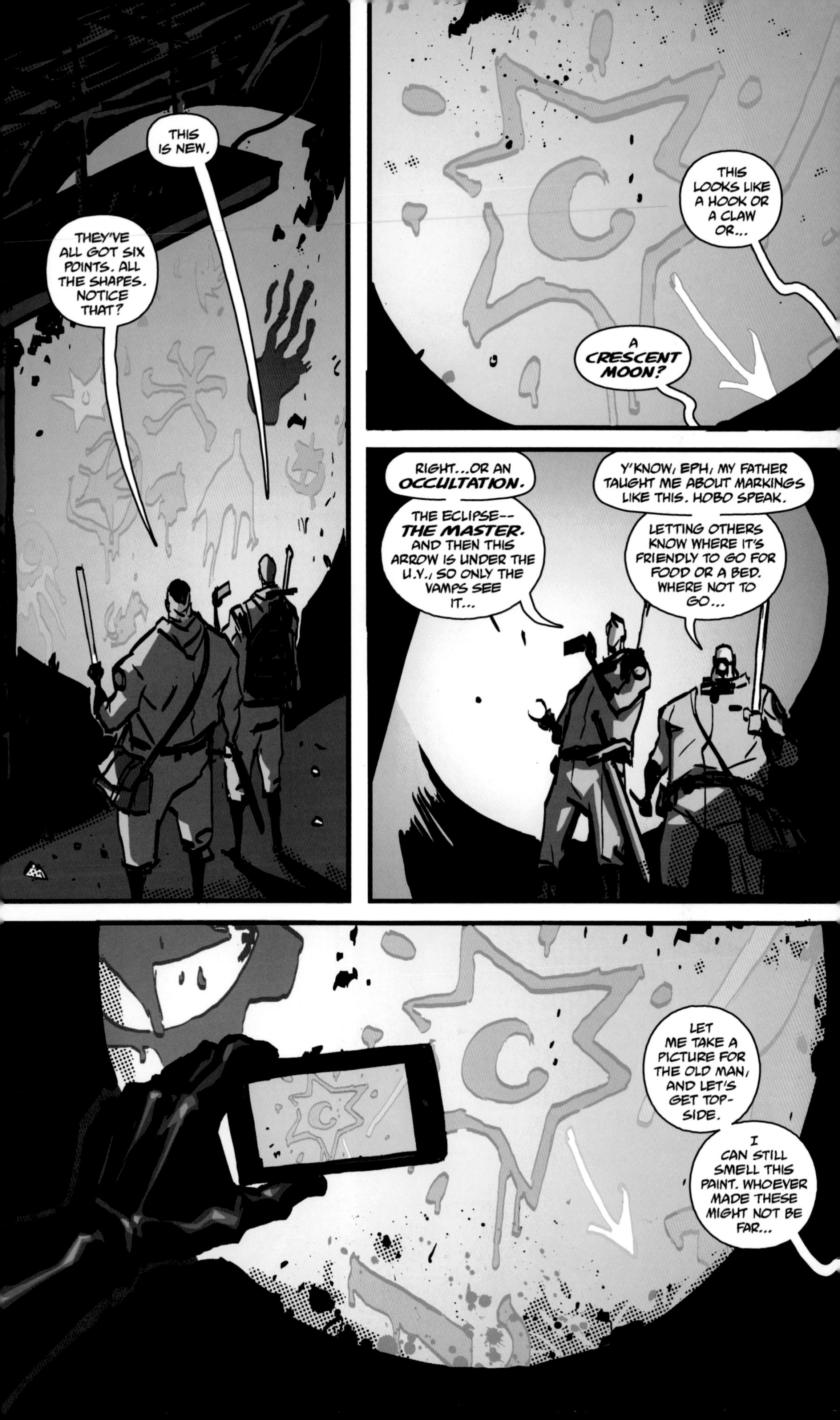
THIS IS NEW.
THEY'VE ALL GOT SIX POINTS. ALL THE SHAPES. NOTICE THAT?
THIS LOOKS LIKE A HOOK OR A CLAW OR...
A CRESCENT MOON?
RIGHT...OR AN OCCULTATION.
THE ECLIPSE-- THE MASTER. AND THEN THIS ARROW IS UNDER THE U.V., SO ONLY THE VAMPS SEE IT...
Y'KNOW, EPH, MY FATHER TAUGHT ME ABOUT MARKINGS LIKE THIS. HOBO SPEAK.
LETTING OTHERS KNOW WHERE IT'S FRIENDLY TO GO FOR FOOD OR A BED. WHERE NOT TO GO...
LET ME TAKE A PICTURE FOR THE OLD MAN, AND LET'S GET TOP-SIDE.
I CAN STILL SMELL THIS PAINT. WHOEVER MADE THESE MIGHT NOT BE FAR...

ARLINGTON PARK,
JERSEY CITY...

THAT HIM,
CREEM?

NOT UNLESS THAT FILTHY MEX HIT THE LOTTERY.

MAYBE HE CALLED THE PARLEY TO BRAG.

COME MORNING I'LL BE BRAGGIN' HOW I KNIFED THE POWER-BALL WINNER, YO.

ALFONSO CREEM. KING OF THE JERSEY SAPPHIRES.

GUS ELIZALDE. KING OF STUPID MOVES.

AM I SUPPOSED TO BE IMPRESSED 'CUZ YOU GOT SOME MONEY IN YOUR POCKET, PUTO?

I GOT A SHITLOAD OF MONEY IN MY POCKET, AND I'M LOOKIN' TO SPREAD THE WEALTH.

HEH...YO GOT SO BALLS RI IN HERE WITH TH THING

MAYBE I BLEED YOU AND TA YOUR POCKE AND YOUR RIDE.

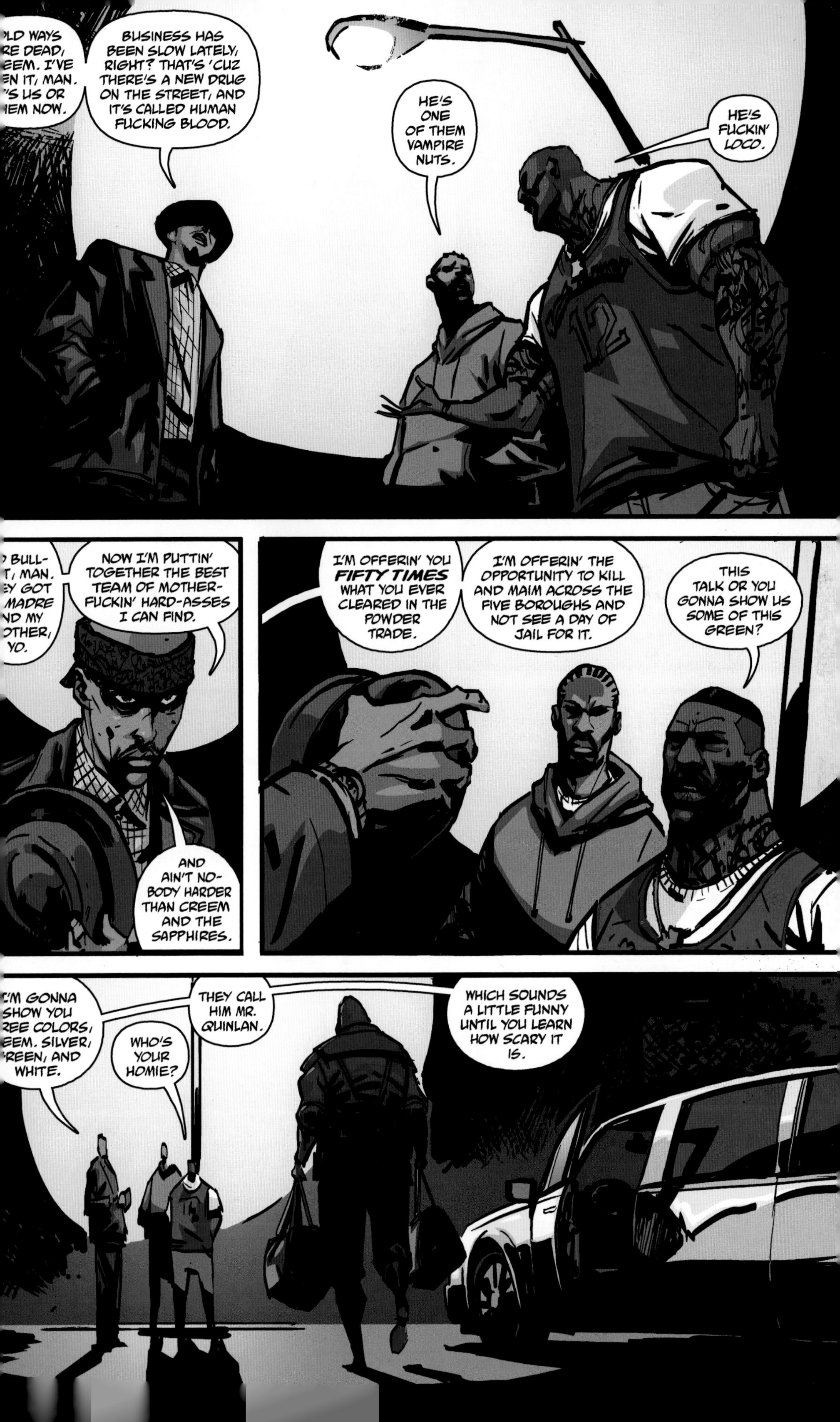

OLD WAYS ARE DEAD, CREEM. I'VE SEEN IT, MAN. IT'S US OR THEM NOW.
BUSINESS HAS BEEN SLOW LATELY, RIGHT? THAT'S 'CUZ THERE'S A NEW DRUG ON THE STREET, AND IT'S CALLED HUMAN FUCKING BLOOD.
HE'S ONE OF THEM VAMPIRE NUTS.
HE'S FUCKIN' LOCO.
BULL- T, MAN. EY GOT MADRE ND MY OTHER, YO.
NOW I'M PUTTIN' TOGETHER THE BEST TEAM OF MOTHER-FUCKIN' HARD-ASSES I CAN FIND.
AND AIN'T NO-BODY HARDER THAN CREEM AND THE SAPPHIRES.
I'M OFFERIN' YOU FIFTY TIMES WHAT YOU EVER CLEARED IN THE POWDER TRADE.
I'M OFFERIN' THE OPPORTUNITY TO KILL AND MAIM ACROSS THE FIVE BOROUGHS AND NOT SEE A DAY OF JAIL FOR IT.
THIS TALK OR YOU GONNA SHOW US SOME OF THIS GREEN?
I'M GONNA SHOW YOU REE COLORS, EEM. SILVER, REEN, AND WHITE.
WHO'S YOUR HOMIE?
THEY CALL HIM MR. QUINLAN.
WHICH SOUNDS A LITTLE FUNNY UNTIL YOU LEARN HOW SCARY IT IS.

GREEN, AND HERE'S YOUR SILVER.

YOU LIKE SILVER, DON'T YOU, CREEM?

IT'S SHOWTIME, MR. QUINLAN.

JESUS. FUCK.

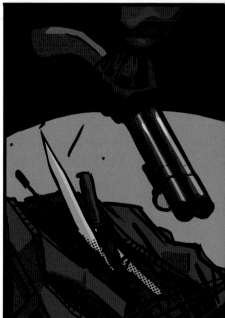

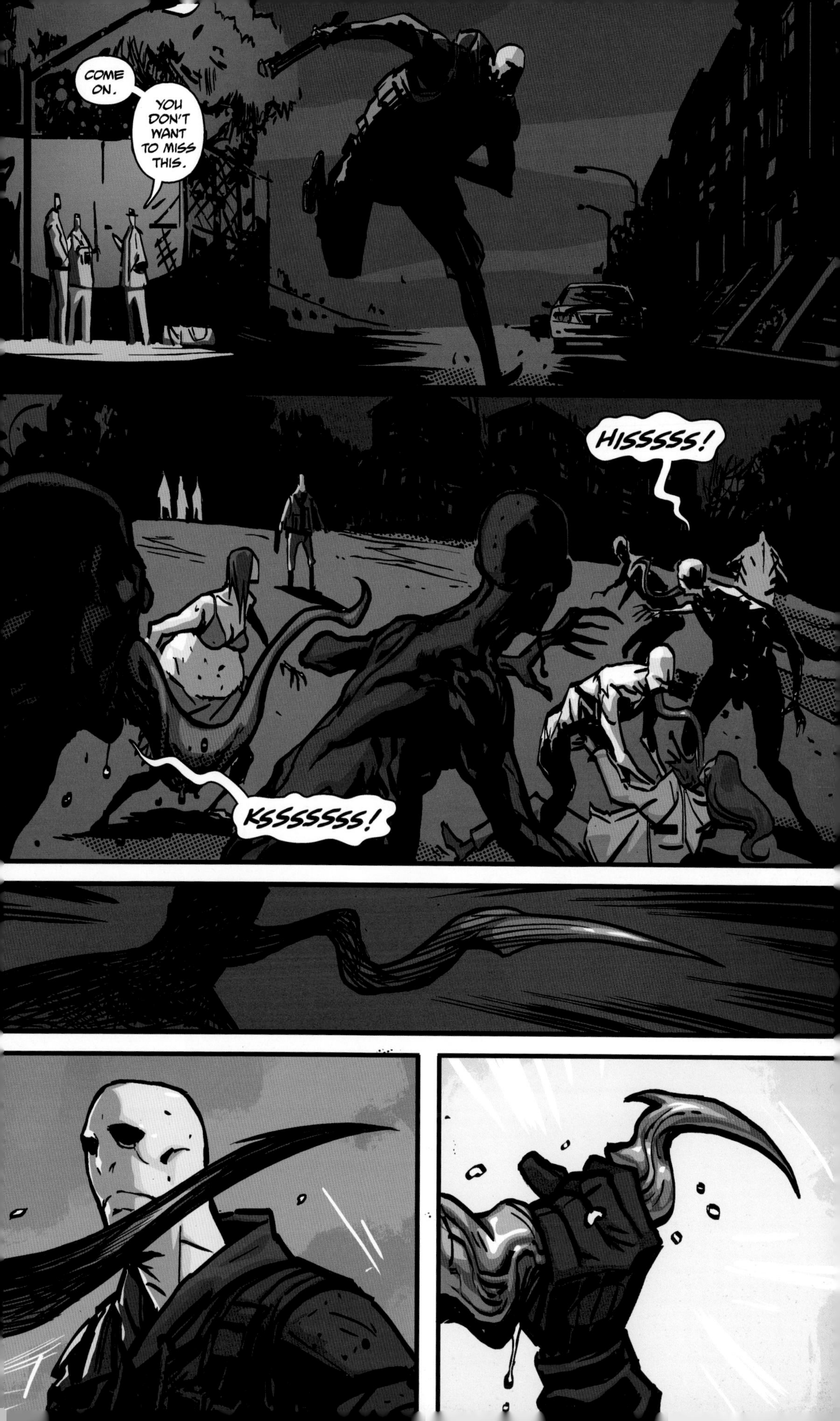
COME ON.
YOU DON'T WANT TO MISS THIS.
HISSSSS!
KSSSSSSS!

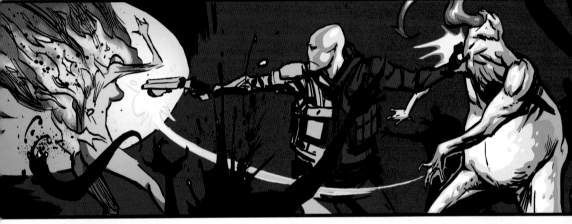

AND THERE'S YOUR WHITE, BRO.

FUCK ME...

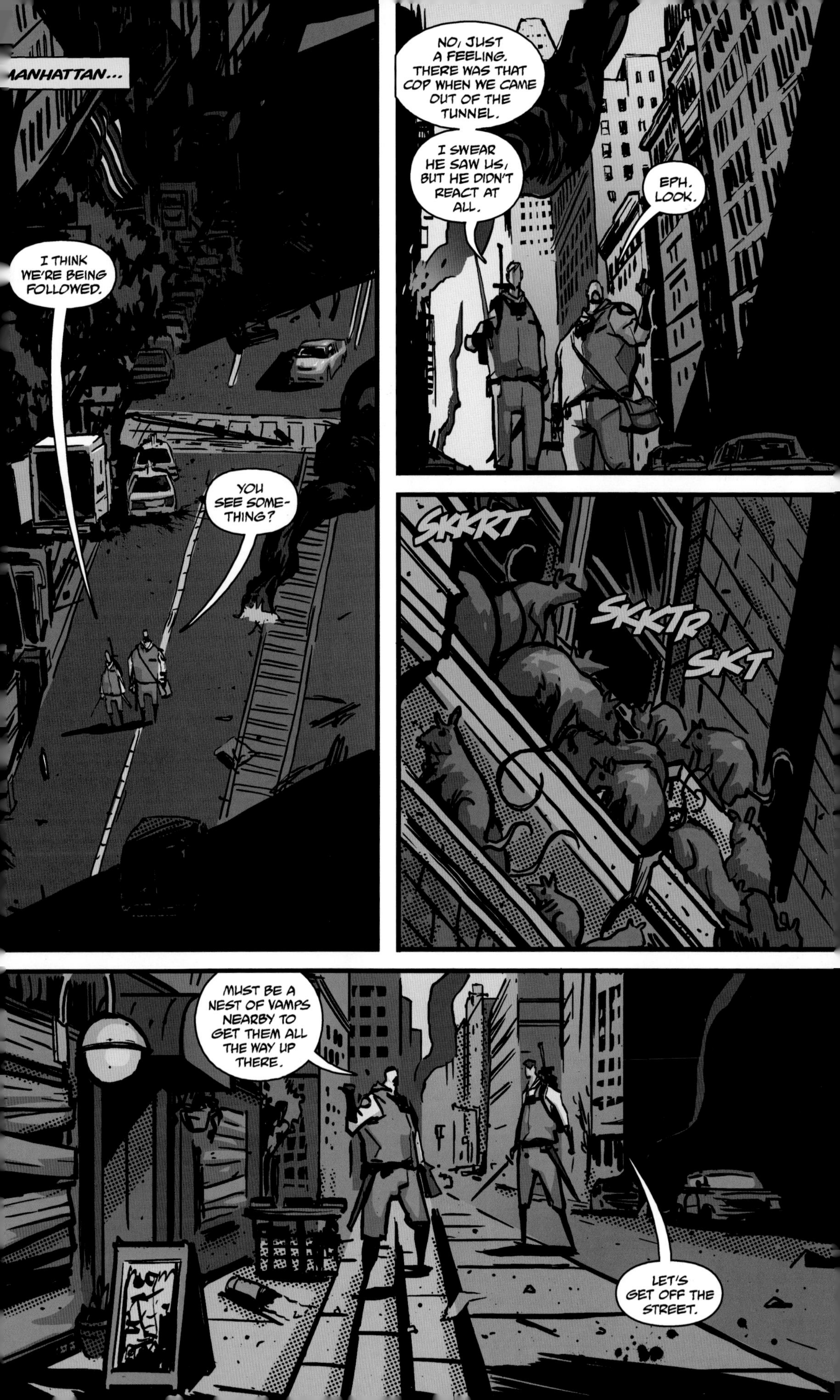
MANHATTAN...
I THINK WE'RE BEING FOLLOWED.
YOU SEE SOME-THING?
NO, JUST A FEELING. THERE WAS THAT COP WHEN WE CAME OUT OF THE TUNNEL.
I SWEAR HE SAW US, BUT HE DIDN'T REACT AT ALL.
EPH. LOOK.
SKKRT
SKKTR
SKT
MUST BE A NEST OF VAMPS NEARBY TO GET THEM ALL THE WAY UP THERE.
LET'S GET OFF THE STREET.

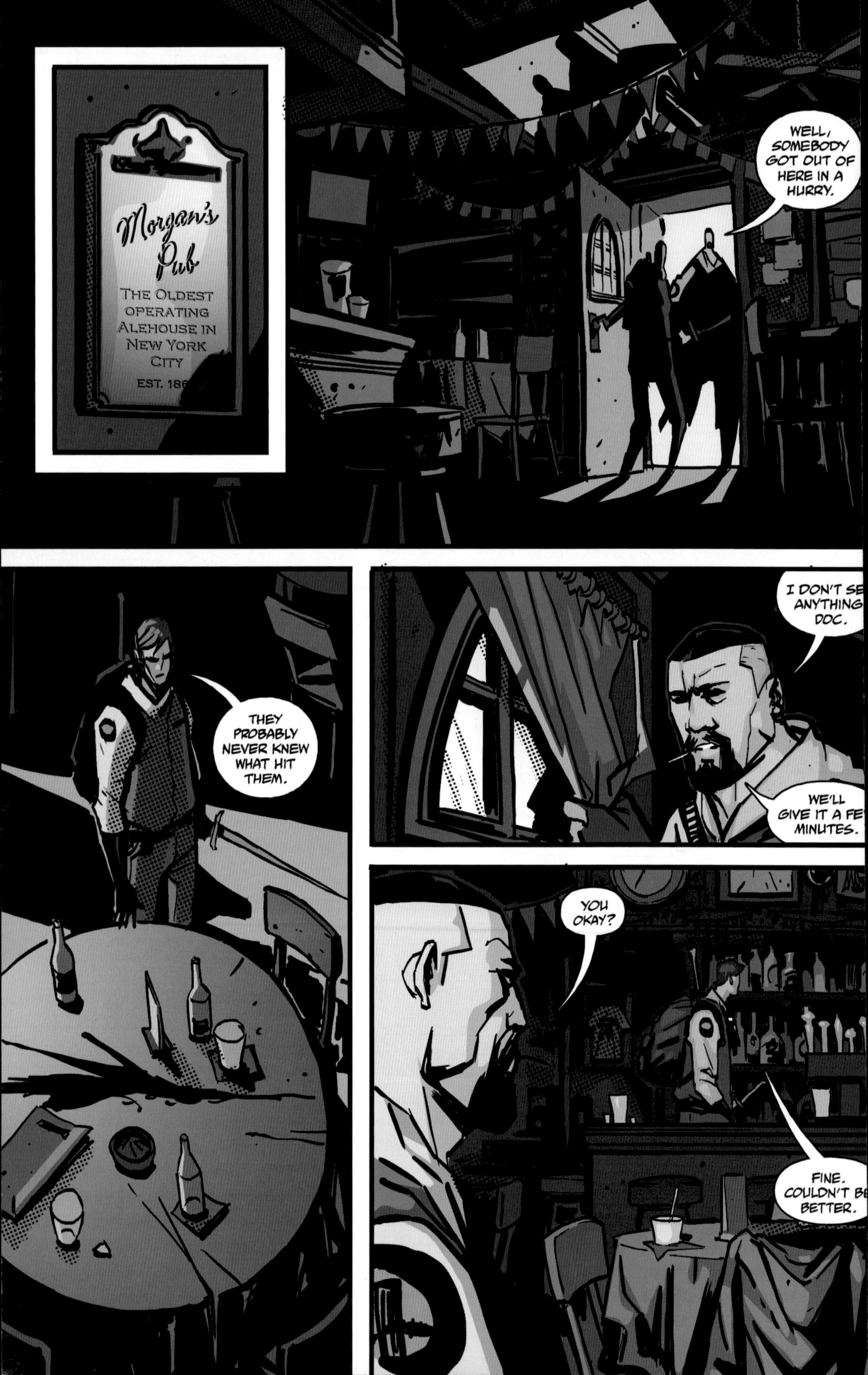
Morgan's Pub
THE OLDEST OPERATING ALEHOUSE IN NEW YORK CITY
EST. 186
WELL, SOMEBODY GOT OUT OF HERE IN A HURRY.
THEY PROBABLY NEVER KNEW WHAT HIT THEM.
I DON'T SE ANYTHING DOC.
WE'LL GIVE IT A FE MINUTES.
YOU OKAY?
FINE. COULDN'T B BETTER.

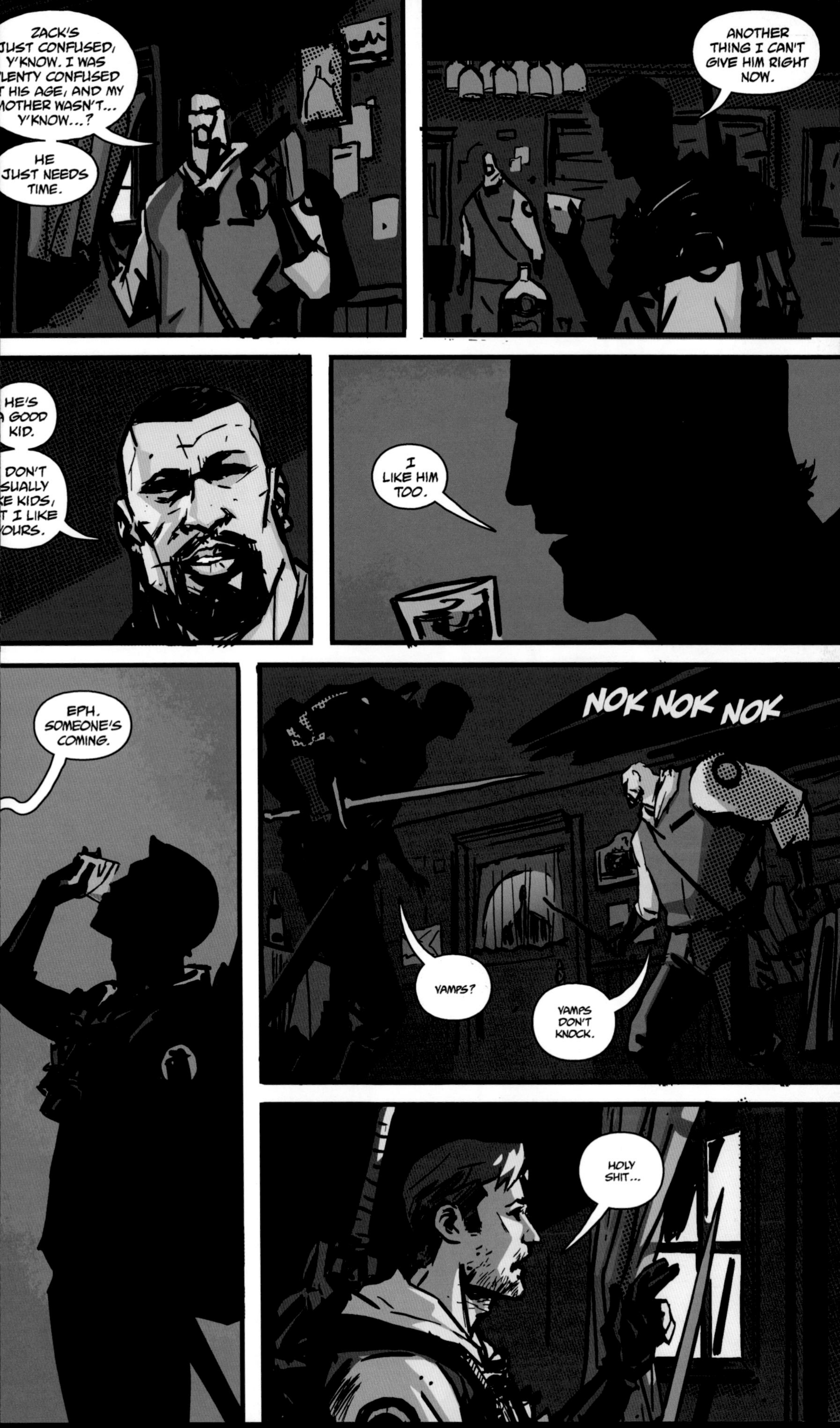
ZACK'S JUST CONFUSED, Y'KNOW. I WAS PLENTY CONFUSED AT HIS AGE, AND MY MOTHER WASN'T... Y'KNOW...?
HE JUST NEEDS TIME.
ANOTHER THING I CAN'T GIVE HIM RIGHT NOW.
HE'S A GOOD KID.
I DON'T USUALLY LIKE KIDS, BUT I LIKE YOURS.
I LIKE HIM TOO.
EPH. SOMEONE'S COMING.
NOK NOK NOK
VAMPS?
VAMPS DON'T KNOCK.
HOLY SHIT...

EPHRAIM?

YOU!

HOW MANY ARE WITH YOU, EVERETT?

THEY ARE ON ORDERS TO STAY WELL BACK.

BUT MAKE NO MISTAKE ABOUT IT, THE AUTHORITIES WILL BE HERE IN A FEW MINUTES, AND WITH FORCE IF I DON'T COME BACK OUT UNHARMED.

I INSISTED I NEEDED FEW MINUT ALONE WI YOU.

JESUS.

WHO IS THIS GUY?

HE'S DR. EVERETT BARNES. DIRECTOR OF THE CENTERS FOR DISEASE CONTROL. MY FORMER BOSS.

EPHRAIM, I STAND BEFORE YOU AS A MAN ADMITTING HIS MISTAKE.

I KNOW NOW THAT WE ARE IN THE GRIP OF SOMETHING ALTOGETHER DEVASTATING AND OTHER-WORLDLY.

I NEED YOU TO COME IN. WE NEED YOUR EXPERTISE.

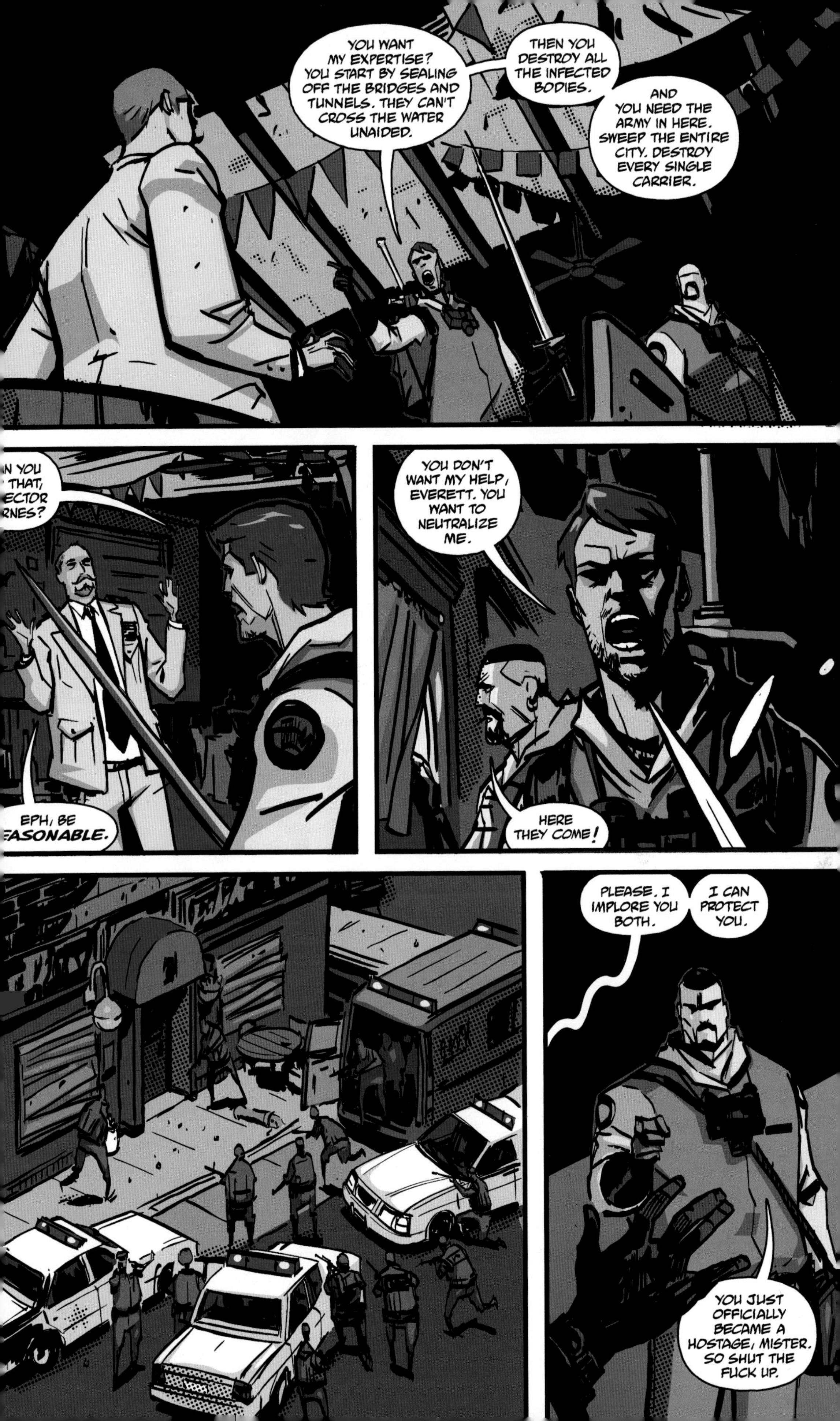
YOU WANT MY EXPERTISE? YOU START BY SEALING OFF THE BRIDGES AND TUNNELS. THEY CAN'T CROSS THE WATER UNAIDED.
THEN YOU DESTROY ALL THE INFECTED BODIES.
AND YOU NEED THE ARMY IN HERE. SWEEP THE ENTIRE CITY. DESTROY EVERY SINGLE CARRIER.
N YOU THAT, ECTOR RNES?
EPH, BE EASONABLE.
YOU DON'T WANT MY HELP, EVERETT. YOU WANT TO NEUTRALIZE ME.
HERE THEY COME!
PLEASE. I IMPLORE YOU BOTH.
I CAN PROTECT YOU.
YOU JUST OFFICIALLY BECAME A HOSTAGE, MISTER. SO SHUT THE FUCK UP.

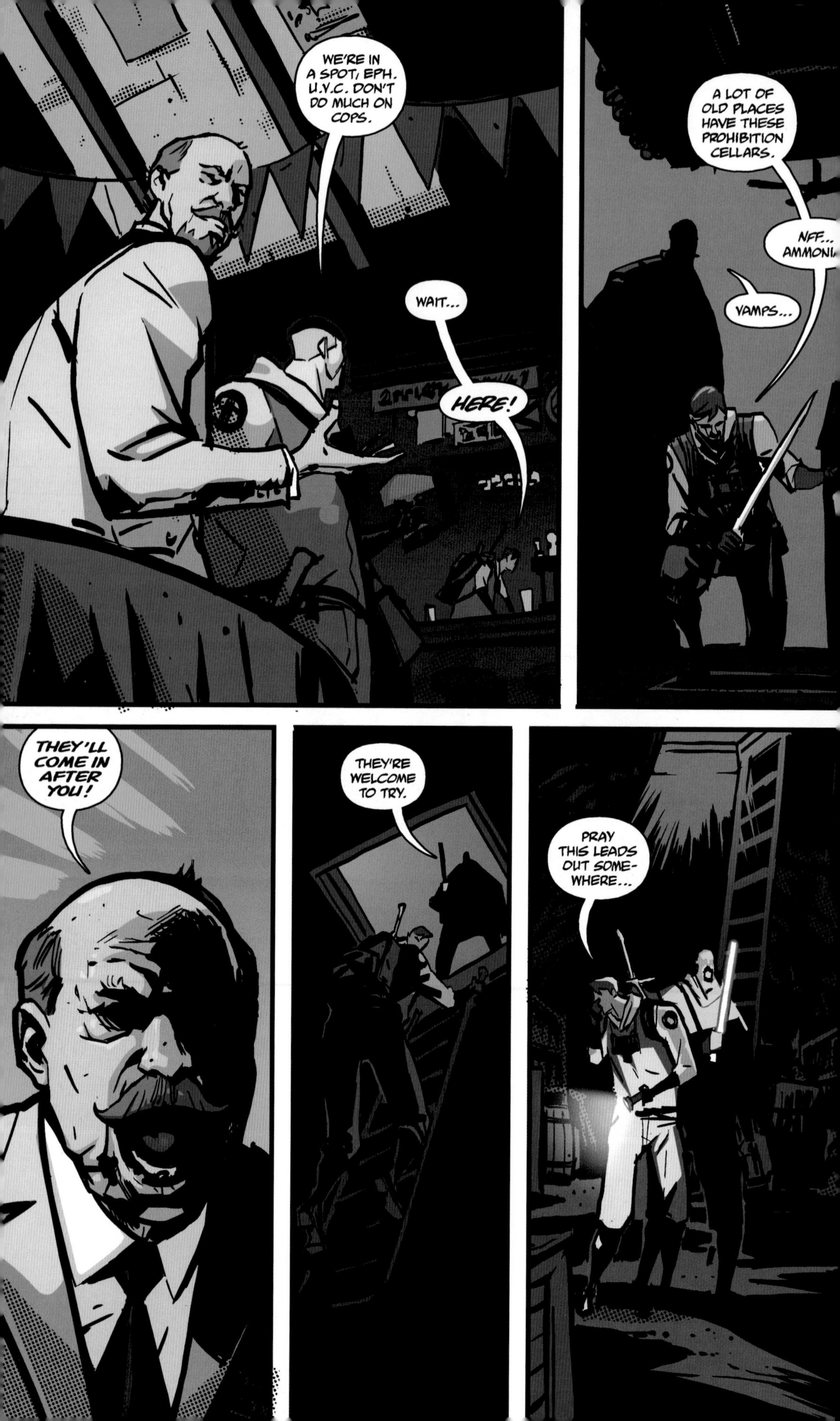
WE'RE IN A SPOT, EPH. U.Y.C. DON'T DO MUCH ON COPS.
WAIT...
HERE!
A LOT OF OLD PLACES HAVE THESE PROHIBITION CELLARS.
NFF... AMMONI
VAMPS...
THEY'LL COME IN AFTER YOU!
THEY'RE WELCOME TO TRY.
PRAY THIS LEADS OUT SOME-WHERE...

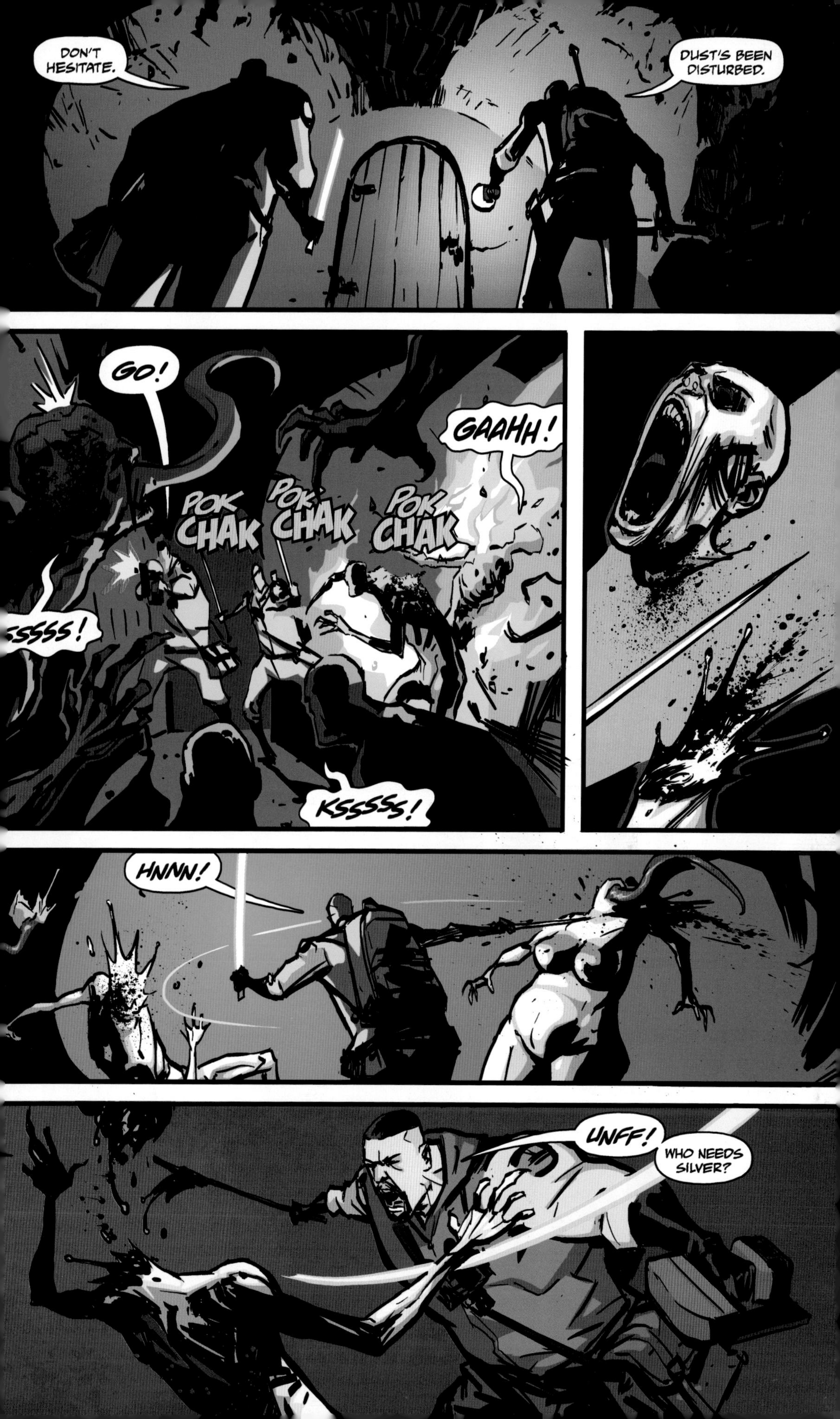

DON'T HESITATE.
DUST'S BEEN DISTURBED.
GO!
POK CHAK
POK CHAK
POK CHAK
GAAHH!
SSSSS!
KSSSSS!
HNNN!
UNFF!
WHO NEEDS SILVER?

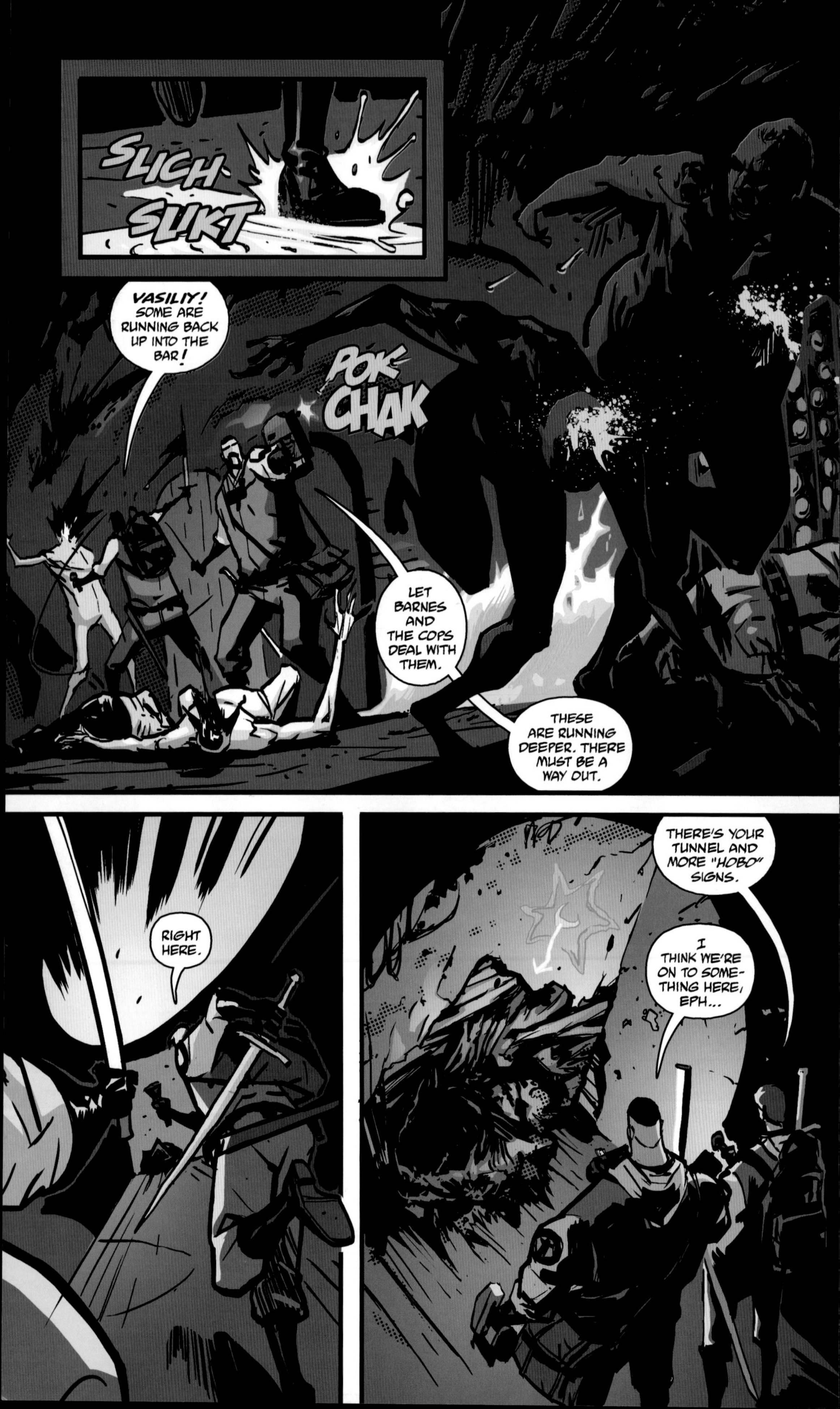
SLICH
SLIKT
VASILIY! SOME ARE RUNNING BACK UP INTO THE BAR!
POK
CHAK
LET BARNES AND THE COPS DEAL WITH THEM.
THESE ARE RUNNING DEEPER. THERE MUST BE A WAY OUT.
RIGHT HERE.
THERE'S YOUR TUNNEL AND MORE "HOBO" SIGNS.
I THINK WE'RE ON TO SOME-THING HERE, EPH...

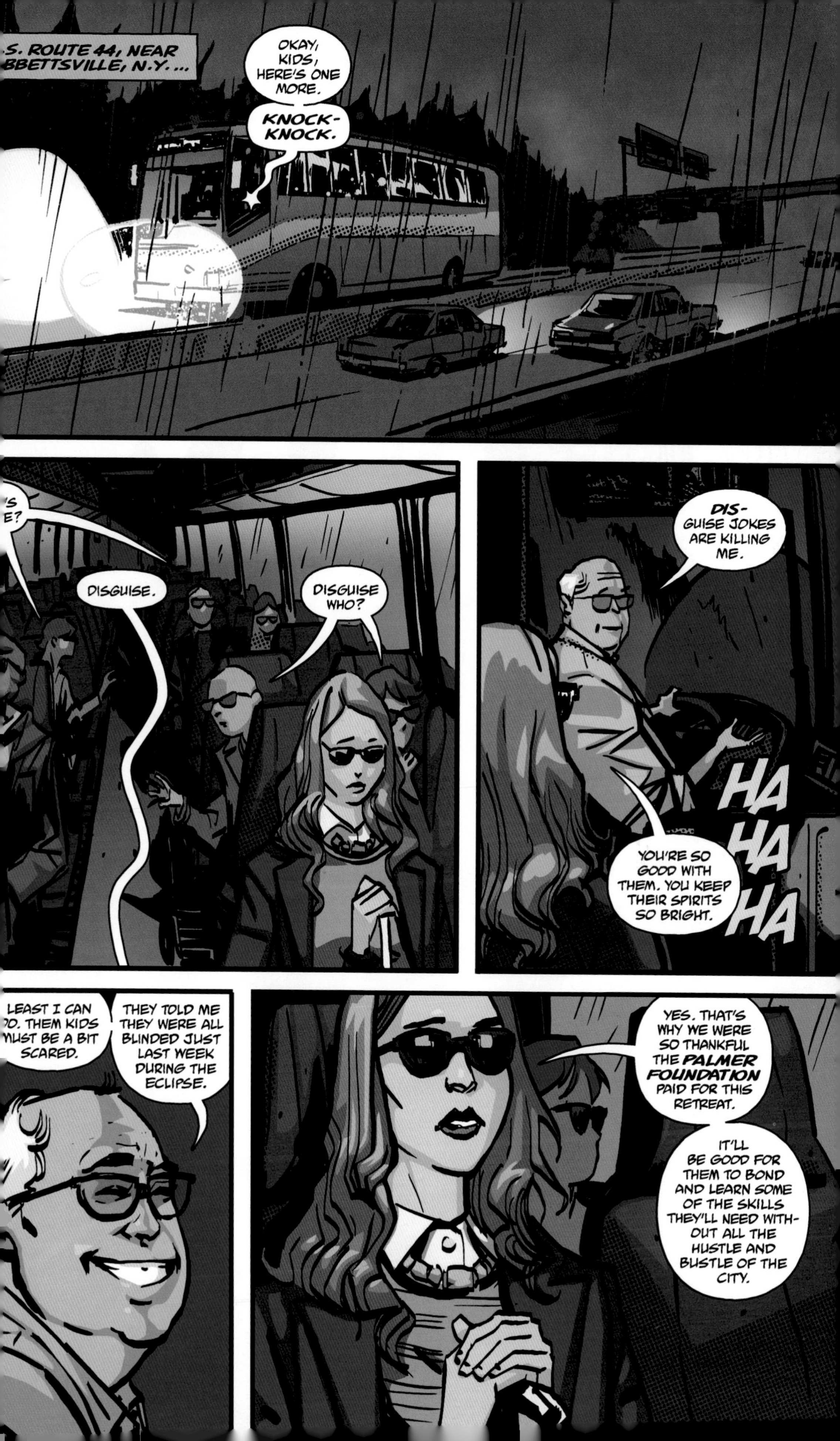
S. ROUTE 44, NEAR
BBETTSVILLE, N.Y. ...
OKAY, KIDS, HERE'S ONE MORE.
KNOCK-KNOCK.
'S
E?
DISGUISE.
DISGUISE WHO?
DIS-GUISE JOKES ARE KILLING ME.
HA HA HA
YOU'RE SO GOOD WITH THEM. YOU KEEP THEIR SPIRITS SO BRIGHT.
LEAST I CAN
O. THEM KIDS
MUST BE A BIT
SCARED.
THEY TOLD ME THEY WERE ALL BLINDED JUST LAST WEEK DURING THE ECLIPSE.
YES. THAT'S WHY WE WERE SO THANKFUL THE PALMER FOUNDATION PAID FOR THIS RETREAT.
IT'LL BE GOOD FOR THEM TO BOND AND LEARN SOME OF THE SKILLS THEY'LL NEED WITH-OUT ALL THE HUSTLE AND BUSTLE OF THE CITY.

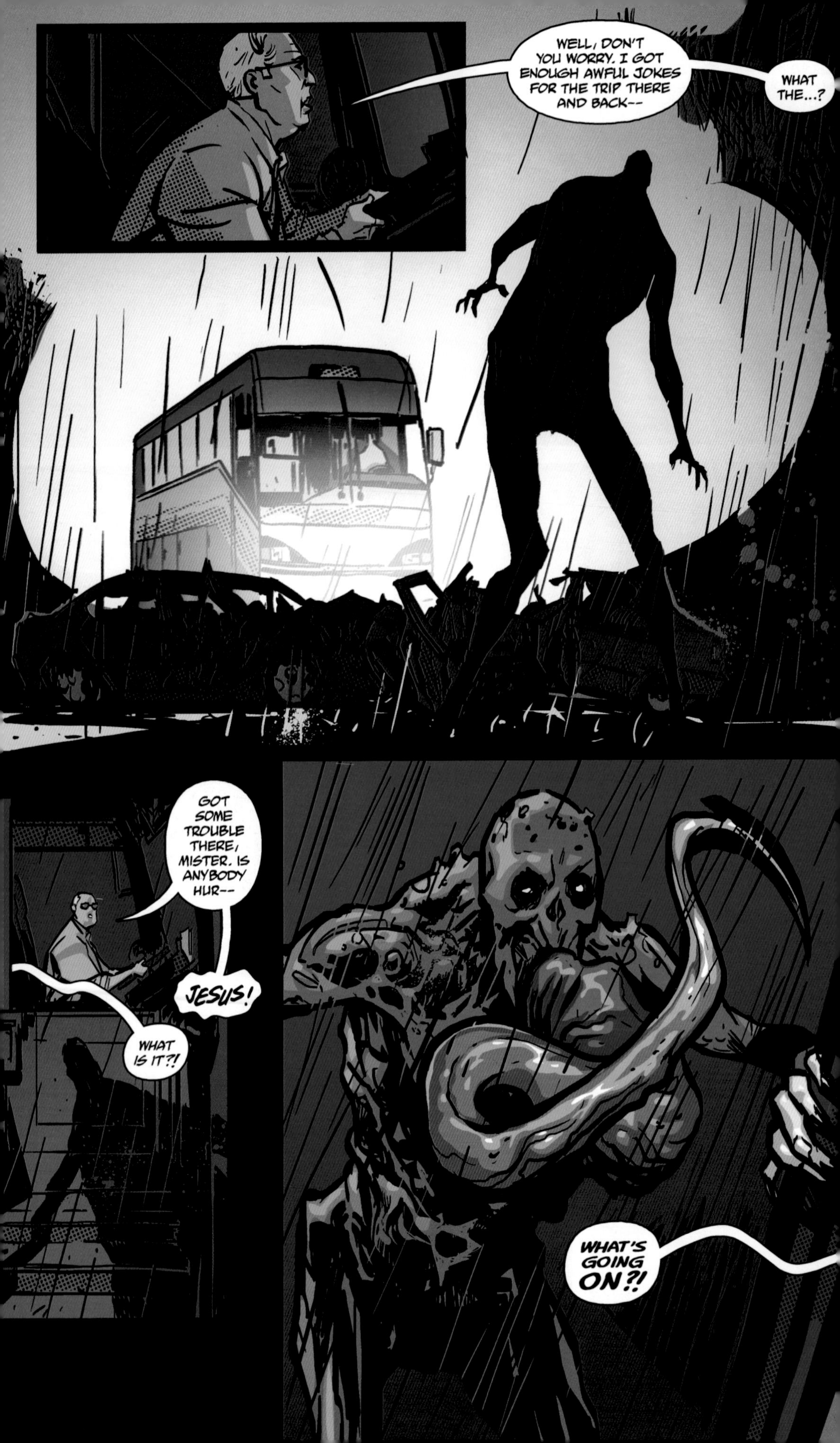
WELL, DON'T YOU WORRY. I GOT ENOUGH AWFUL JOKES FOR THE TRIP THERE AND BACK--
WHAT THE...?
GOT SOME TROUBLE THERE, MISTER. IS ANYBODY HUR--
JESUS!
WHAT IS IT?!
WHAT'S GOING ON?!

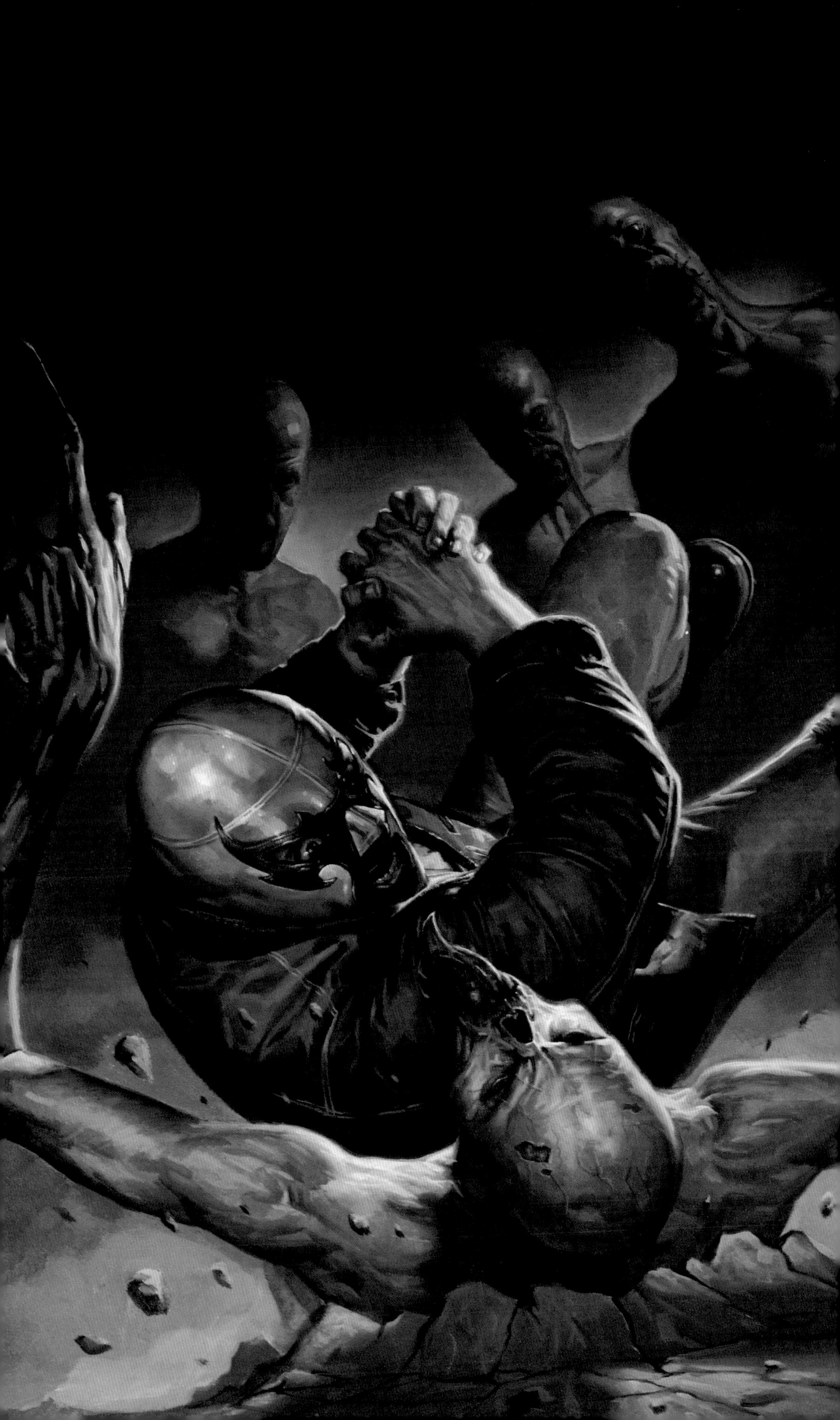

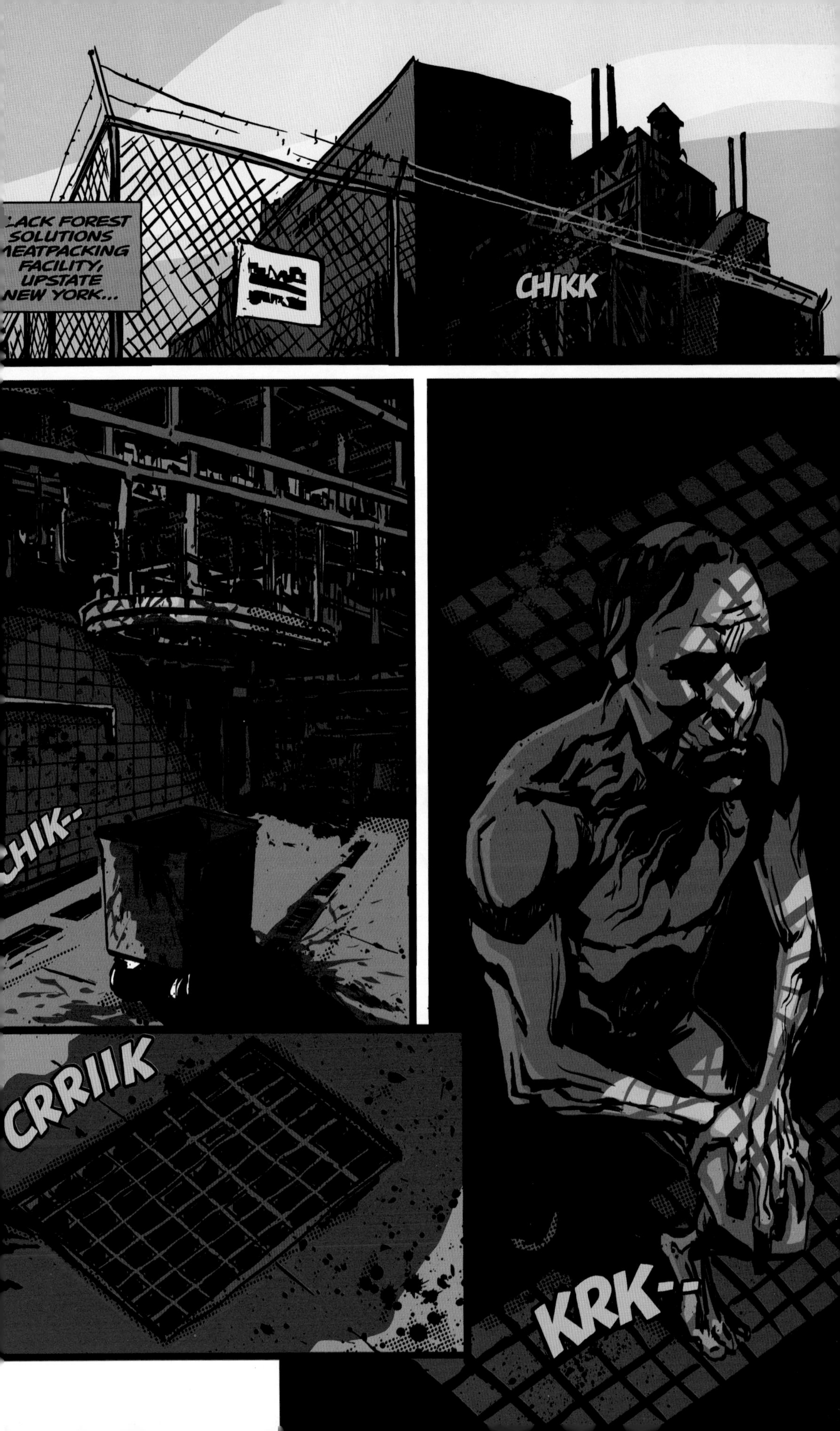
LACK FOREST SOLUTIONS MEATPACKING FACILITY, UPSTATE NEW YORK...
CHIKK
CHIK-
CRRIIK
KRK-

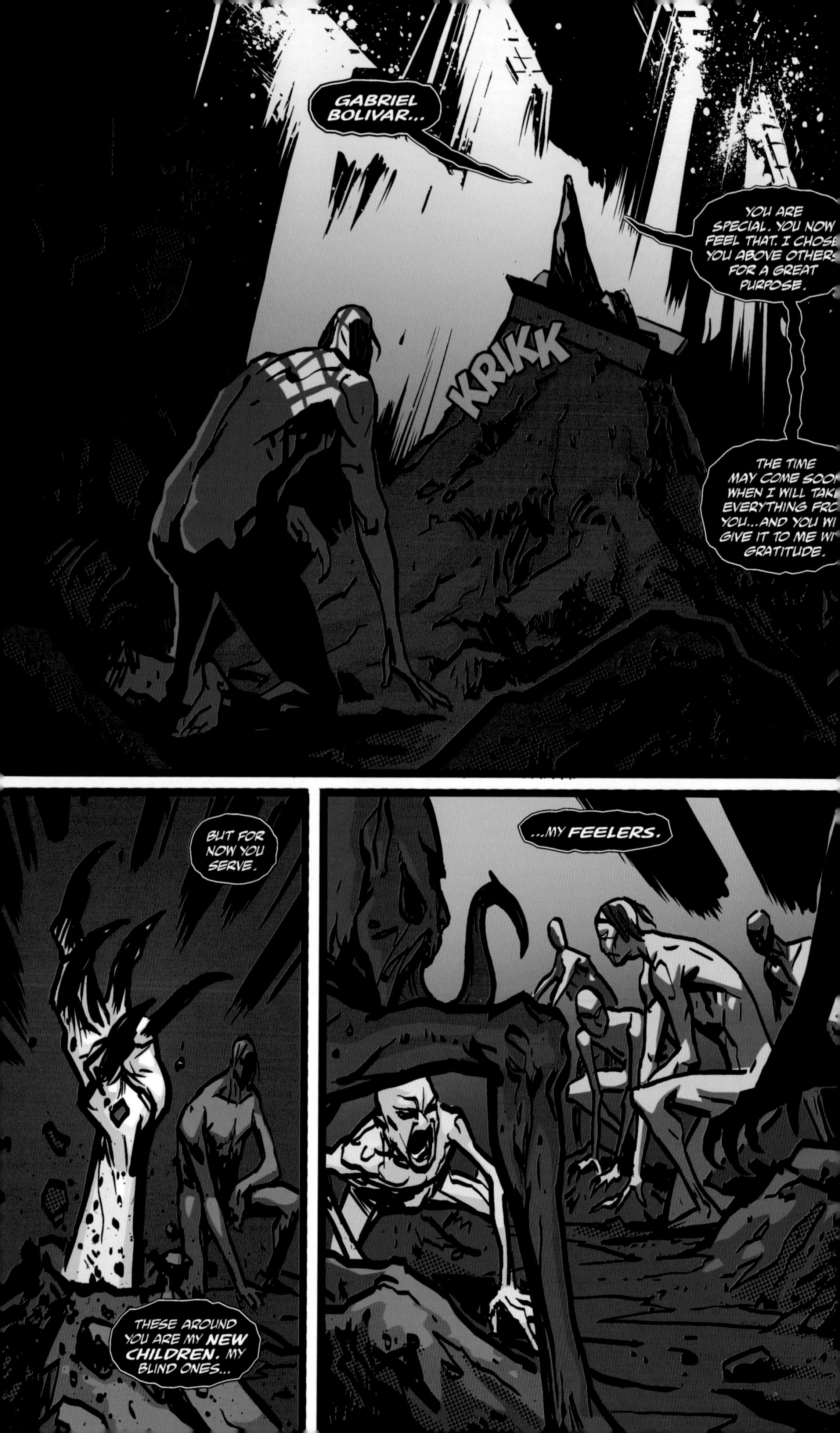
GABRIEL BOLIVAR...
YOU ARE SPECIAL. YOU NOW FEEL THAT. I CHOSE YOU ABOVE OTHERS FOR A GREAT PURPOSE.
KRIKK
THE TIME MAY COME SOO WHEN I WILL TAK EVERYTHING FRO YOU...AND YOU WI GIVE IT TO ME WI GRATITUDE.
BUT FOR NOW YOU SERVE.
THESE AROUND YOU ARE MY **NEW CHILDREN.** MY BLIND ONES...
...MY **FEELERS.**

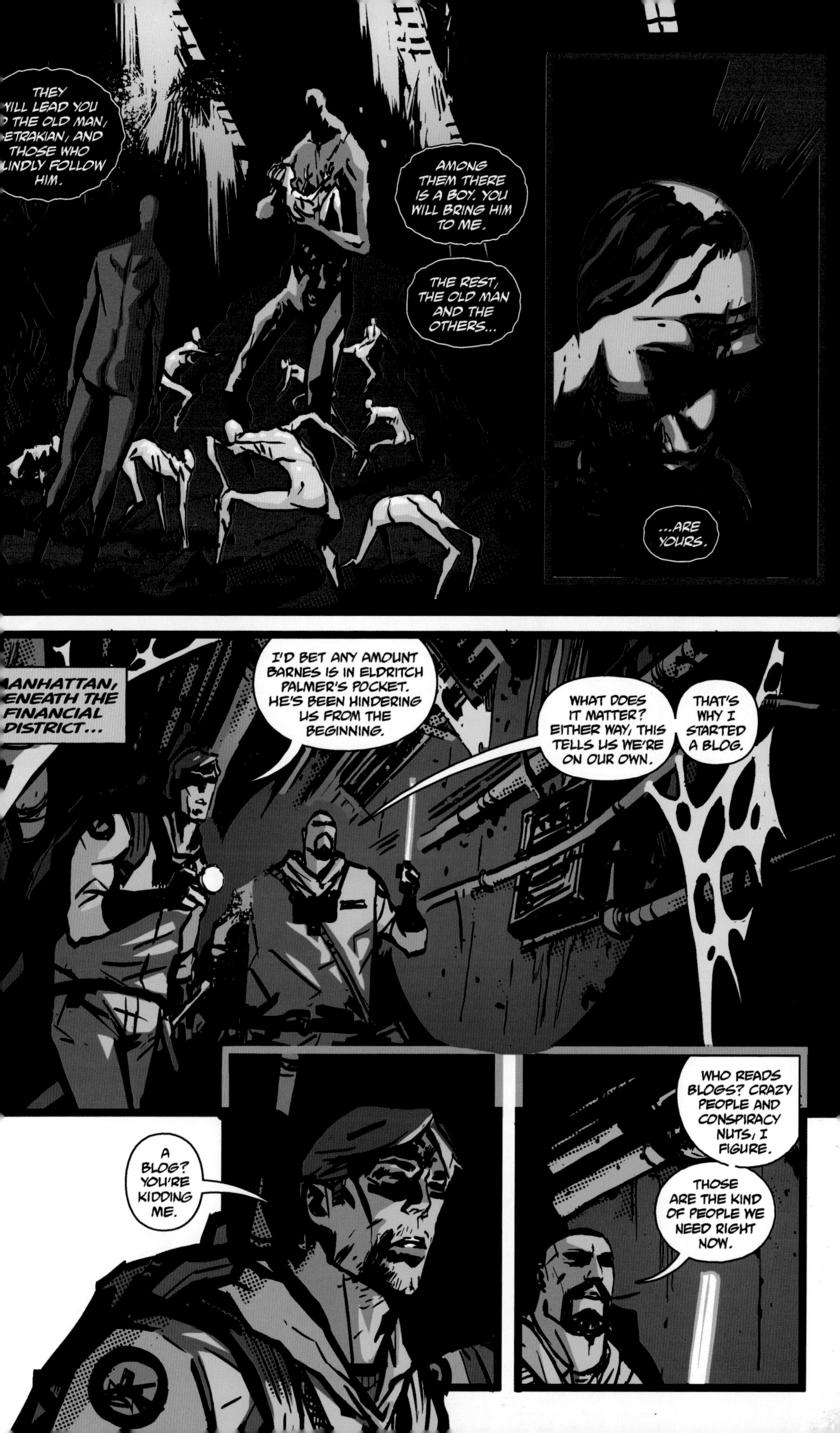
THEY VILL LEAD YOU D THE OLD MAN, ETRAKIAN, AND THOSE WHO LINDLY FOLLOW HIM.
AMONG THEM THERE IS A BOY. YOU WILL BRING HIM TO ME.
THE REST, THE OLD MAN AND THE OTHERS...
...ARE YOURS.
ANHATTAN, ENEATH THE FINANCIAL DISTRICT...
I'D BET ANY AMOUNT BARNES IS IN ELDRITCH PALMER'S POCKET. HE'S BEEN HINDERING US FROM THE BEGINNING.
WHAT DOES IT MATTER? EITHER WAY, THIS TELLS US WE'RE ON OUR OWN.
THAT'S WHY I STARTED A BLOG.
A BLOG? YOU'RE KIDDING ME.
WHO READS BLOGS? CRAZY PEOPLE AND CONSPIRACY NUTS, I FIGURE.
THOSE ARE THE KIND OF PEOPLE WE NEED RIGHT NOW.

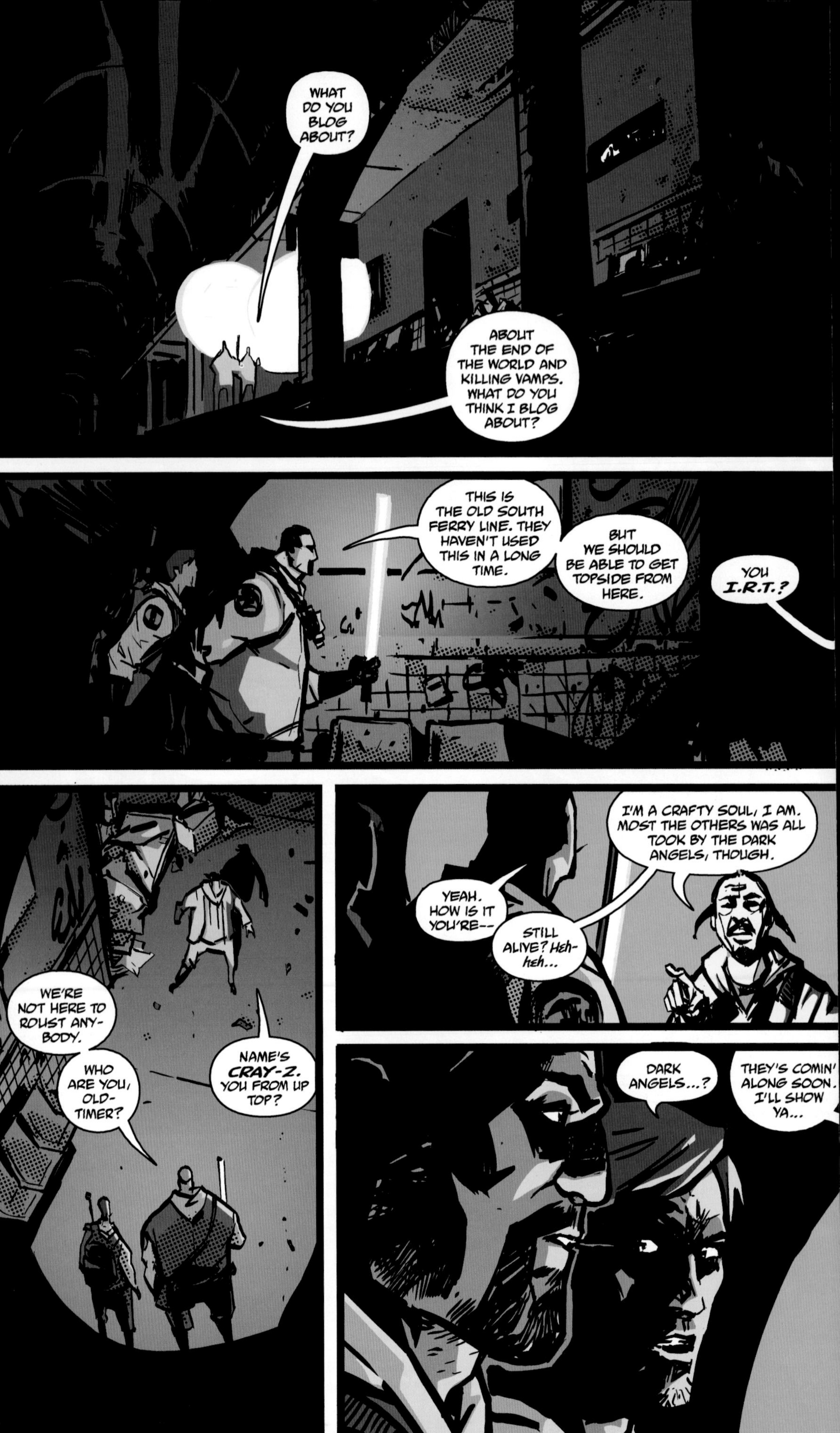
WHAT DO YOU BLOG ABOUT?
ABOUT THE END OF THE WORLD AND KILLING VAMPS. WHAT DO YOU THINK I BLOG ABOUT?
THIS IS THE OLD SOUTH FERRY LINE. THEY HAVEN'T USED THIS IN A LONG TIME.
BUT WE SHOULD BE ABLE TO GET TOPSIDE FROM HERE.
YOU *I.R.T.?*
WE'RE NOT HERE TO ROUST ANY-BODY.
WHO ARE YOU, OLD-TIMER?
NAME'S *CRAY-Z.* YOU FROM UP TOP?
I'M A CRAFTY SOUL, I AM. MOST THE OTHERS WAS ALL TOOK BY THE DARK ANGELS, THOUGH.
YEAH. HOW IS IT YOU'RE--
STILL ALIVE? *Heh-heh...*
DARK ANGELS...?
THEY'S COMIN' ALONG SOON. I'LL SHOW YA...

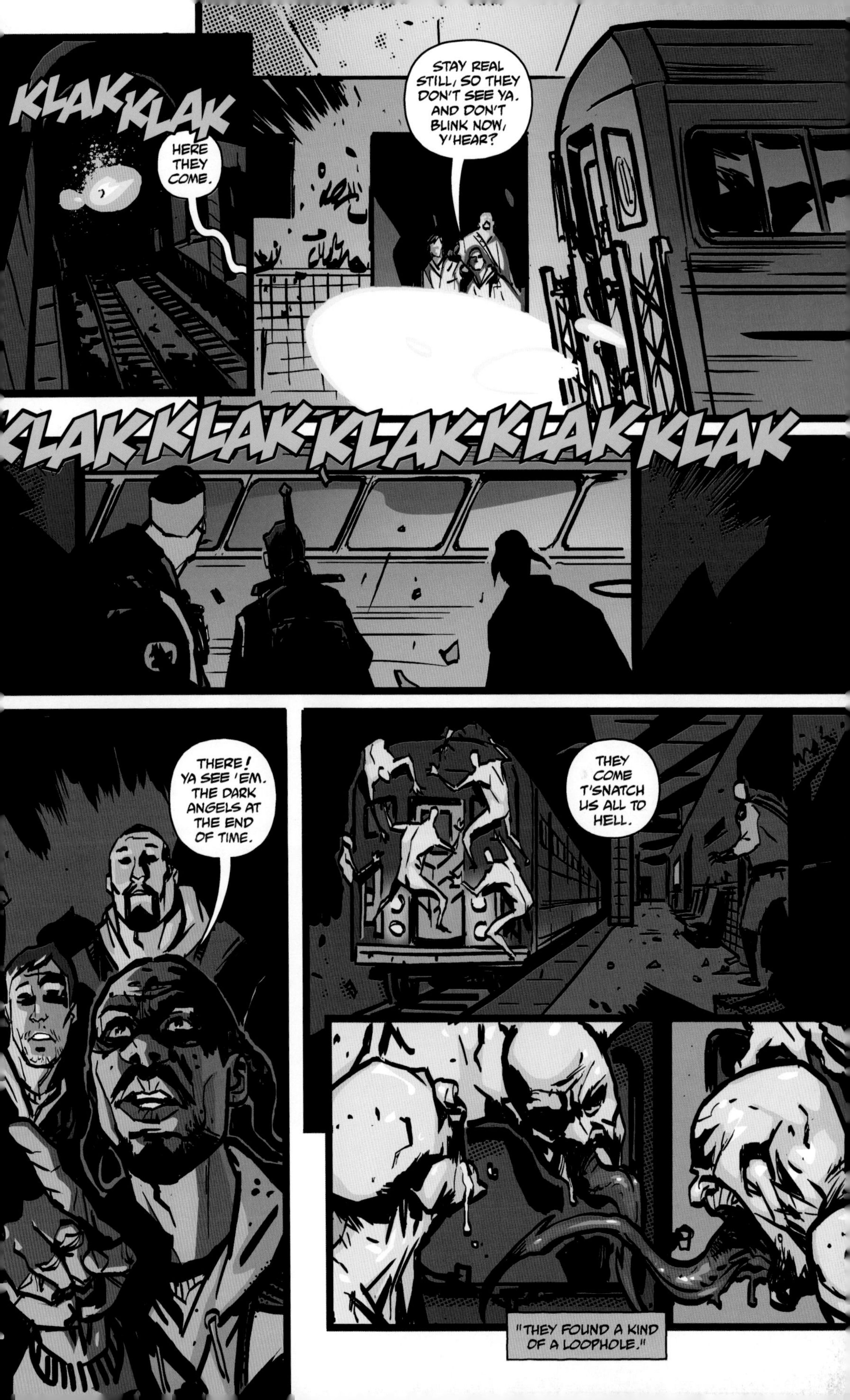

KLAK KLAK
HERE THEY COME.
STAY REAL STILL, SO THEY DON'T SEE YA. AND DON'T BLINK NOW, Y'HEAR?
KLAK KLAK KLAK KLAK KLAK
THERE! YA SEE 'EM. THE DARK ANGELS AT THE END OF TIME.
THEY COME T'SNATCH US ALL TO HELL.
"THEY FOUND A KIND OF A LOOPHOLE."

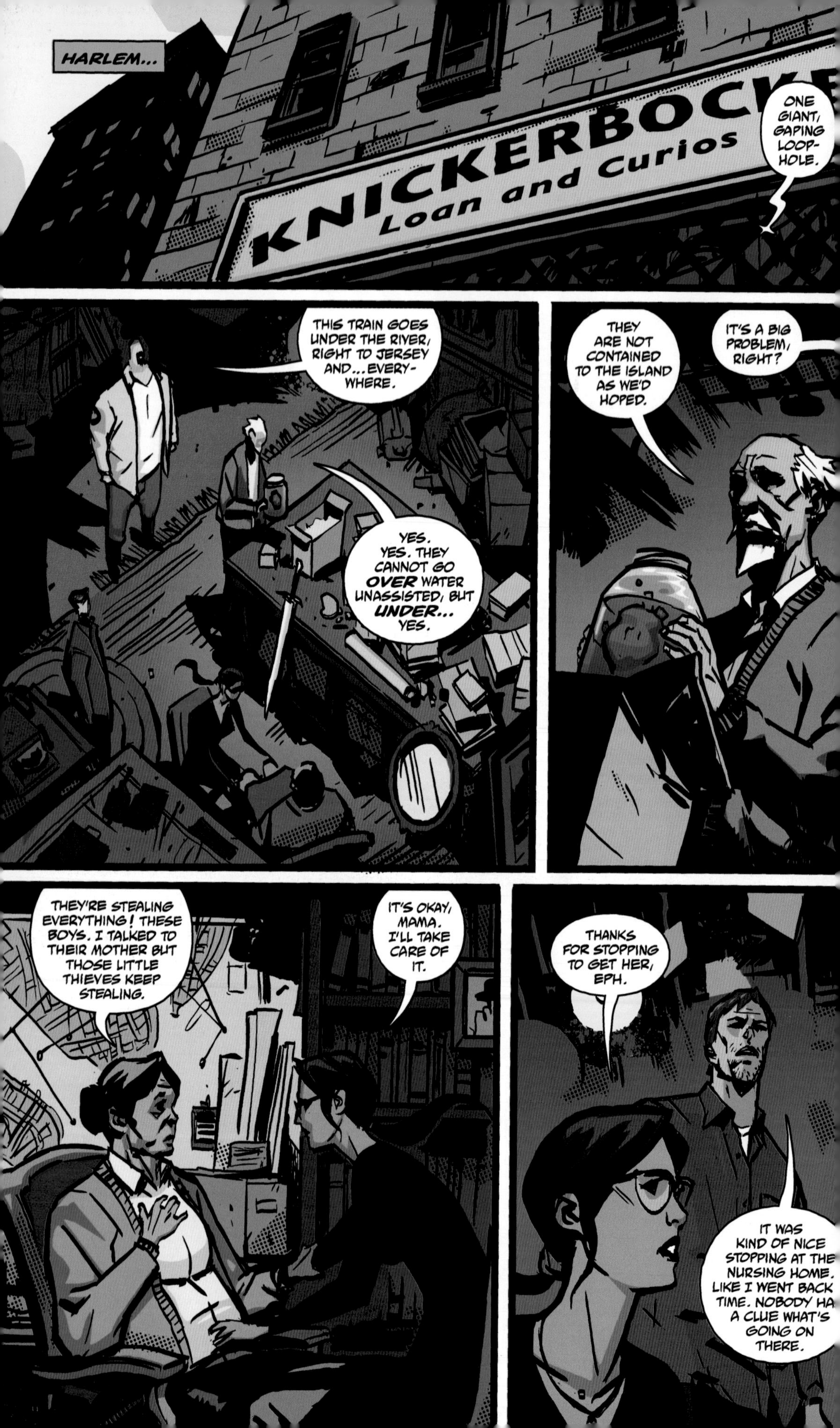
HARLEM...
KNICKERBOCKE
Loan and Curios
ONE GIANT, GAPING LOOP-HOLE.
THIS TRAIN GOES UNDER THE RIVER, RIGHT TO JERSEY AND... EVERY-WHERE.
YES. YES. THEY CANNOT GO OVER WATER UNASSISTED, BUT UNDER... YES.
THEY ARE NOT CONTAINED TO THE ISLAND AS WE'D HOPED.
IT'S A BIG PROBLEM, RIGHT?
THEY'RE STEALING EVERYTHING! THESE BOYS. I TALKED TO THEIR MOTHER BUT THOSE LITTLE THIEVES KEEP STEALING.
IT'S OKAY, MAMA. I'LL TAKE CARE OF IT.
THANKS FOR STOPPING TO GET HER, EPH.
IT WAS KIND OF NICE STOPPING AT THE NURSING HOME. LIKE I WENT BACK TIME. NOBODY HA A CLUE WHAT'S GOING ON THERE.

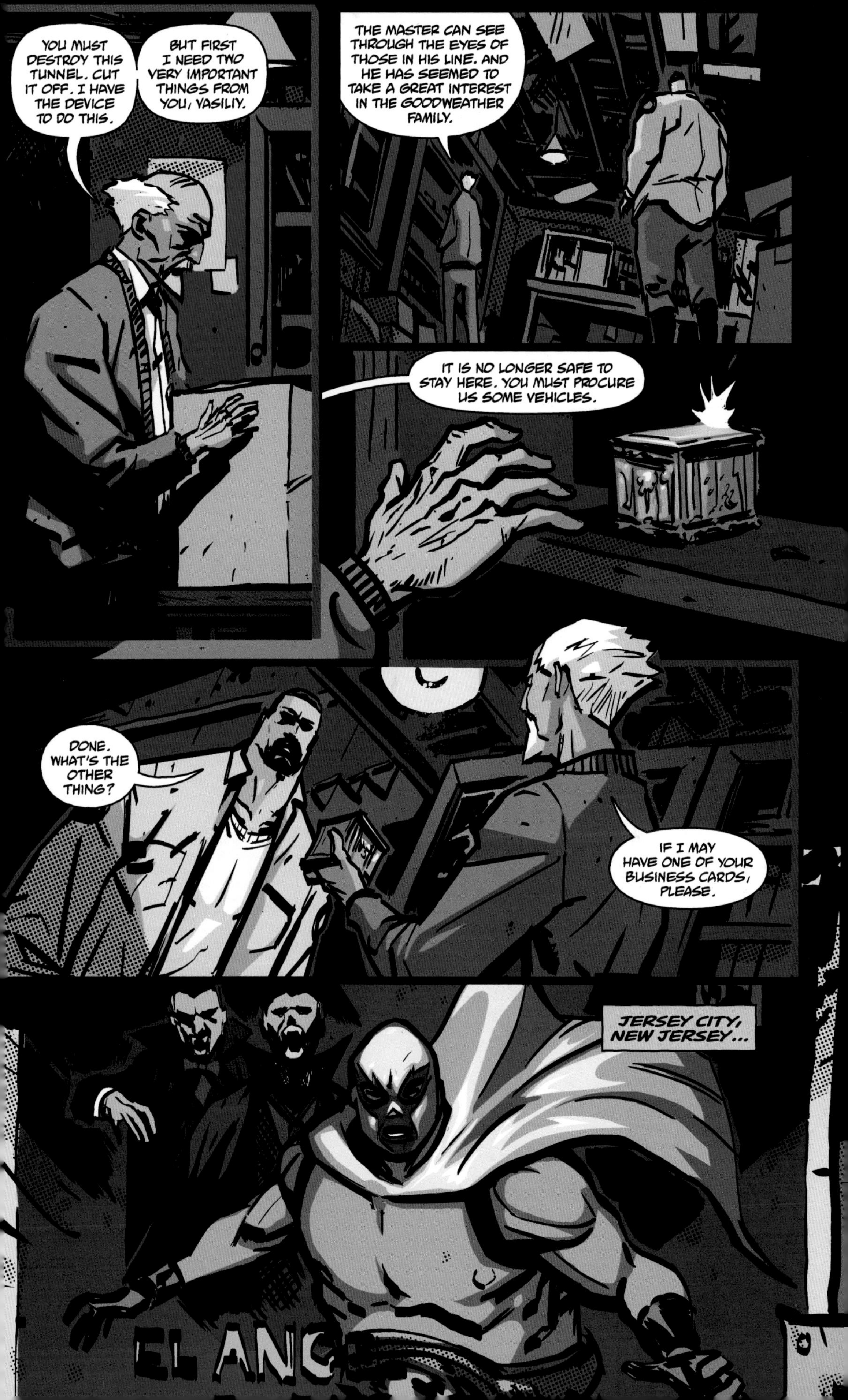
YOU MUST DESTROY THIS TUNNEL. CUT IT OFF. I HAVE THE DEVICE TO DO THIS.
BUT FIRST I NEED TWO VERY IMPORTANT THINGS FROM YOU, VASILIY.
THE MASTER CAN SEE THROUGH THE EYES OF THOSE IN HIS LINE. AND HE HAS SEEMED TO TAKE A GREAT INTEREST IN THE GOODWEATHER FAMILY.
IT IS NO LONGER SAFE TO STAY HERE. YOU MUST PROCURE US SOME VEHICLES.
DONE. WHAT'S THE OTHER THING?
IF I MAY HAVE ONE OF YOUR BUSINESS CARDS, PLEASE.
JERSEY CITY, NEW JERSEY...
EL ANG

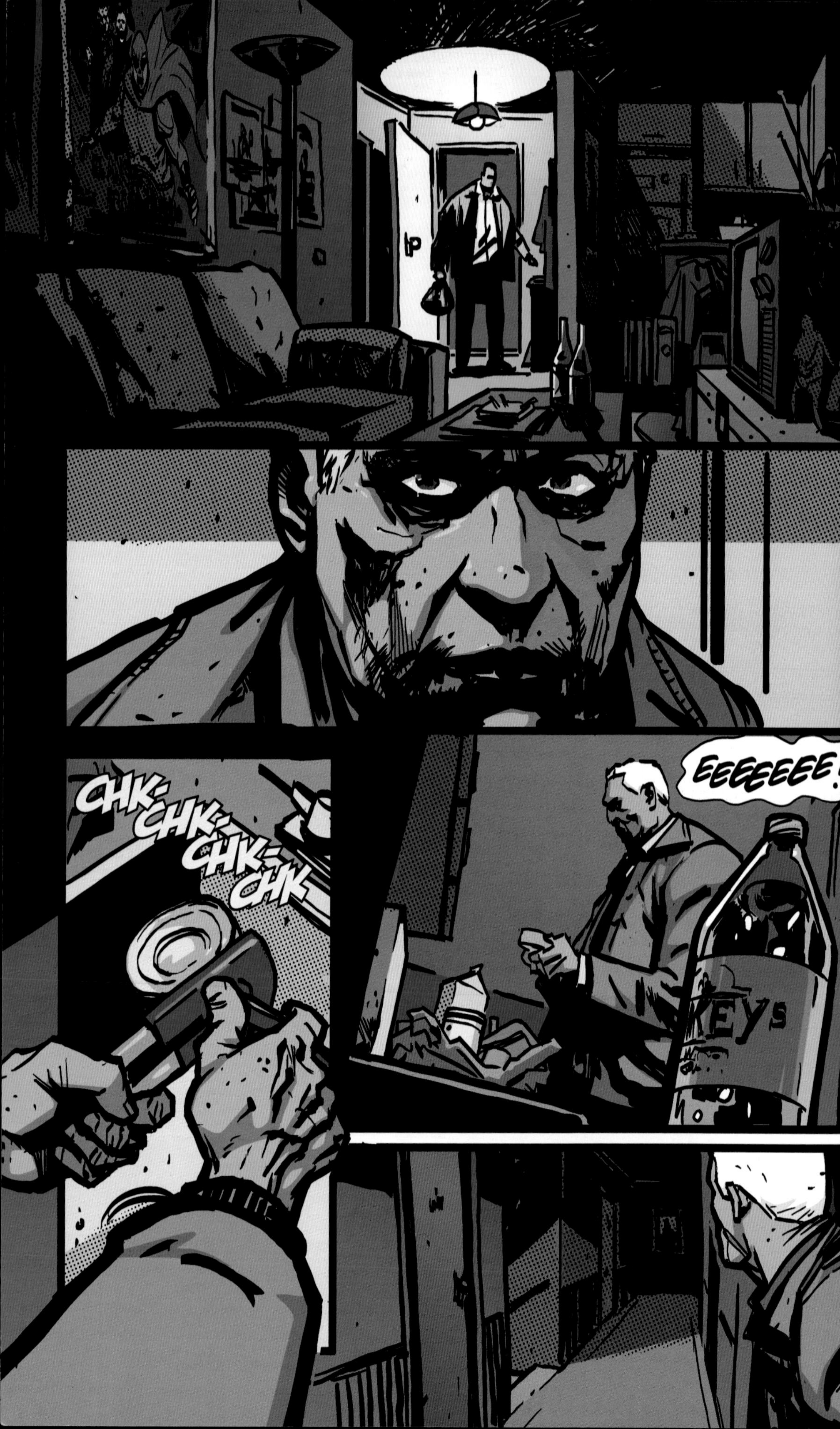
CHK-CHK-CHK-CHK
EEEEEEE!
KEYs

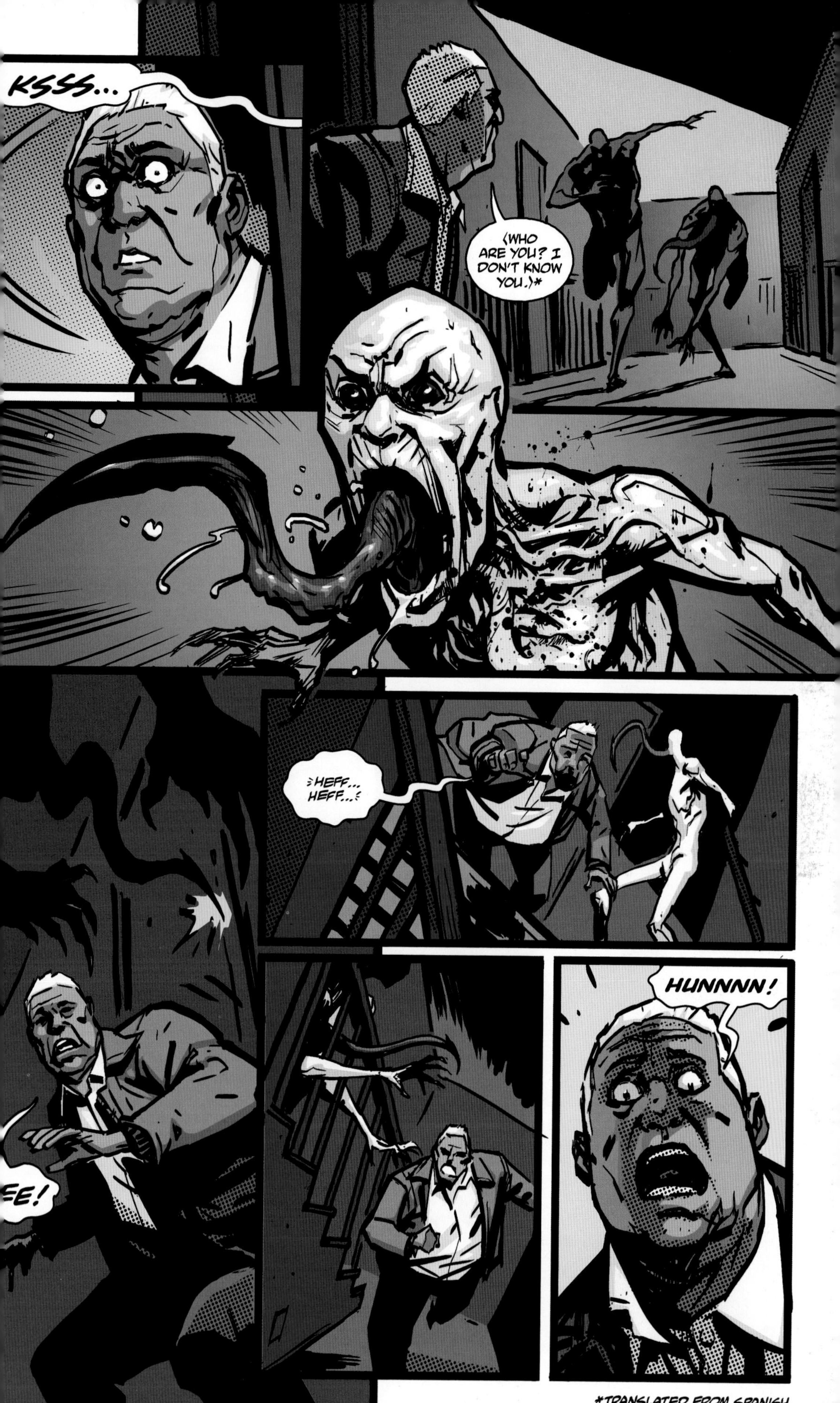
KSSS...
⟨WHO ARE YOU? I DON'T KNOW YOU.⟩*
HEFF... HEFF...
EE!
HUNNNN!

*TRANSLATED FROM SPANISH

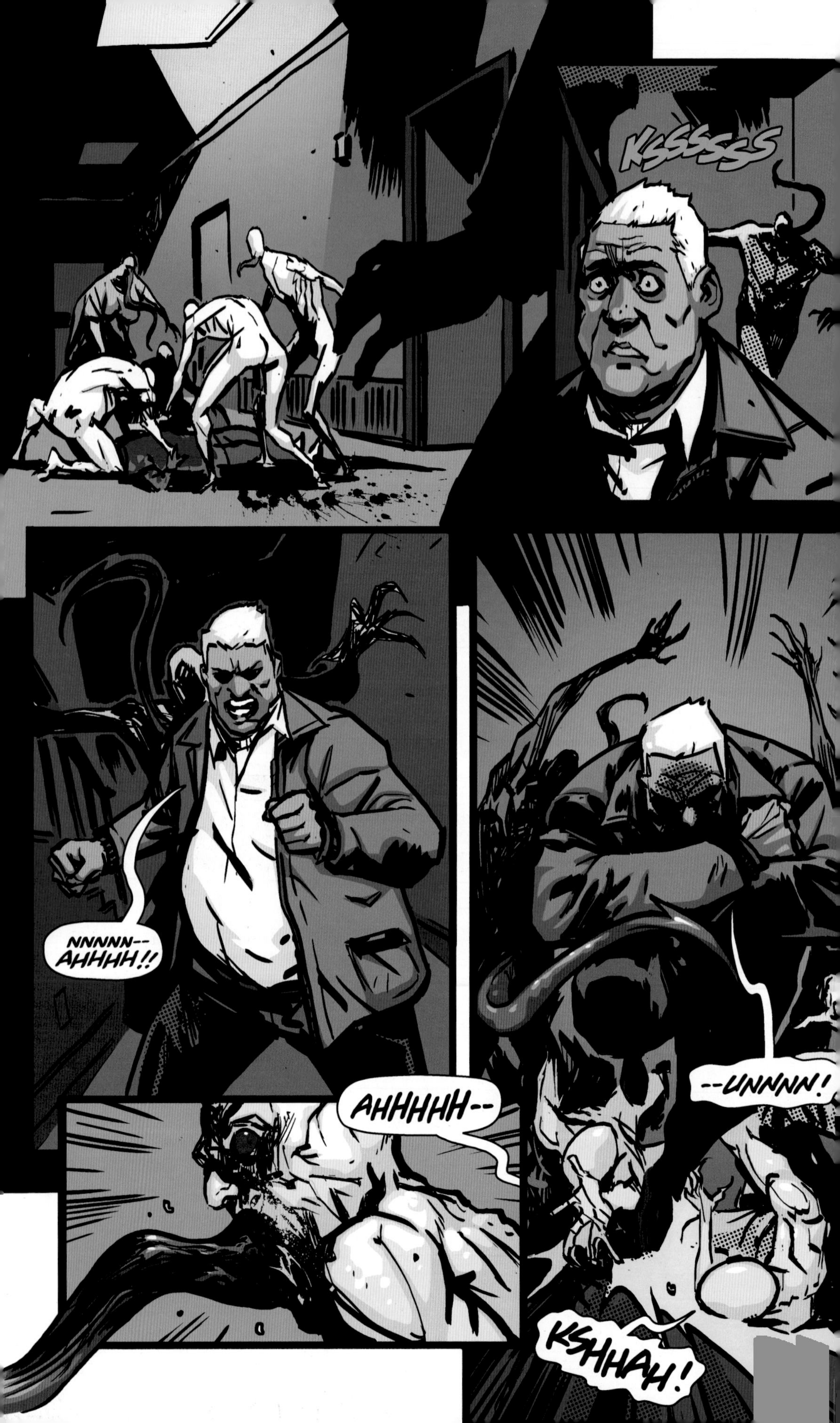
KSSSSSS
NNNNN--
AHHHH!!
AHHHHH--
--UNNNN!
KSHHAH!

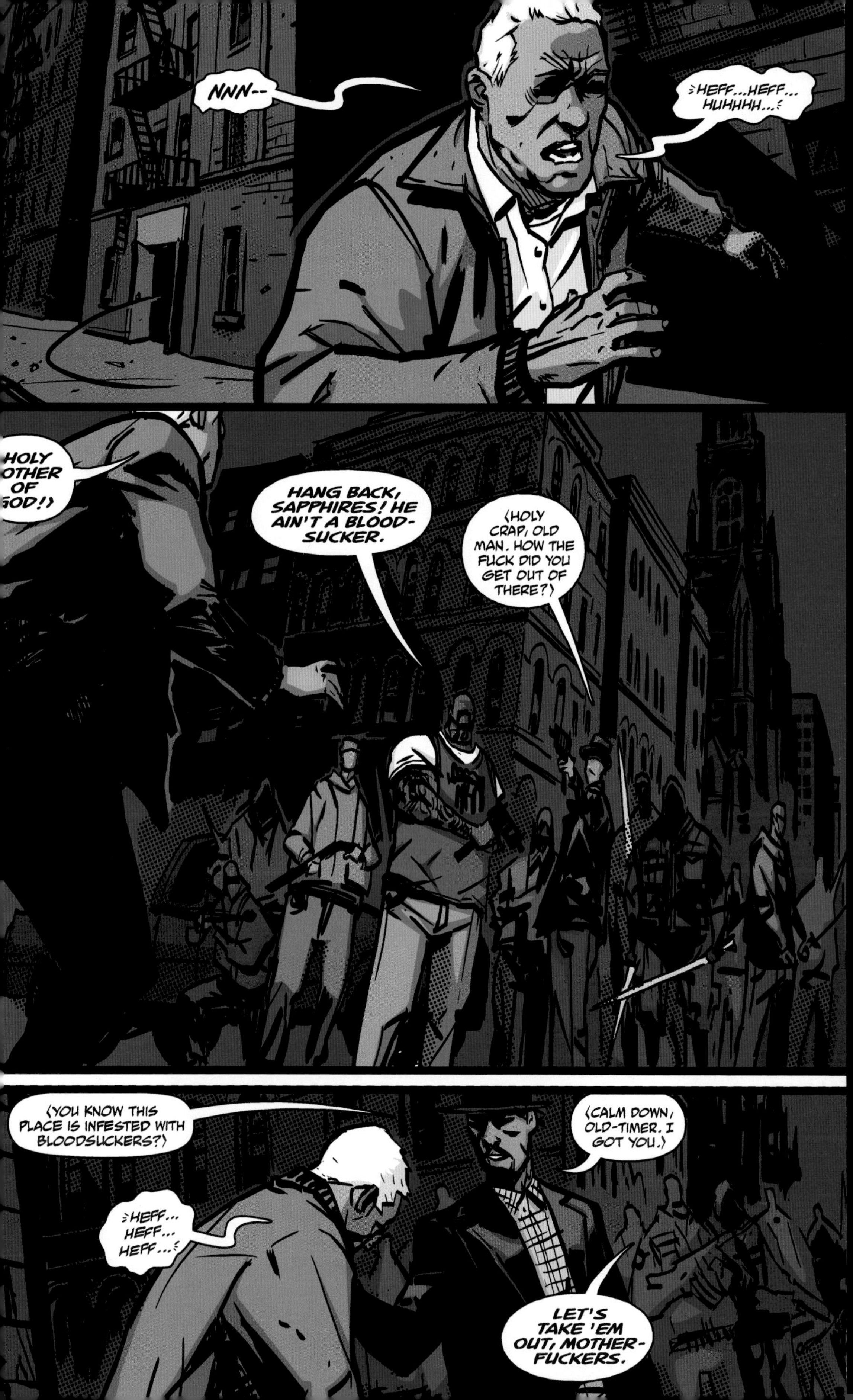
NNN--
HEFF...HEFF... HUHHHH...
HOLY MOTHER OF GOD!
HANG BACK, SAPPHIRES! HE AIN'T A BLOOD-SUCKER.
HOLY CRAP, OLD MAN. HOW THE FUCK DID YOU GET OUT OF THERE?
YOU KNOW THIS PLACE IS INFESTED WITH BLOODSUCKERS?
CALM DOWN, OLD-TIMER. I GOT YOU.
HEFF... HEFF... HEFF...
LET'S TAKE 'EM OUT, MOTHER-FUCKERS.

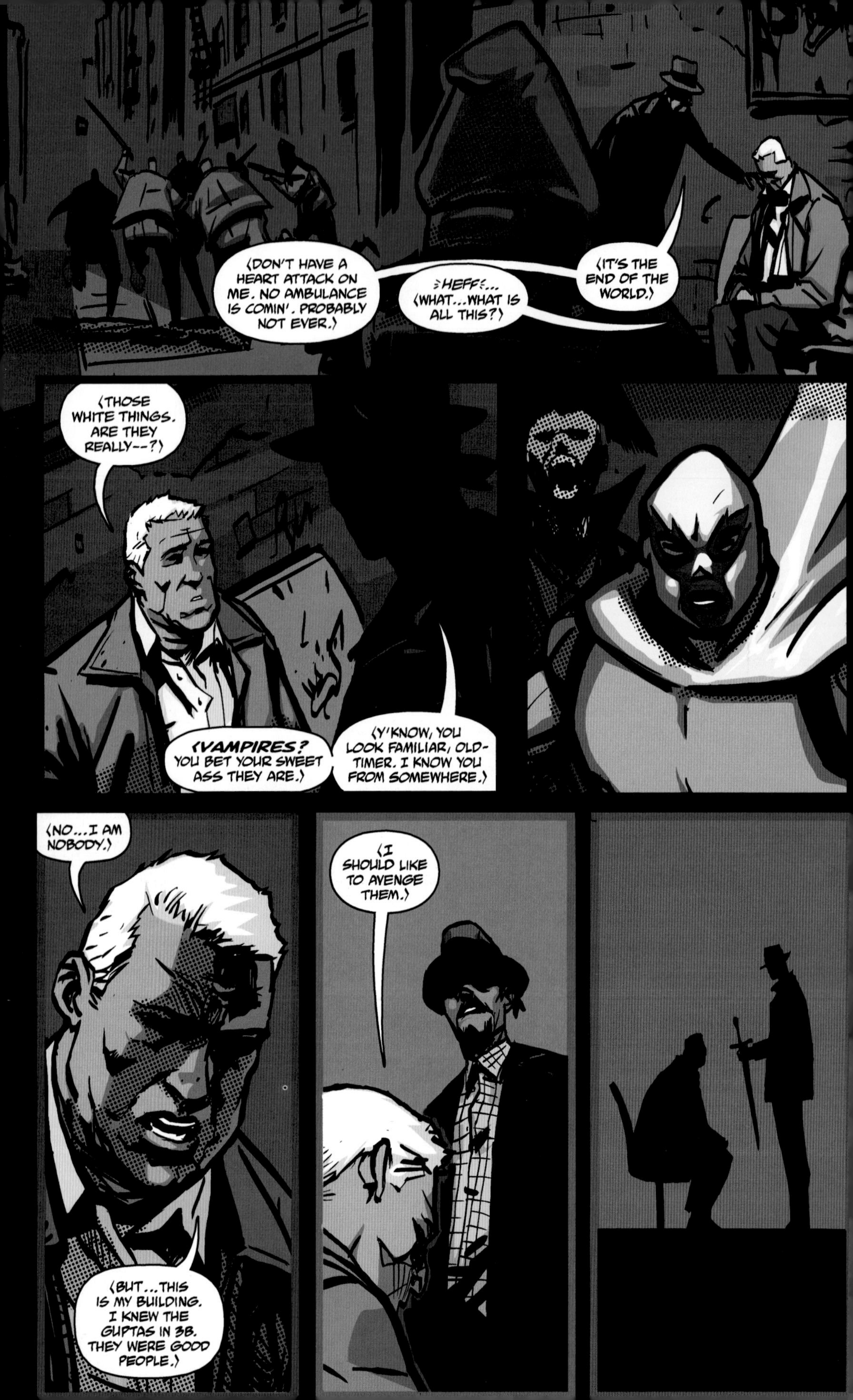
⟨DON'T HAVE A HEART ATTACK ON ME. NO AMBULANCE IS COMIN'. PROBABLY NOT EVER.⟩
≶HEFF≶... ⟨WHAT...WHAT IS ALL THIS?⟩
⟨IT'S THE END OF THE WORLD.⟩
⟨THOSE WHITE THINGS. ARE THEY REALLY--?⟩
⟨*VAMPIRES?* YOU BET YOUR SWEET ASS THEY ARE.⟩
⟨Y'KNOW, YOU LOOK FAMILIAR, OLD-TIMER. I KNOW YOU FROM SOMEWHERE.⟩
⟨NO...I AM NOBODY.⟩
⟨BUT...THIS IS MY BUILDING. I KNEW THE GUPTAS IN 3B. THEY WERE GOOD PEOPLE.⟩
⟨I SHOULD LIKE TO AVENGE THEM.⟩

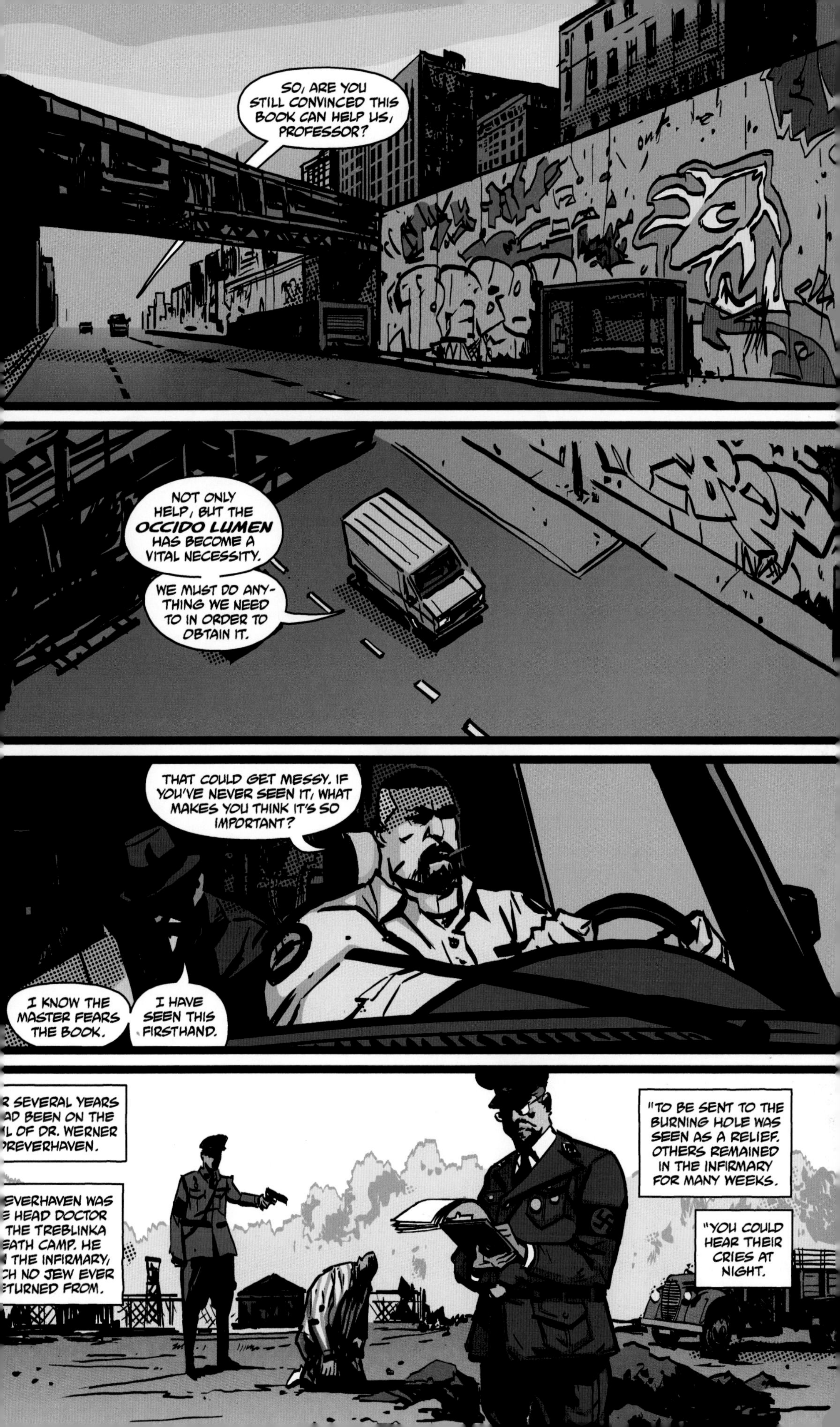
SO, ARE YOU STILL CONVINCED THIS BOOK CAN HELP US, PROFESSOR?
NOT ONLY HELP, BUT THE OCCIDO LUMEN HAS BECOME A VITAL NECESSITY.
WE MUST DO ANYTHING WE NEED TO IN ORDER TO OBTAIN IT.
THAT COULD GET MESSY. IF YOU'VE NEVER SEEN IT, WHAT MAKES YOU THINK IT'S SO IMPORTANT?
I KNOW THE MASTER FEARS THE BOOK.
I HAVE SEEN THIS FIRSTHAND.
R SEVERAL YEARS AD BEEN ON THE L OF DR. WERNER PREVERHAVEN.
EVERHAVEN WAS E HEAD DOCTOR THE TREBLINKA EATH CAMP. HE THE INFIRMARY, CH NO JEW EVER ETURNED FROM.
"TO BE SENT TO THE BURNING HOLE WAS SEEN AS A RELIEF. OTHERS REMAINED IN THE INFIRMARY FOR MANY WEEKS.
"YOU COULD HEAR THEIR CRIES AT NIGHT.

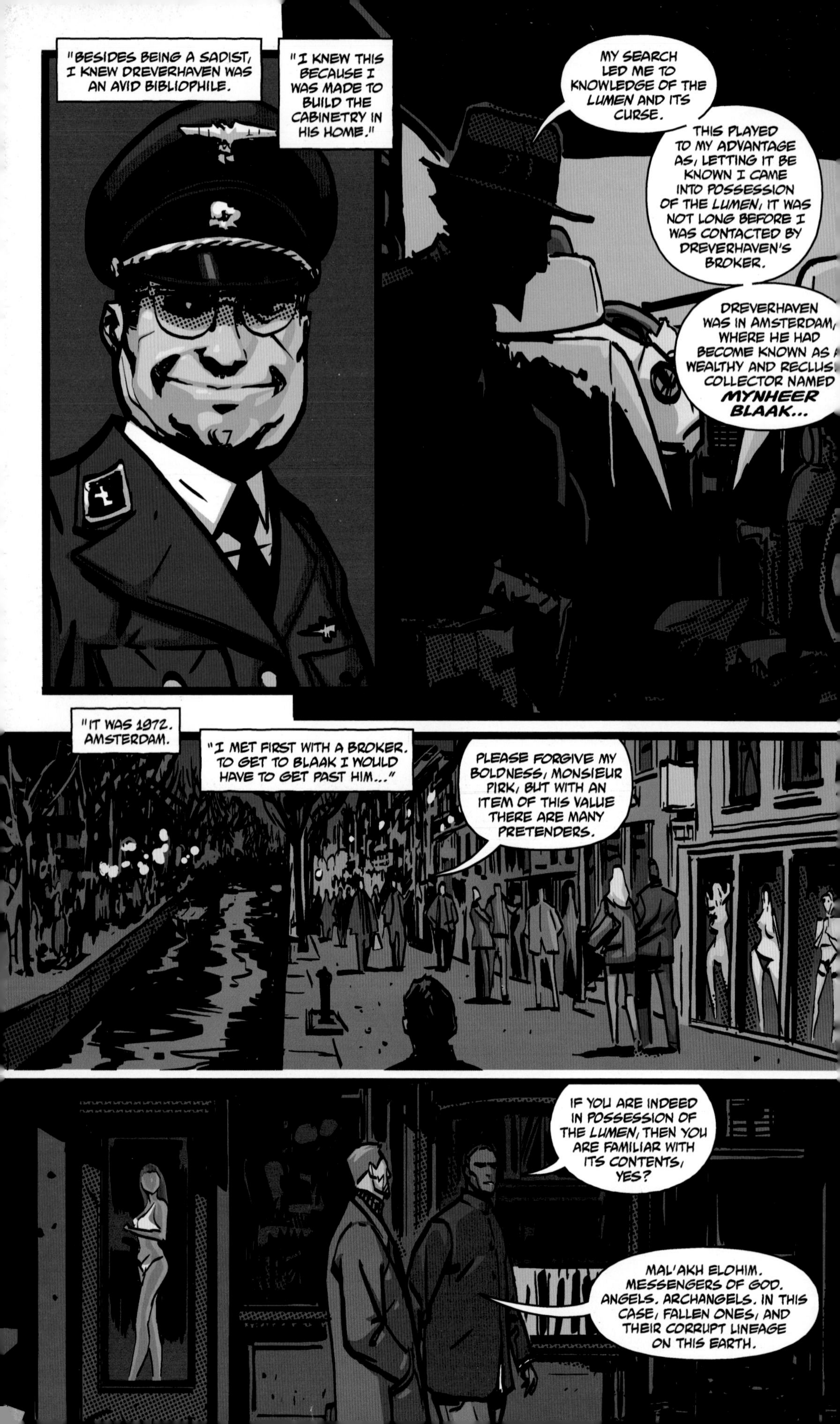
"BESIDES BEING A SADIST, I KNEW DREVERHAVEN WAS AN AVID BIBLIOPHILE.
"I KNEW THIS BECAUSE I WAS MADE TO BUILD THE CABINETRY IN HIS HOME."
MY SEARCH LED ME TO KNOWLEDGE OF THE *LUMEN* AND ITS CURSE.
THIS PLAYED TO MY ADVANTAGE AS, LETTING IT BE KNOWN I CAME INTO POSSESSION OF THE *LUMEN*, IT WAS NOT LONG BEFORE I WAS CONTACTED BY DREVERHAVEN'S BROKER.
DREVERHAVEN WAS IN AMSTERDAM, WHERE HE HAD BECOME KNOWN AS A WEALTHY AND RECLUSIVE COLLECTOR NAMED ***MYNHEER BLAAK...***
"IT WAS 1972. AMSTERDAM.
"I MET FIRST WITH A BROKER. TO GET TO BLAAK I WOULD HAVE TO GET PAST HIM..."
PLEASE FORGIVE MY BOLDNESS, MONSIEUR PIRK, BUT WITH AN ITEM OF THIS VALUE THERE ARE MANY PRETENDERS.
IF YOU ARE INDEED IN POSSESSION OF THE *LUMEN*, THEN YOU ARE FAMILIAR WITH ITS CONTENTS, YES?
MAL'AKH ELOHIM. MESSENGERS OF GOD. ANGELS. ARCHANGELS. IN THIS CASE, FALLEN ONES, AND THEIR CORRUPT LINEAGE ON THIS EARTH.

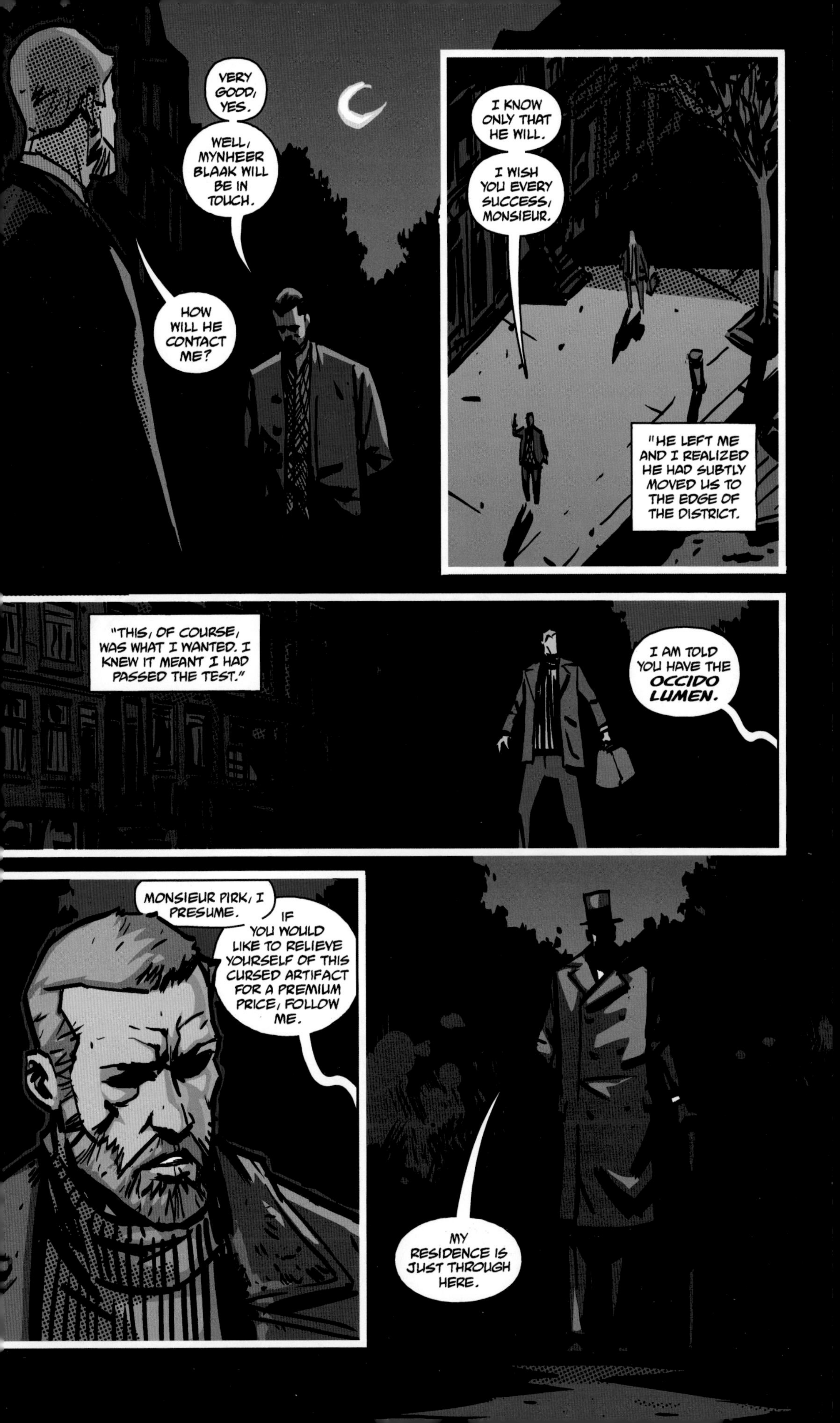
VERY GOOD, YES.
WELL, MYNHEER BLAAK WILL BE IN TOUCH.
HOW WILL HE CONTACT ME?
I KNOW ONLY THAT HE WILL.
I WISH YOU EVERY SUCCESS, MONSIEUR.
"HE LEFT ME AND I REALIZED HE HAD SUBTLY MOVED US TO THE EDGE OF THE DISTRICT.
"THIS, OF COURSE, WAS WHAT I WANTED. I KNEW IT MEANT I HAD PASSED THE TEST."
I AM TOLD YOU HAVE THE *OCCIDO LUMEN.*
MONSIEUR PIRK, I PRESUME.
IF YOU WOULD LIKE TO RELIEVE YOURSELF OF THIS CURSED ARTIFACT FOR A PREMIUM PRICE, FOLLOW ME.
MY RESIDENCE IS JUST THROUGH HERE.

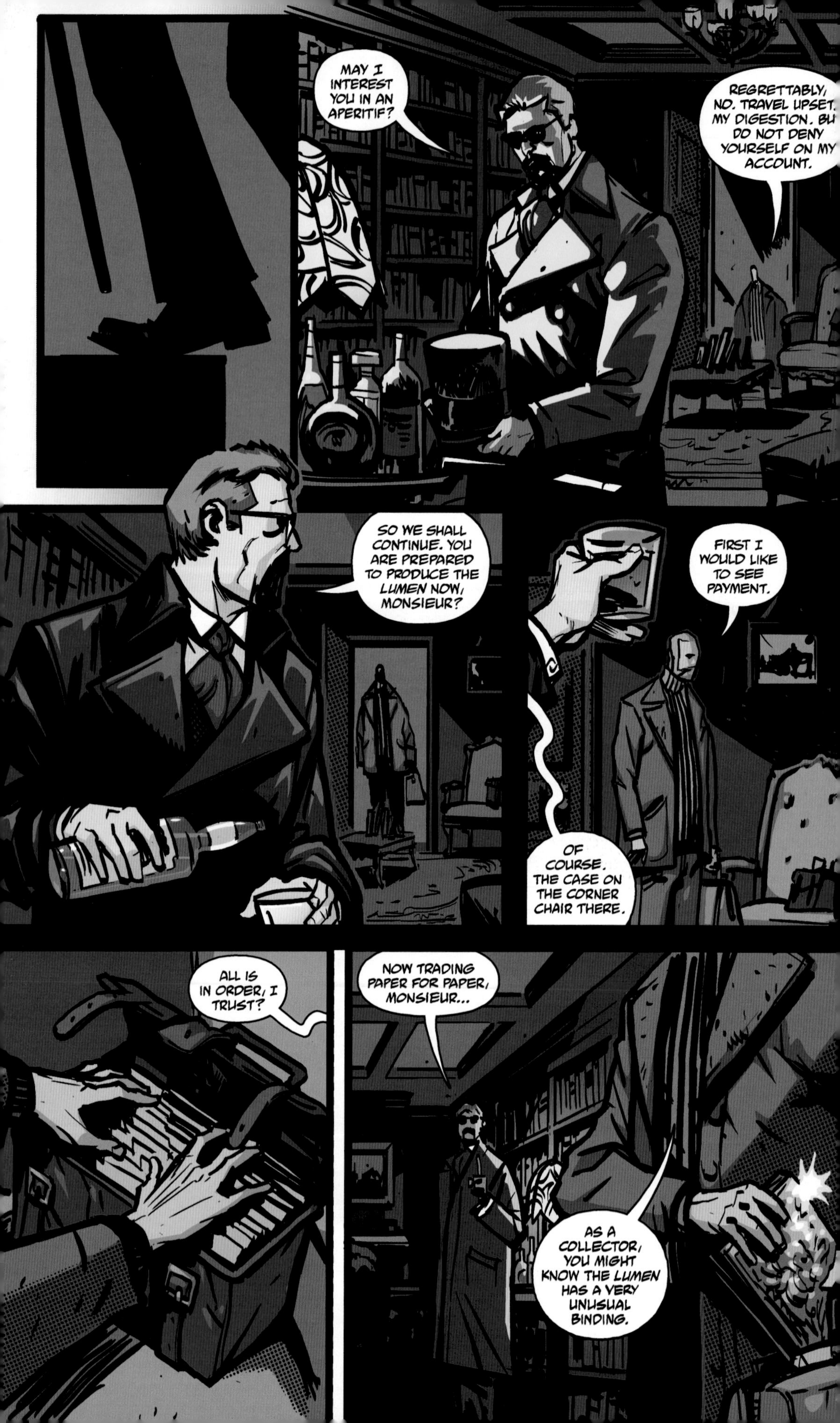
MAY I INTEREST YOU IN AN APERITIF?
REGRETTABLY, NO. TRAVEL UPSET MY DIGESTION. BU DO NOT DENY YOURSELF ON MY ACCOUNT.
SO WE SHALL CONTINUE. YOU ARE PREPARED TO PRODUCE THE *LUMEN* NOW, MONSIEUR?
FIRST I WOULD LIKE TO SEE PAYMENT.
OF COURSE. THE CASE ON THE CORNER CHAIR THERE.
ALL IS IN ORDER, I TRUST?
NOW TRADING PAPER FOR PAPER, MONSIEUR...
AS A COLLECTOR, YOU MIGHT KNOW THE *LUMEN* HAS A VERY UNUSUAL BINDING.

COVERS MADE OF PURE SILVER. ADDING PARTLY TO ITS UNIQUENESS AND VALUE.

YOU WOULD LIKE TO INSPECT IT, OF COURSE.

PUT IT DOWN ON THE TABLE.

BUT SURELY YOU'D LIKE TO INSPECT IT...

I DO NOT NEED TO.

THE BOOK IS A FAKE.

BUT THE SILVER.

I ASSURE YOU, STRIGOI, THE SILVER IS VERY REAL.

YOUR SCENT IS FAMILIAR, JEW.

KSSSSSSS!

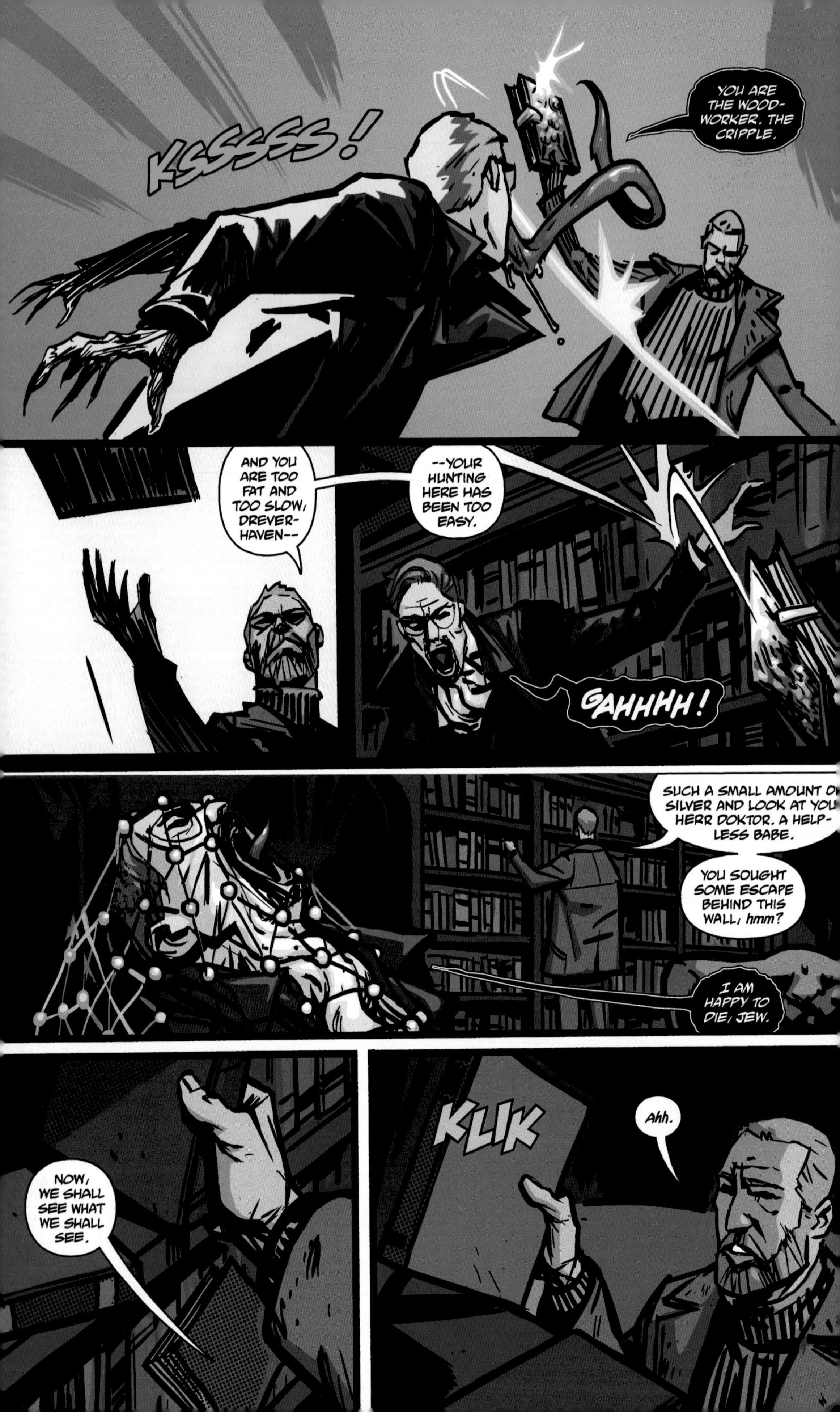
KSSSSSS!
YOU ARE THE WOOD-WORKER. THE CRIPPLE.
AND YOU ARE TOO FAT AND TOO SLOW, DREVER-HAVEN--
--YOUR HUNTING HERE HAS BEEN TOO EASY.
GAHHHH!
SUCH A SMALL AMOUNT OF SILVER AND LOOK AT YOU HERR DOKTOR. A HELP-LESS BABE.
YOU SOUGHT SOME ESCAPE BEHIND THIS WALL, hmm?
I AM HAPPY TO DIE, JEW.
NOW, WE SHALL SEE WHAT WE SHALL SEE.
KLIK
Ahh.

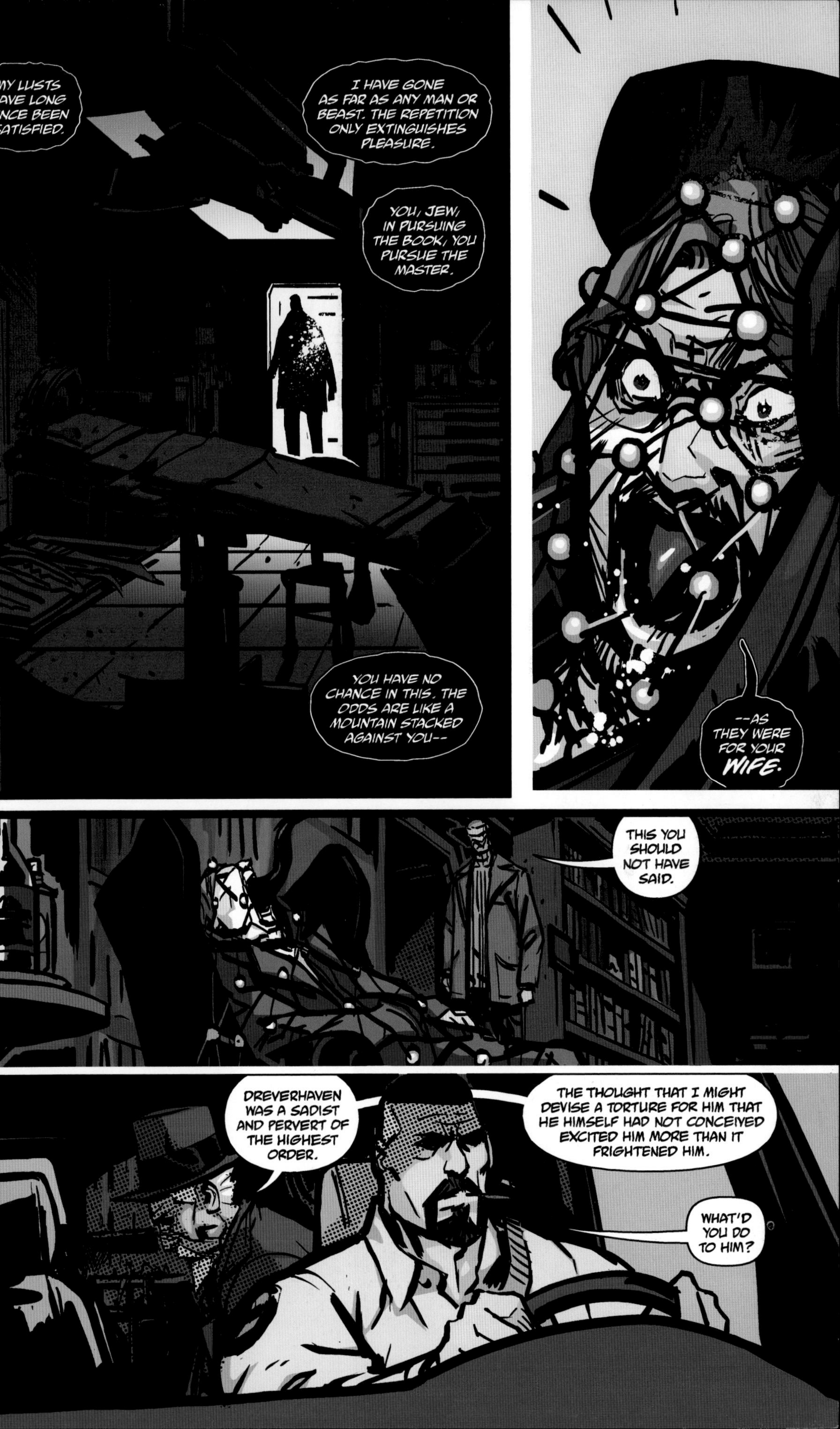
MY LUSTS HAVE LONG SINCE BEEN SATISFIED.
I HAVE GONE AS FAR AS ANY MAN OR BEAST. THE REPETITION ONLY EXTINGUISHES PLEASURE.
YOU, JEW, IN PURSUING THE BOOK, YOU PURSUE THE MASTER.
YOU HAVE NO CHANCE IN THIS. THE ODDS ARE LIKE A MOUNTAIN STACKED AGAINST YOU--
--AS THEY WERE FOR YOUR WIFE.
THIS YOU SHOULD NOT HAVE SAID.
DREVERHAVEN WAS A SADIST AND PERVERT OF THE HIGHEST ORDER.
THE THOUGHT THAT I MIGHT DEVISE A TORTURE FOR HIM THAT HE HIMSELF HAD NOT CONCEIVED EXCITED HIM MORE THAN IT FRIGHTENED HIM.
WHAT'D YOU DO TO HIM?

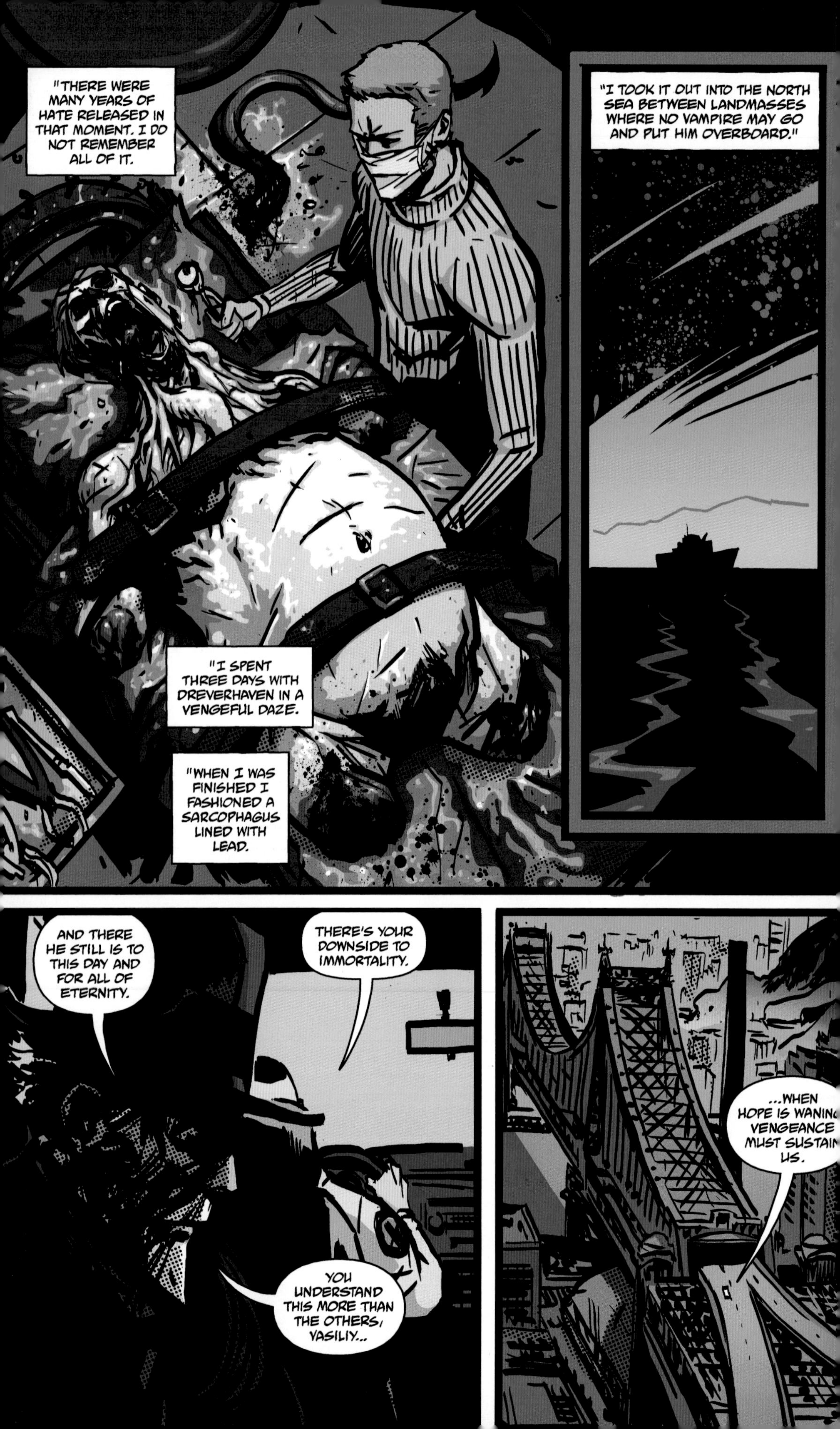
"THERE WERE MANY YEARS OF HATE RELEASED IN THAT MOMENT. I DO NOT REMEMBER ALL OF IT.
"I SPENT THREE DAYS WITH DREVERHAVEN IN A VENGEFUL DAZE.
"WHEN I WAS FINISHED I FASHIONED A SARCOPHAGUS LINED WITH LEAD.
"I TOOK IT OUT INTO THE NORTH SEA BETWEEN LANDMASSES WHERE NO VAMPIRE MAY GO AND PUT HIM OVERBOARD."
AND THERE HE STILL IS TO THIS DAY AND FOR ALL OF ETERNITY.
THERE'S YOUR DOWNSIDE TO IMMORTALITY.
YOU UNDERSTAND THIS MORE THAN THE OTHERS, VASILIY...
...WHEN HOPE IS WANING VENGEANCE MUST SUSTAIN US.

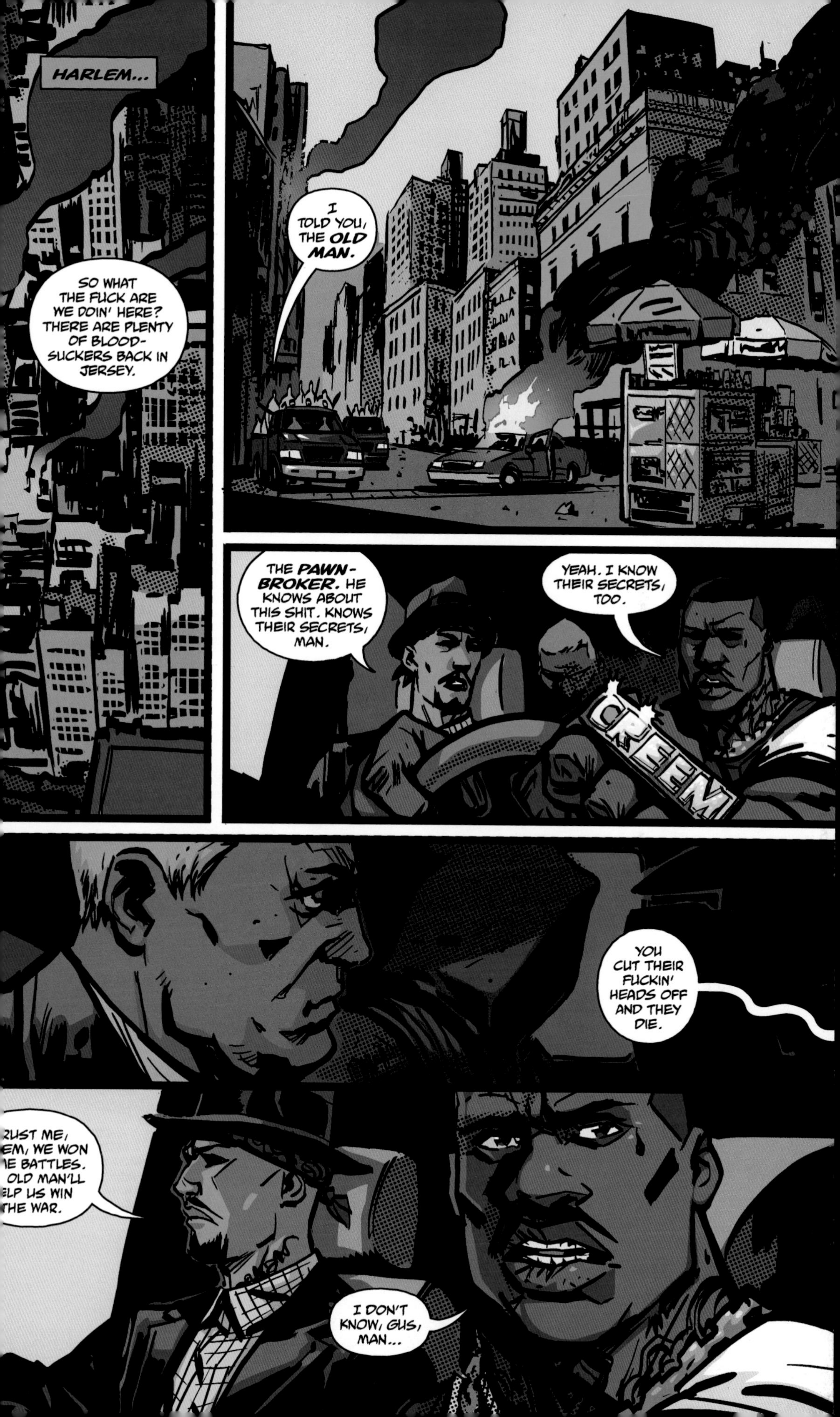
HARLEM...
SO WHAT THE FUCK ARE WE DOIN' HERE? THERE ARE PLENTY OF BLOOD-SUCKERS BACK IN JERSEY.
I TOLD YOU, THE OLD MAN.
THE PAWN-BROKER. HE KNOWS ABOUT THIS SHIT. KNOWS THEIR SECRETS, MAN.
YEAH. I KNOW THEIR SECRETS, TOO.
CREEM
YOU CUT THEIR FUCKIN' HEADS OFF AND THEY DIE.
RUST ME, EM, WE WON E BATTLES. OLD MAN'LL ELP US WIN THE WAR.
I DON'T KNOW, GUS, MAN...

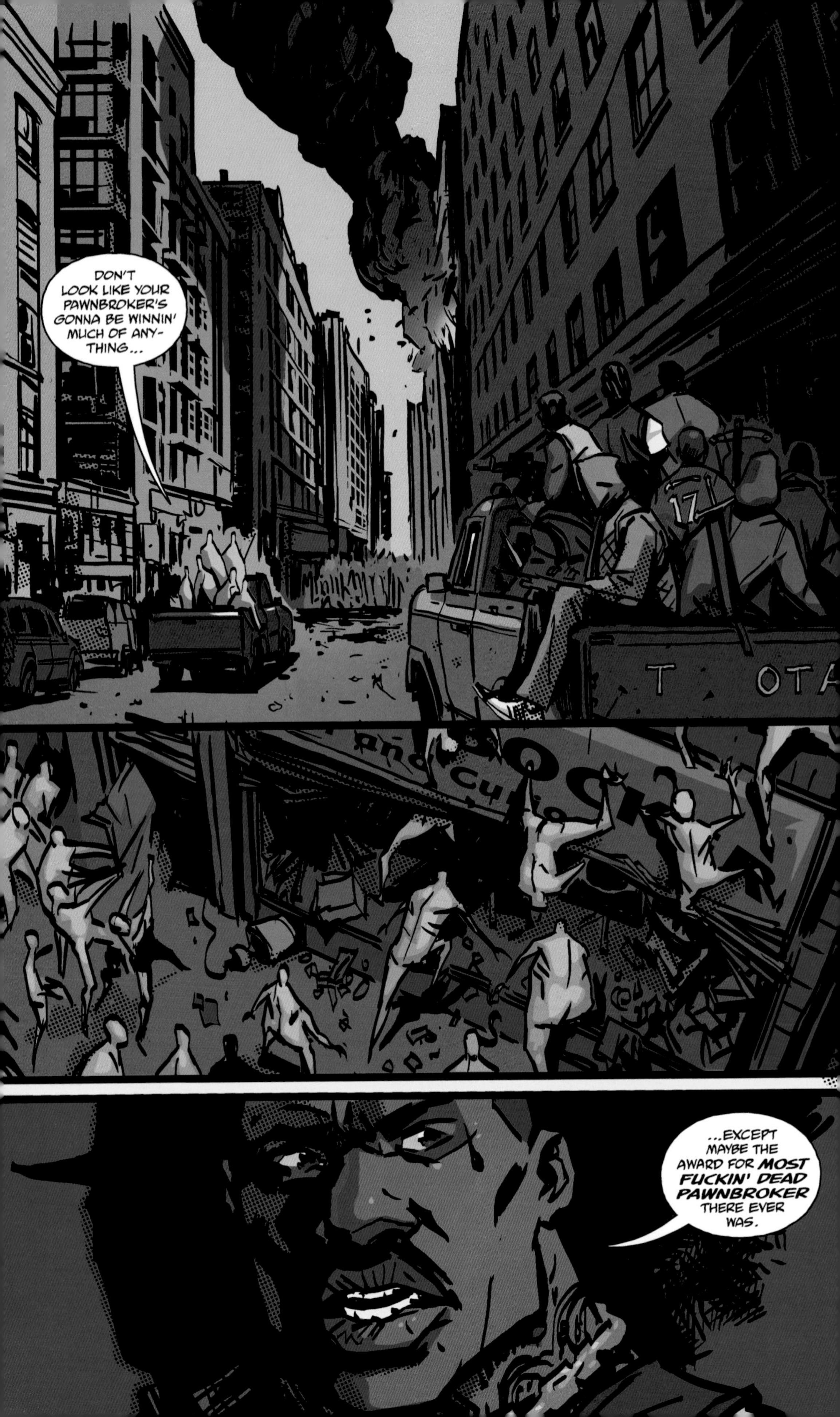
DON'T LOOK LIKE YOUR PAWNBROKER'S GONNA BE WINNIN' MUCH OF ANY-THING...
...EXCEPT MAYBE THE AWARD FOR **MOST FUCKIN' DEAD PAWNBROKER** THERE EVER WAS.

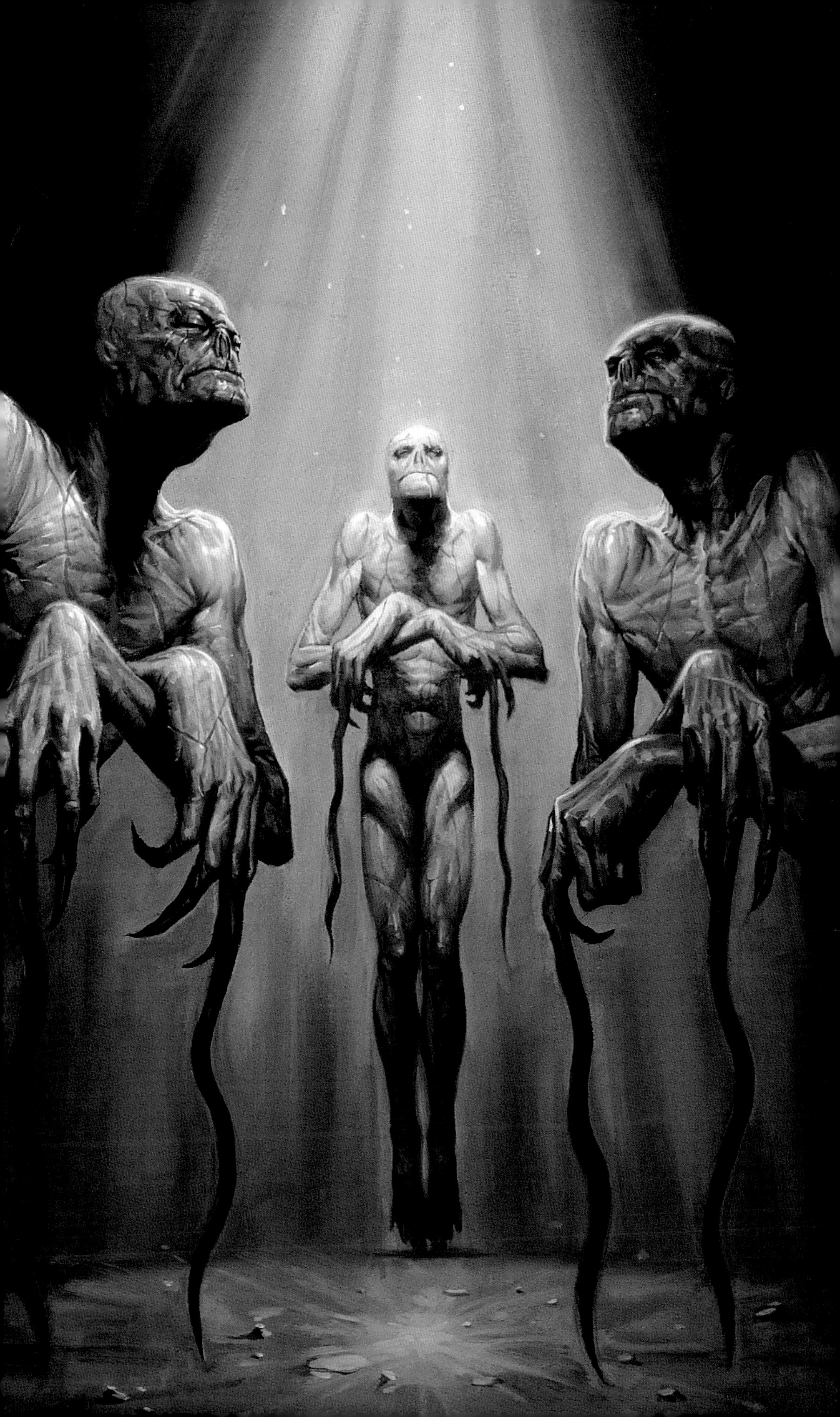

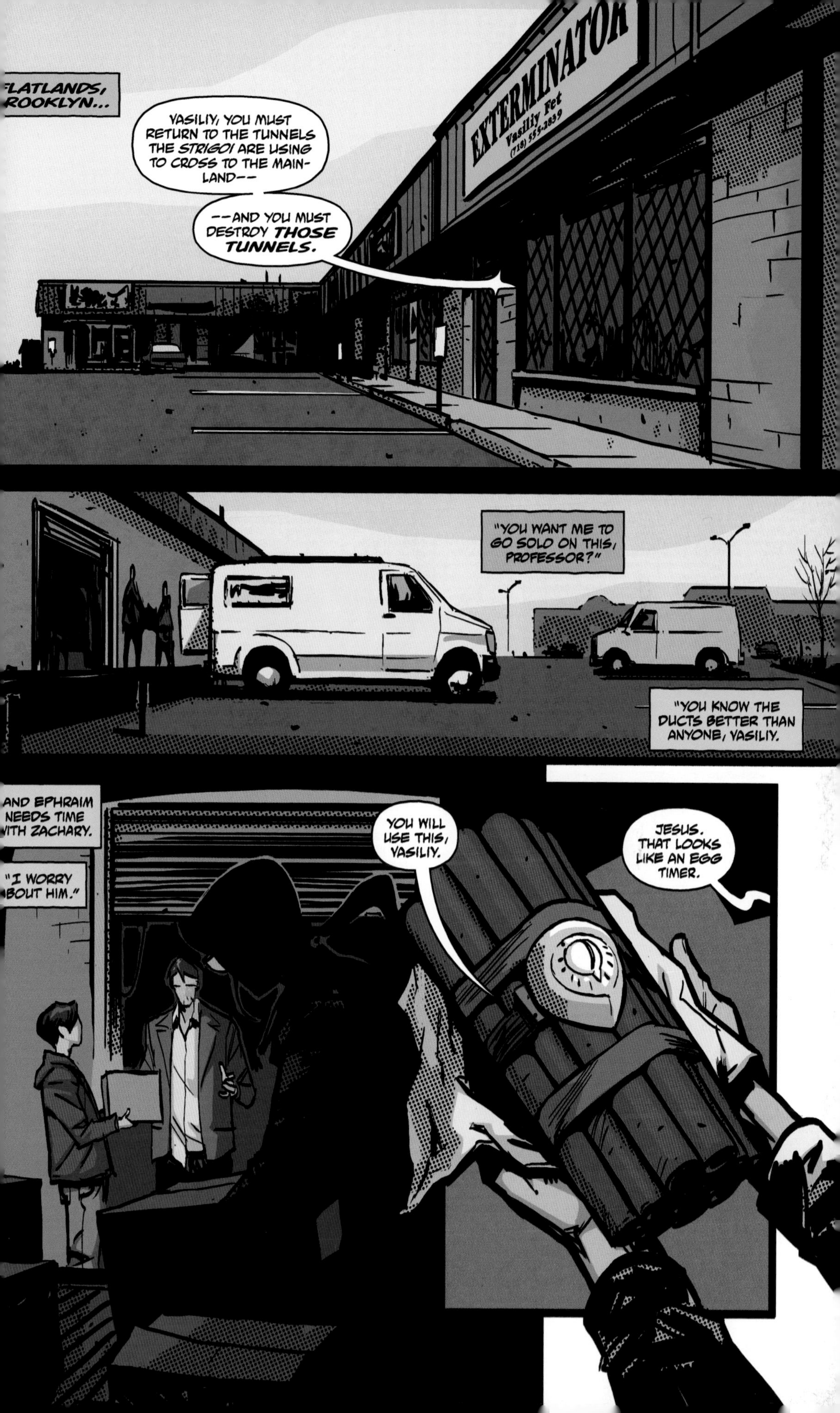
FLATLANDS, BROOKLYN...
EXTERMINATOR
Vasiliy Fet
(718) 555-2839
VASILIY, YOU MUST RETURN TO THE TUNNELS THE STRIGOI ARE USING TO CROSS TO THE MAIN-LAND--
--AND YOU MUST DESTROY THOSE TUNNELS.
"YOU WANT ME TO GO SOLO ON THIS, PROFESSOR?"
"YOU KNOW THE DUCTS BETTER THAN ANYONE, VASILIY.
AND EPHRAIM NEEDS TIME WITH ZACHARY.
"I WORRY ABOUT HIM."
YOU WILL USE THIS, VASILIY.
JESUS. THAT LOOKS LIKE AN EGG TIMER.

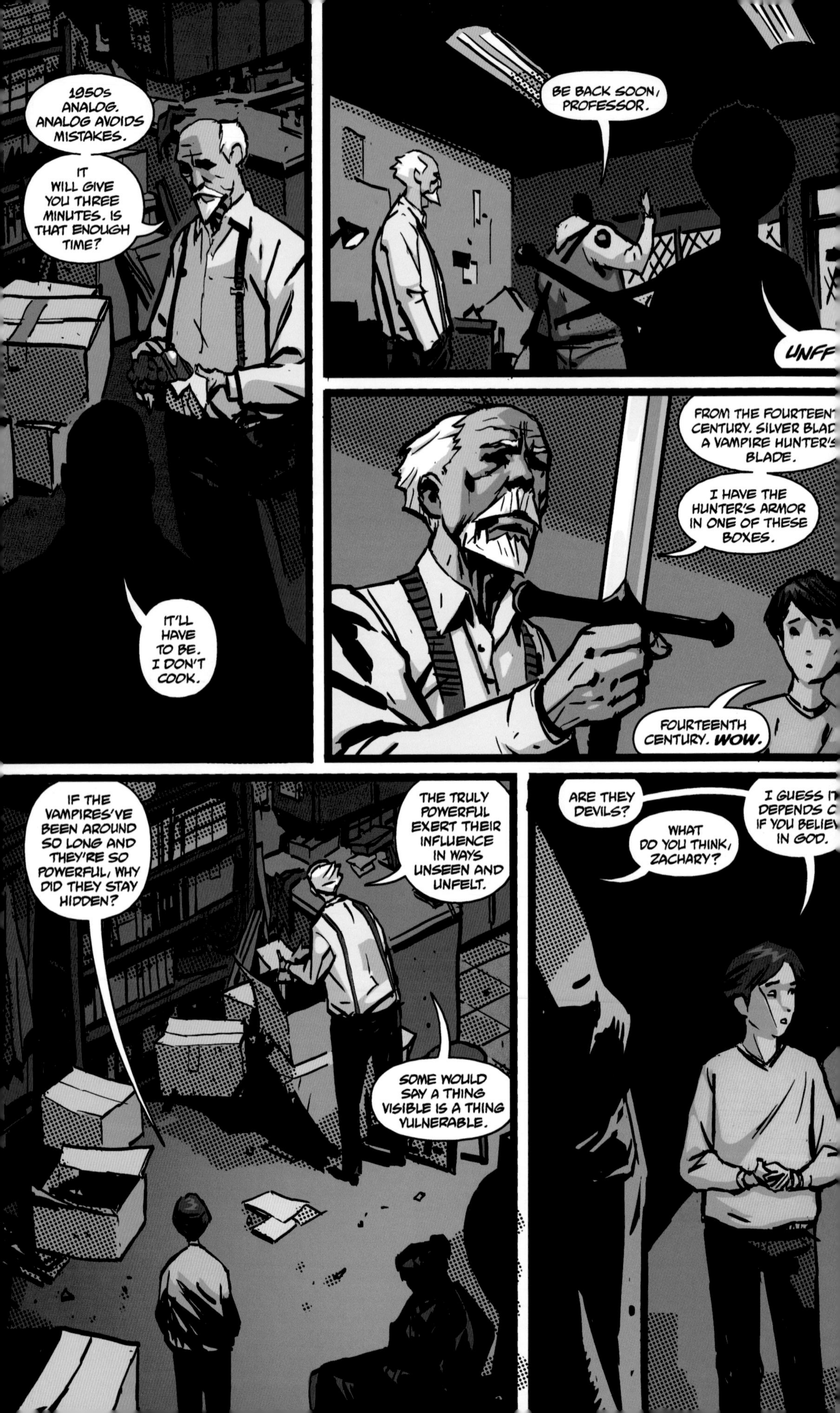
1950s ANALOG. ANALOG AVOIDS MISTAKES.
IT WILL GIVE YOU THREE MINUTES. IS THAT ENOUGH TIME?
IT'LL HAVE TO BE. I DON'T COOK.
BE BACK SOON, PROFESSOR.
UNFF
FROM THE FOURTEENT CENTURY. SILVER BLAD A VAMPIRE HUNTER'S BLADE.
I HAVE THE HUNTER'S ARMOR IN ONE OF THESE BOXES.
FOURTEENTH CENTURY. WOW.
IF THE VAMPIRES'VE BEEN AROUND SO LONG AND THEY'RE SO POWERFUL, WHY DID THEY STAY HIDDEN?
THE TRULY POWERFUL EXERT THEIR INFLUENCE IN WAYS UNSEEN AND UNFELT.
SOME WOULD SAY A THING VISIBLE IS A THING VULNERABLE.
ARE THEY DEVILS?
WHAT DO YOU THINK, ZACHARY?
I GUESS IT DEPENDS C IF YOU BELIEV IN GOD.

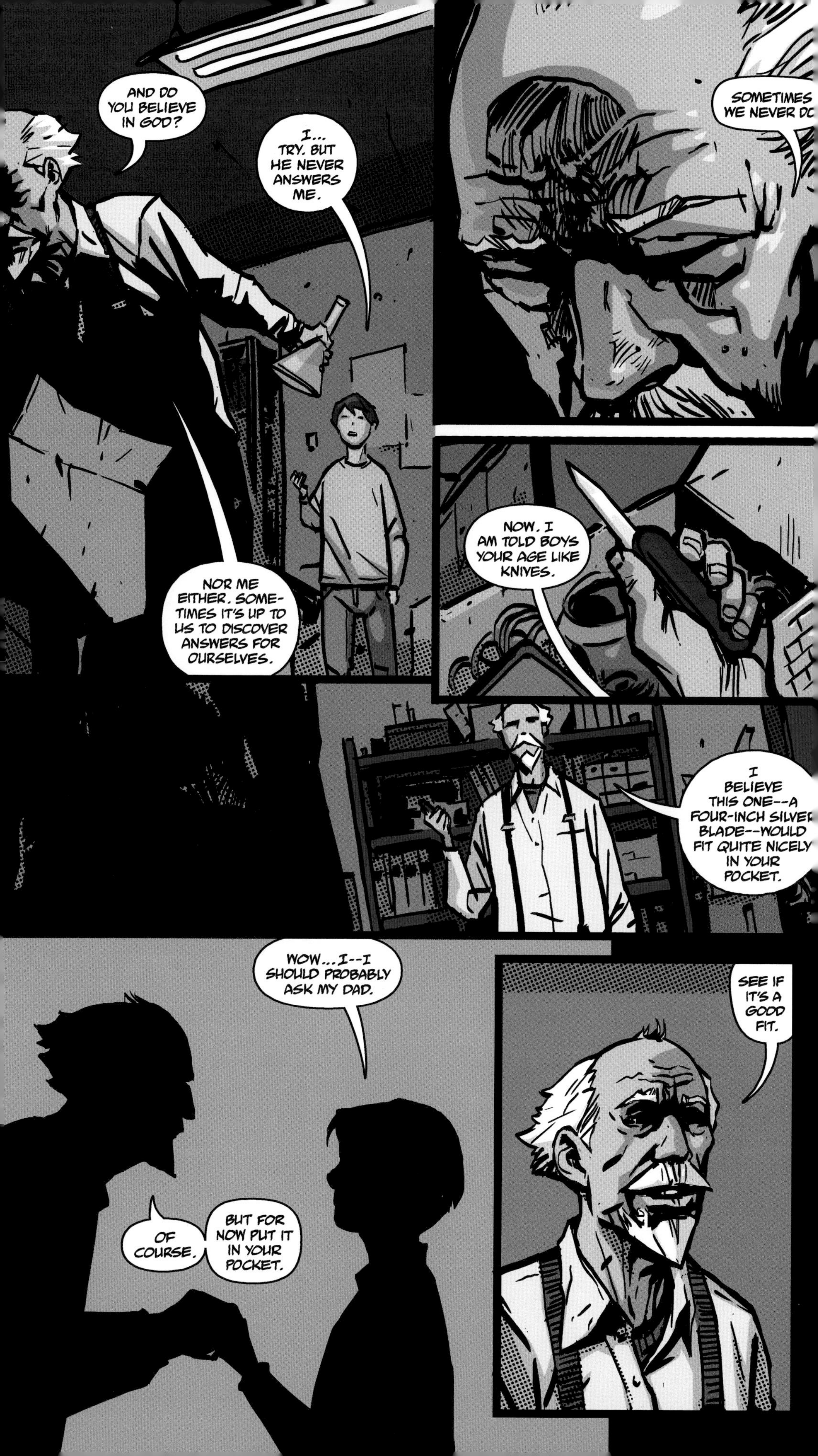
AND DO YOU BELIEVE IN GOD?
I... TRY. BUT HE NEVER ANSWERS ME.
NOR ME EITHER. SOMETIMES IT'S UP TO US TO DISCOVER ANSWERS FOR OURSELVES.
SOMETIMES WE NEVER DO
NOW. I AM TOLD BOYS YOUR AGE LIKE KNIVES.
I BELIEVE THIS ONE--A FOUR-INCH SILVER BLADE--WOULD FIT QUITE NICELY IN YOUR POCKET.
WOW...I--I SHOULD PROBABLY ASK MY DAD.
OF COURSE.
BUT FOR NOW PUT IT IN YOUR POCKET.
SEE IF IT'S A GOOD FIT.

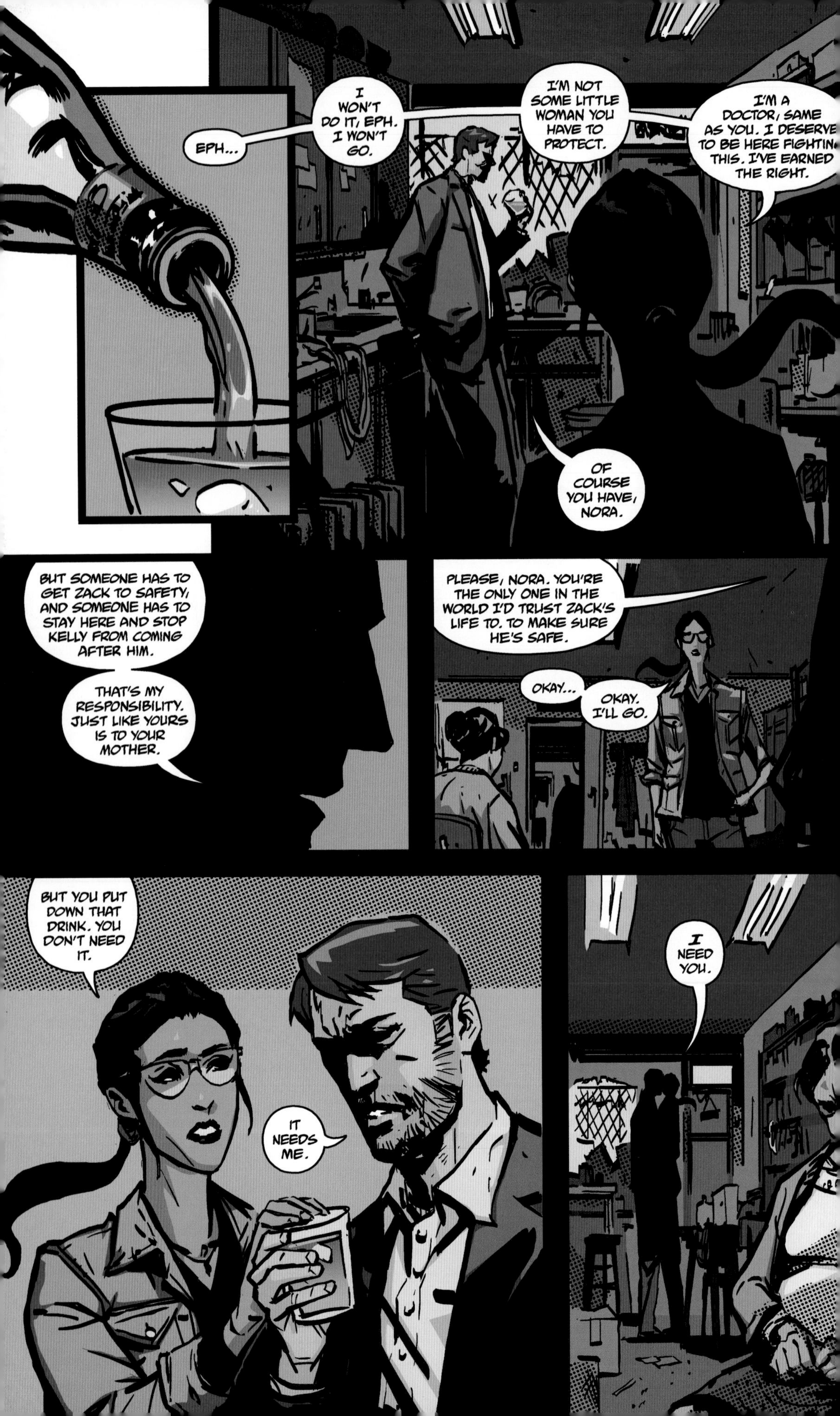
EPH...
I WON'T DO IT, EPH. I WON'T GO.
I'M NOT SOME LITTLE WOMAN YOU HAVE TO PROTECT.
I'M A DOCTOR, SAME AS YOU. I DESERVE TO BE HERE FIGHTIN THIS. I'VE EARNED THE RIGHT.
OF COURSE YOU HAVE, NORA.
BUT SOMEONE HAS TO GET ZACK TO SAFETY, AND SOMEONE HAS TO STAY HERE AND STOP KELLY FROM COMING AFTER HIM.
THAT'S MY RESPONSIBILITY. JUST LIKE YOURS IS TO YOUR MOTHER.
PLEASE, NORA. YOU'RE THE ONLY ONE IN THE WORLD I'D TRUST ZACK'S LIFE TO. TO MAKE SURE HE'S SAFE.
OKAY...
OKAY. I'LL GO.
BUT YOU PUT DOWN THAT DRINK. YOU DON'T NEED IT.
IT NEEDS ME.
I NEED YOU.

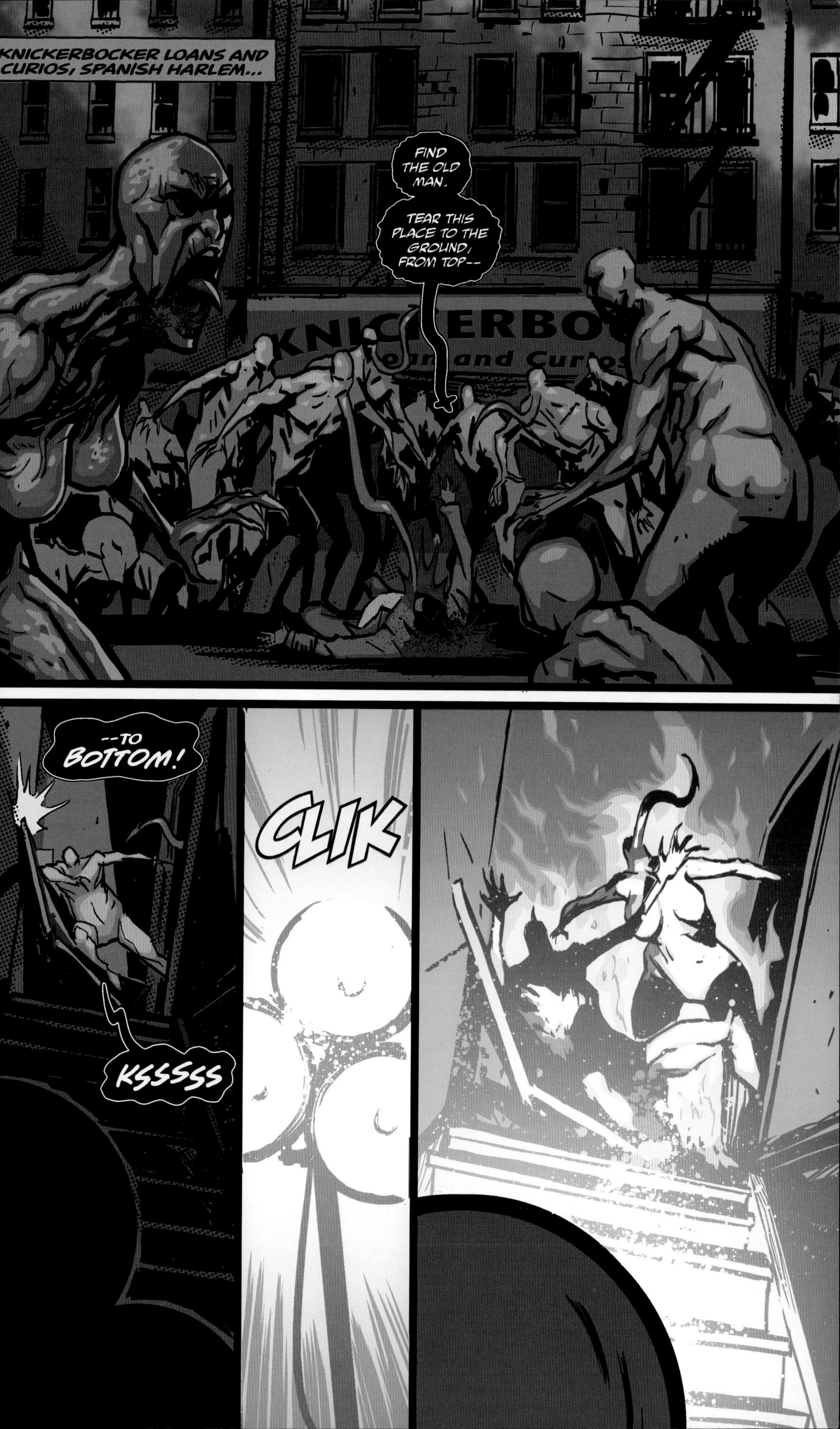
KNICKERBOCKER LOANS AND CURIOS, SPANISH HARLEM...
FIND THE OLD MAN.
TEAR THIS PLACE TO THE GROUND, FROM TOP--
KNICKERBO
Loans and Curios
--TO BOTTOM!
KSSSSS
CLIK

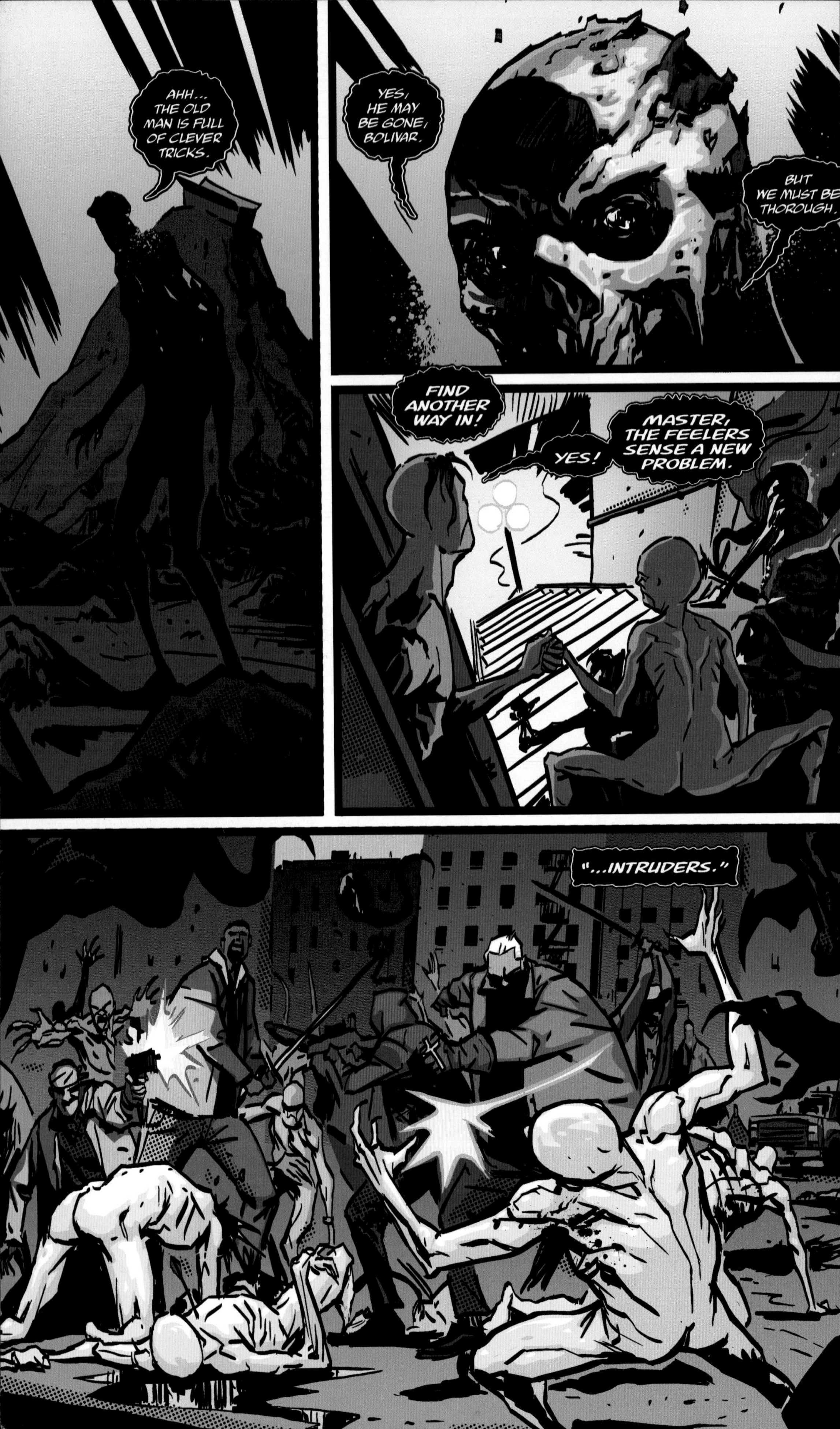
AHH... THE OLD MAN IS FULL OF CLEVER TRICKS.
YES, HE MAY BE GONE, BOLIVAR.
BUT WE MUST BE THOROUGH.
FIND ANOTHER WAY IN!
YES!
MASTER, THE FEELERS SENSE A NEW PROBLEM.
"...INTRUDERS."

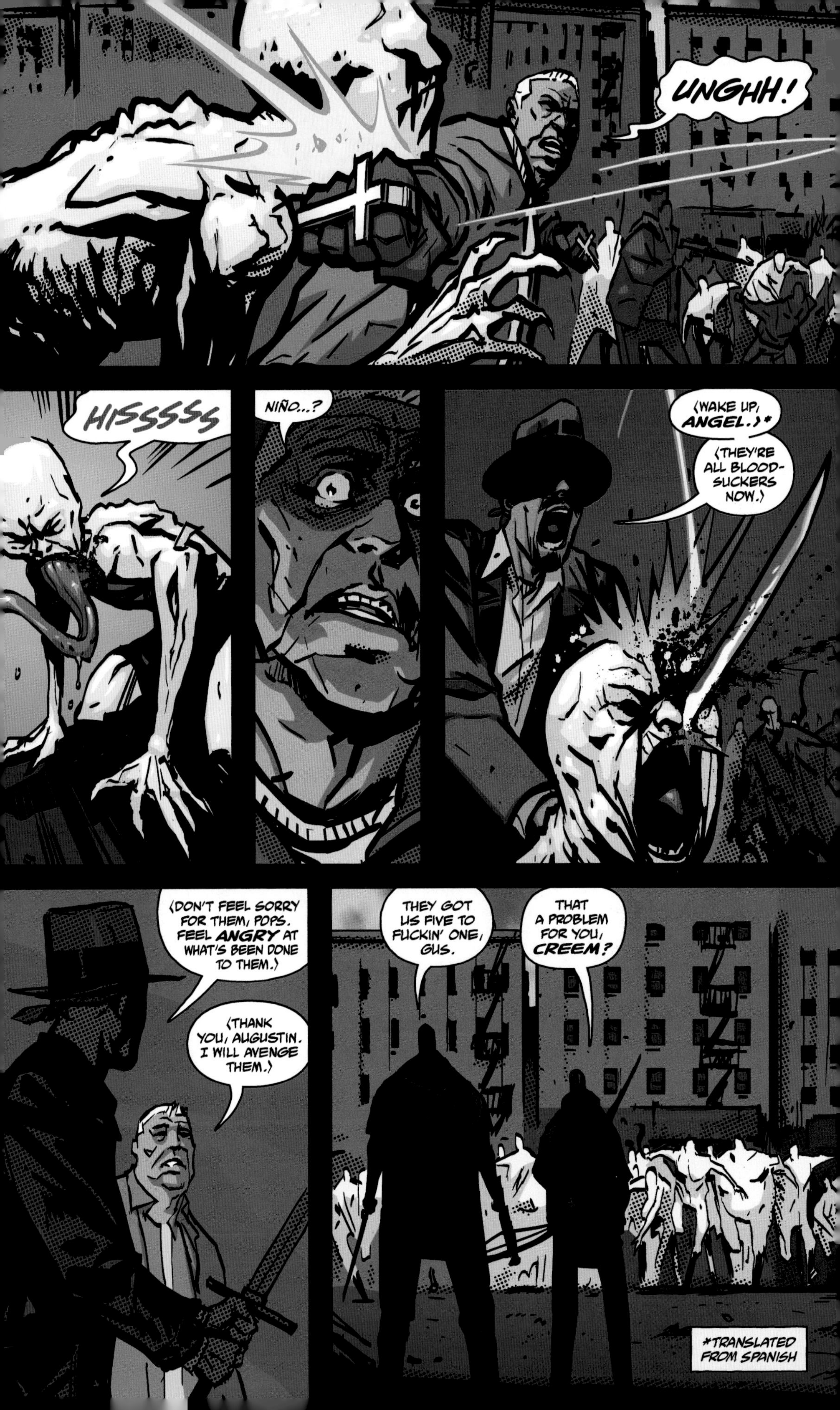
UNGHH!
HISSSSS
NIÑO...?
⟨WAKE UP, ANGEL.⟩*
⟨THEY'RE ALL BLOOD-SUCKERS NOW.⟩
⟨DON'T FEEL SORRY FOR THEM, POPS. FEEL ANGRY AT WHAT'S BEEN DONE TO THEM.⟩
⟨THANK YOU, AUGUSTIN. I WILL AVENGE THEM.⟩
THEY GOT US FIVE TO FUCKIN' ONE, GUS.
THAT A PROBLEM FOR YOU, CREEM?
*TRANSLATED FROM SPANISH

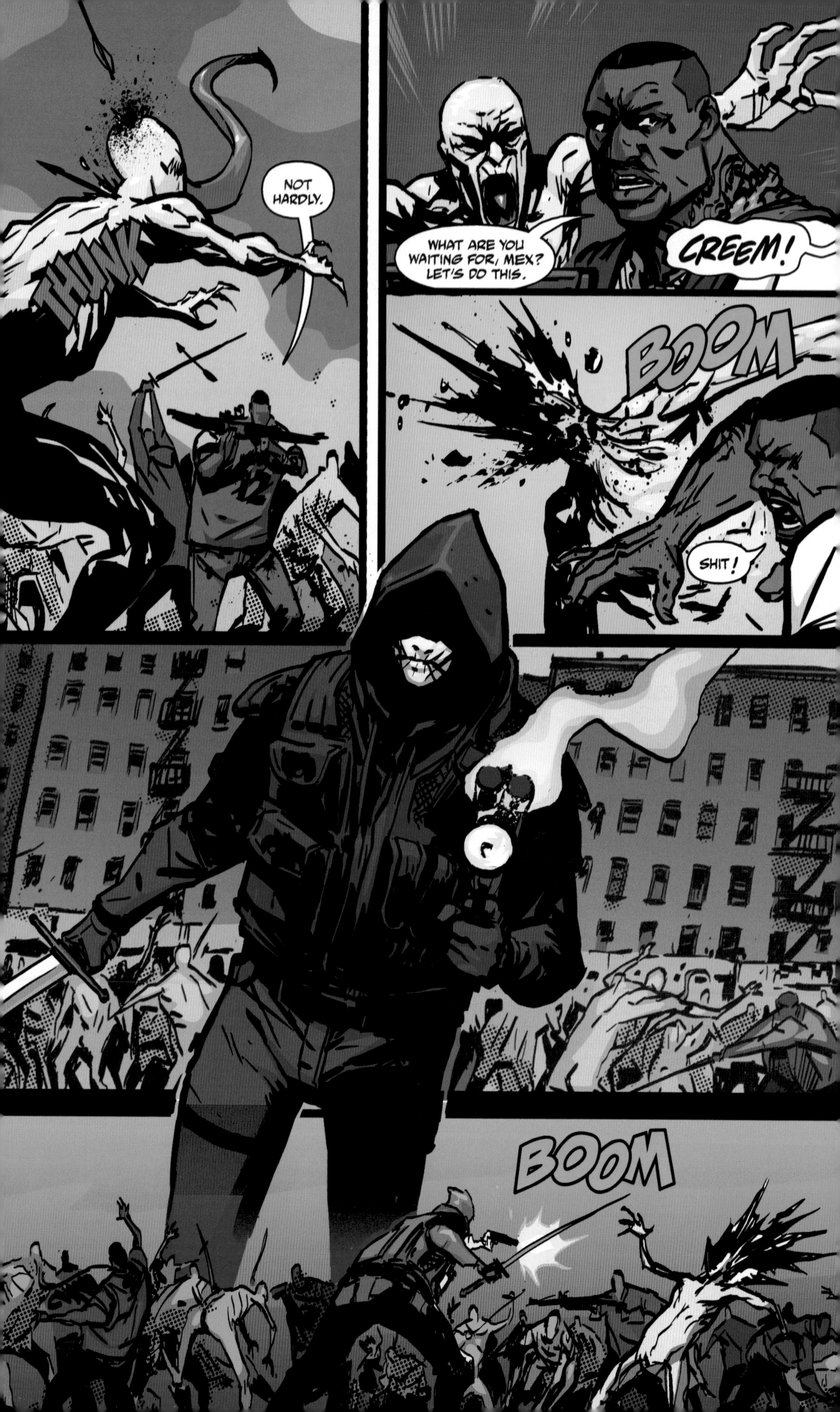
NOT HARDLY.
THUNK
WHAT ARE YOU WAITING FOR, MEX? LET'S DO THIS.
CREEM!
BOOM
SHIT!
BOOM

KISSSS BOOM

THAT'S ONE SCARY-ASS MOTHER-FUCKER.

BROOKLYN

WHAT... ...IS THAT?

HEY, OLD MAN! PAWNBROKER!

WHERE YOU HIDIN' AT?

YOU HOLED UP DOWN HERE, PAWN-BROKER?

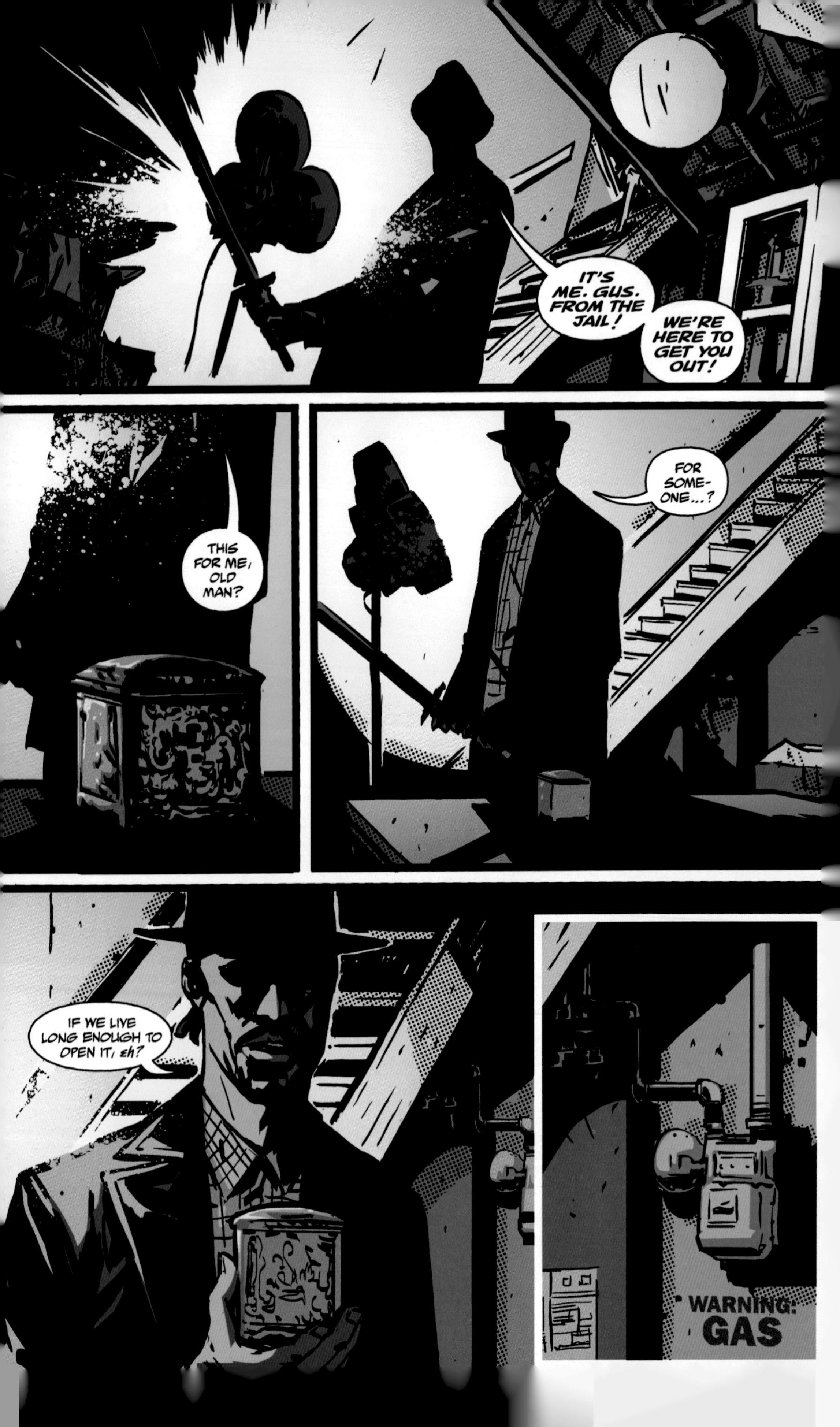
IT'S ME. GUS. FROM THE JAIL!
WE'RE HERE TO GET YOU OUT!
THIS FOR ME, OLD MAN?
FOR SOME-ONE...?
IF WE LIVE LONG ENOUGH TO OPEN IT, eh?
WARNING: GAS

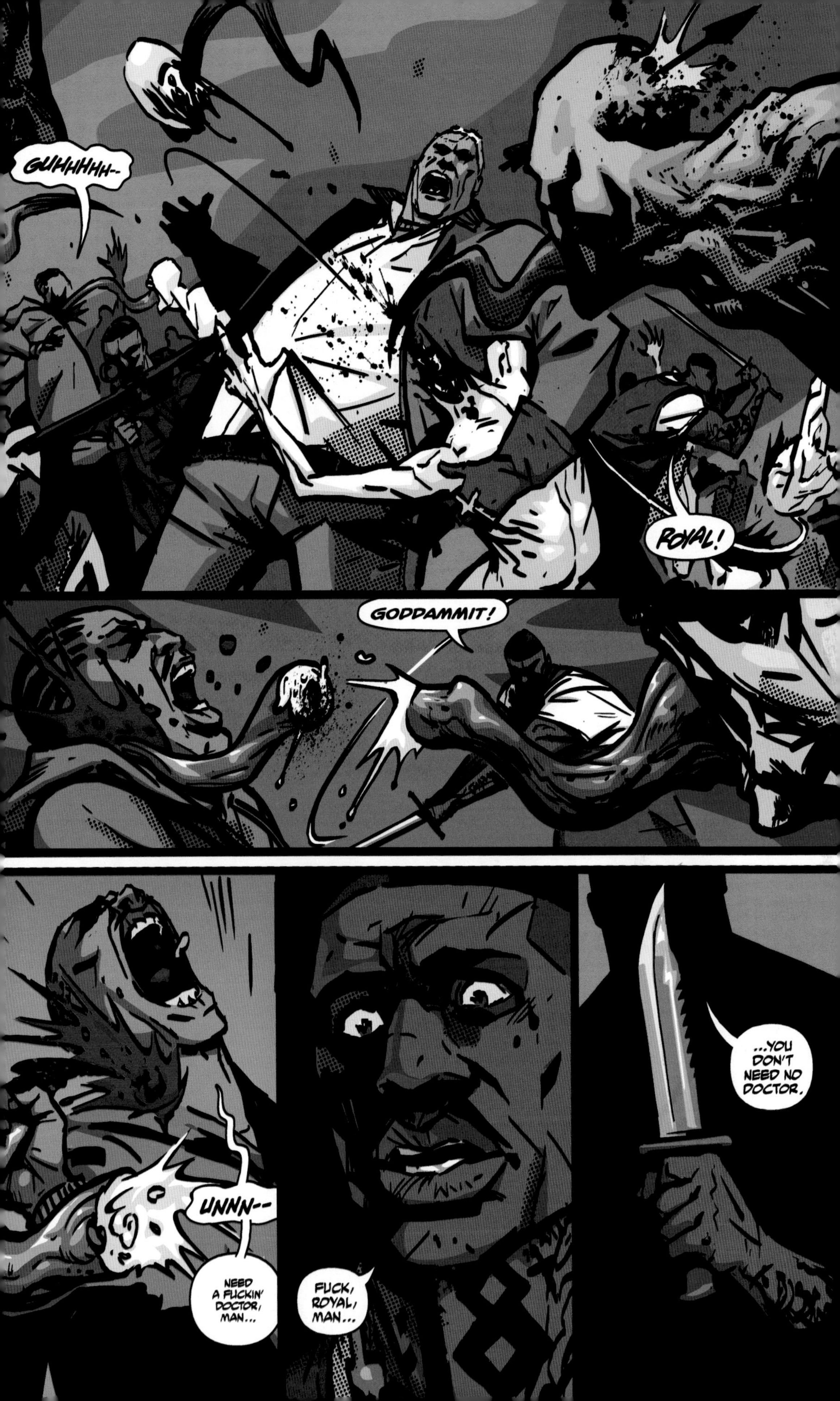
GUHHHHH--
ROYAL!
GODDAMMIT!
UNNN--
NEED A FUCKIN' DOCTOR, MAN...
FUCK, ROYAL, MAN...
...YOU DON'T NEED NO DOCTOR.

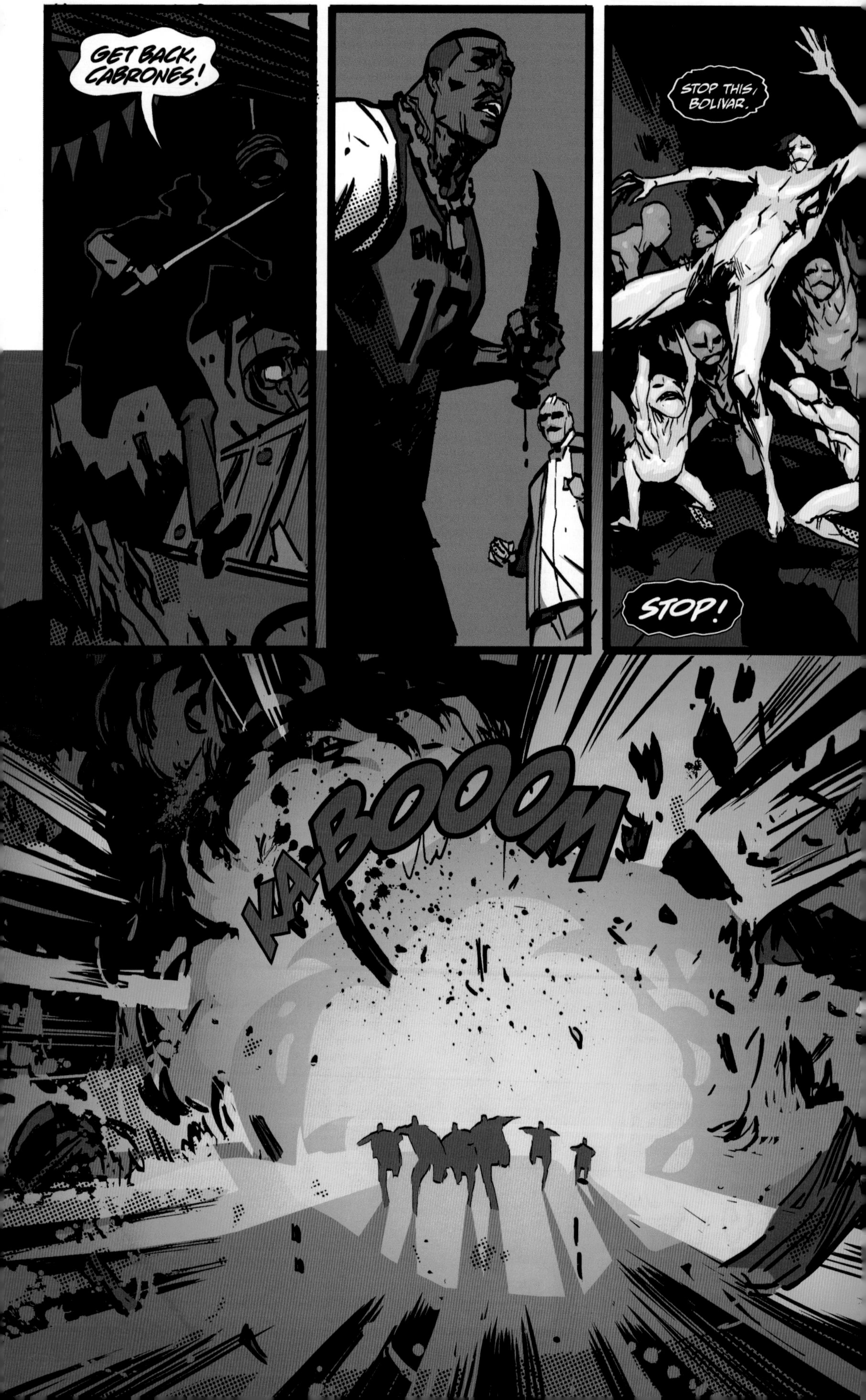
GET BACK, CABRONES!
STOP THIS, BOLIVAR.
STOP!
KA-BOOOM

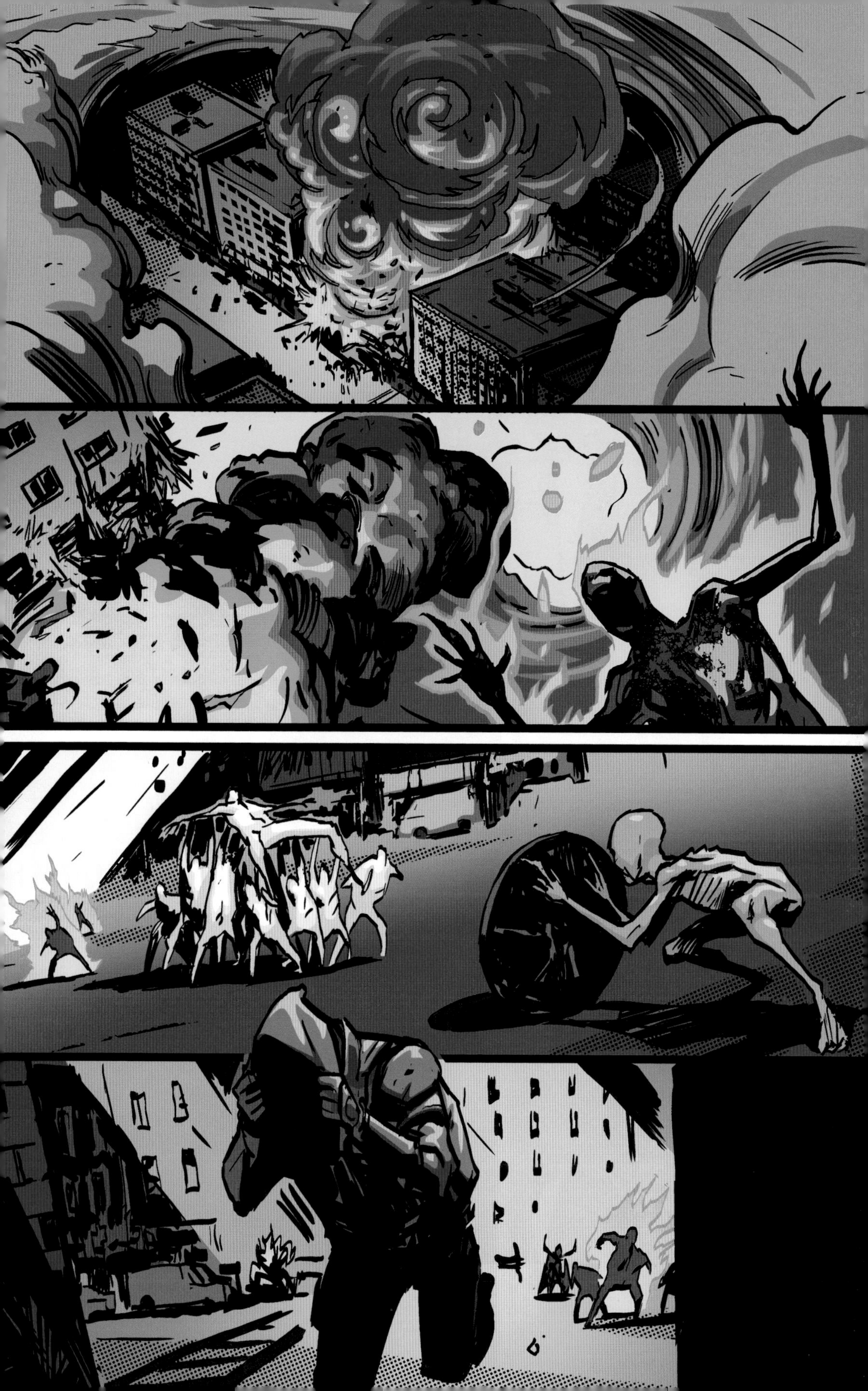

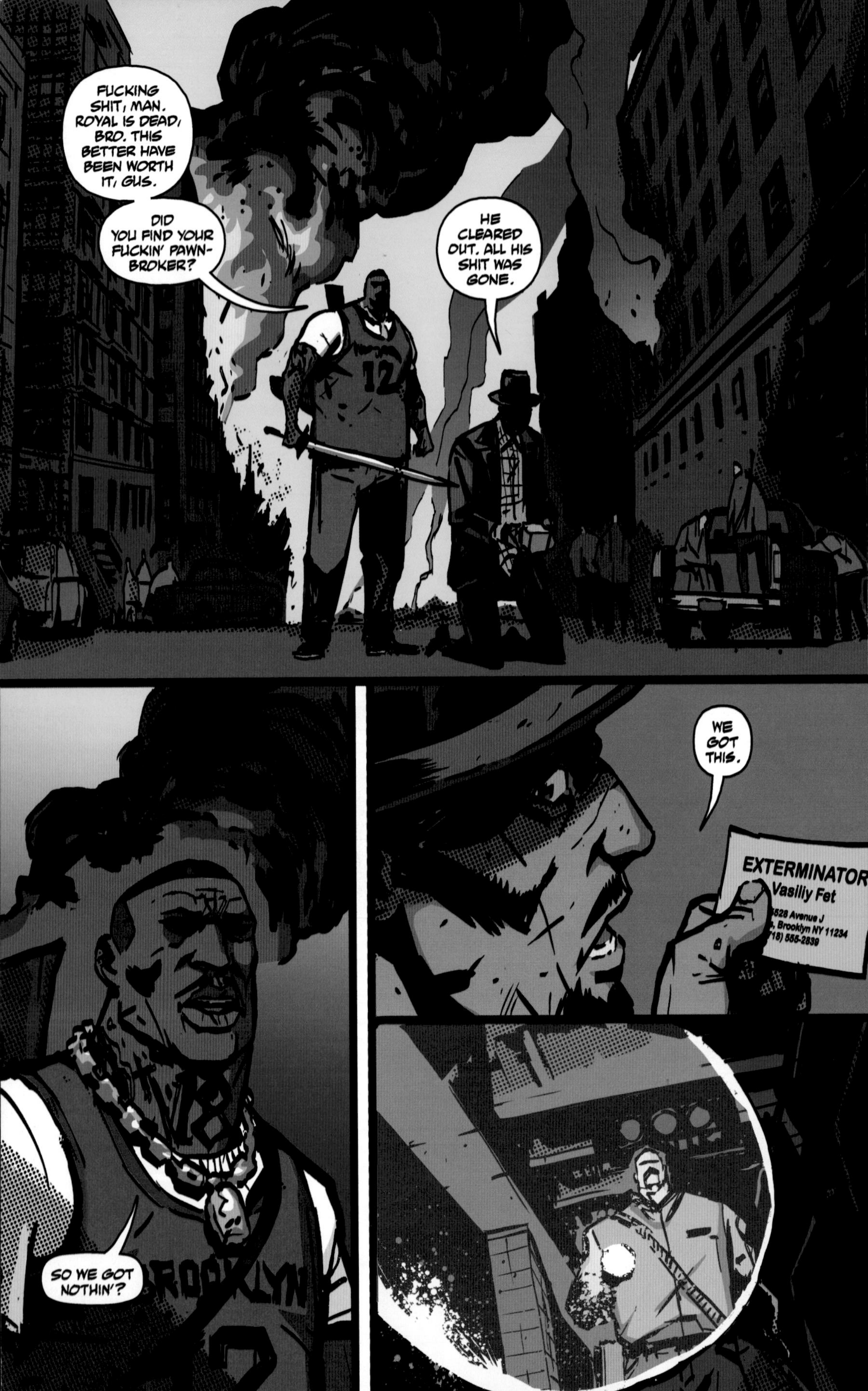
FUCKING SHIT, MAN. ROYAL IS DEAD, BRO. THIS BETTER HAVE BEEN WORTH IT, GUS.
DID YOU FIND YOUR FUCKIN' PAWN-BROKER?
HE CLEARED OUT. ALL HIS SHIT WAS GONE.
12
BROOKLYN
SO WE GOT NOTHIN'?
WE GOT THIS.
EXTERMINATOR
Vasiliy Fet
Brooklyn NY 11234

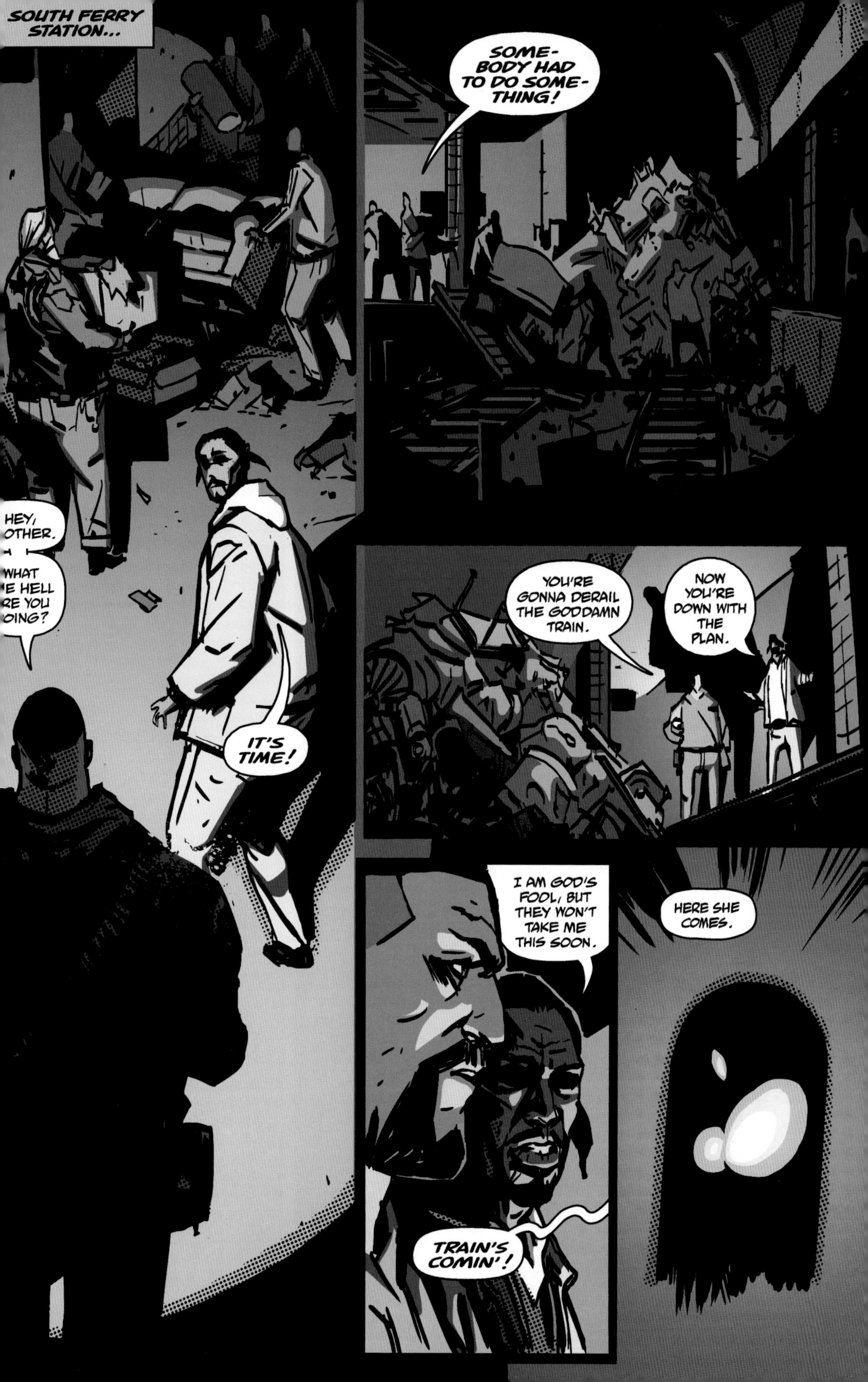
SOUTH FERRY STATION...
SOME-BODY HAD TO DO SOME-THING!
HEY, OTHER.
WHAT E HELL RE YOU OING?
IT'S TIME!
YOU'RE GONNA DERAIL THE GODDAMN TRAIN.
NOW YOU'RE DOWN WITH THE PLAN.
I AM GOD'S FOOL, BUT THEY WON'T TAKE ME THIS SOON.
TRAIN'S COMIN'!
HERE SHE COMES.

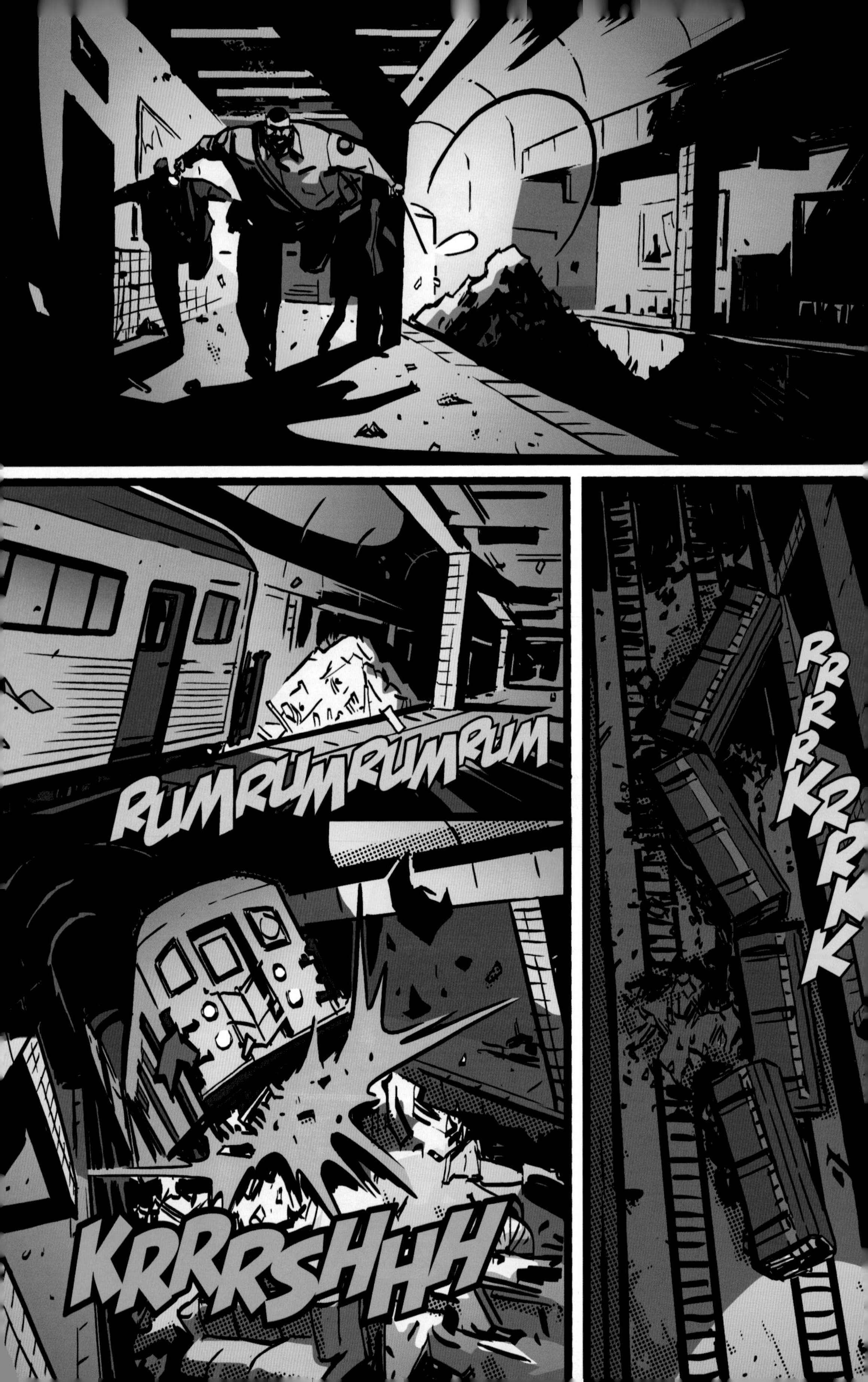
RUMRUMRUMRUM
KRRRSHHH
RRRRKRRRK

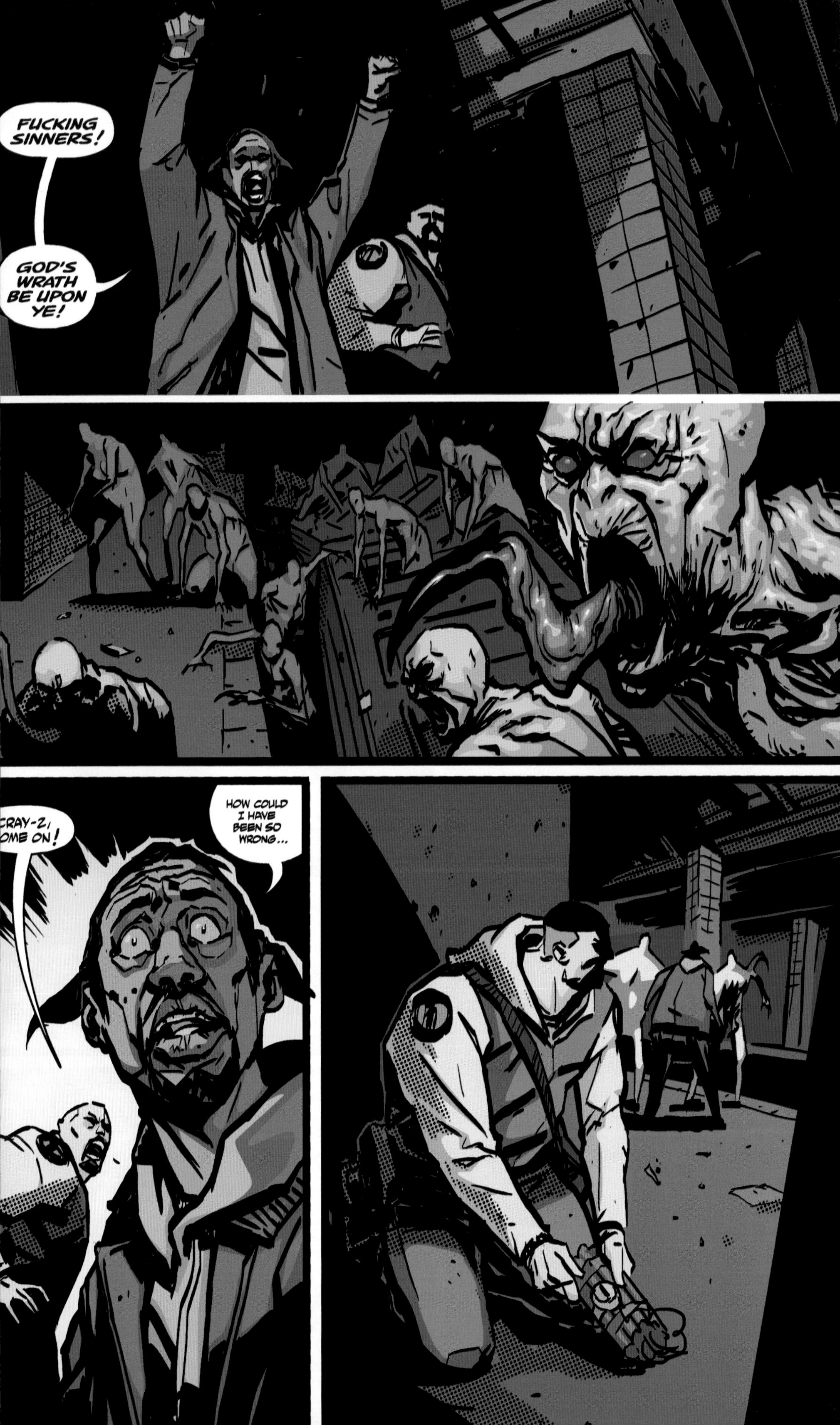
FUCKING SINNERS!
GOD'S WRATH BE UPON YE!
CRAY-Z, OME ON!
HOW COULD I HAVE BEEN SO WRONG...

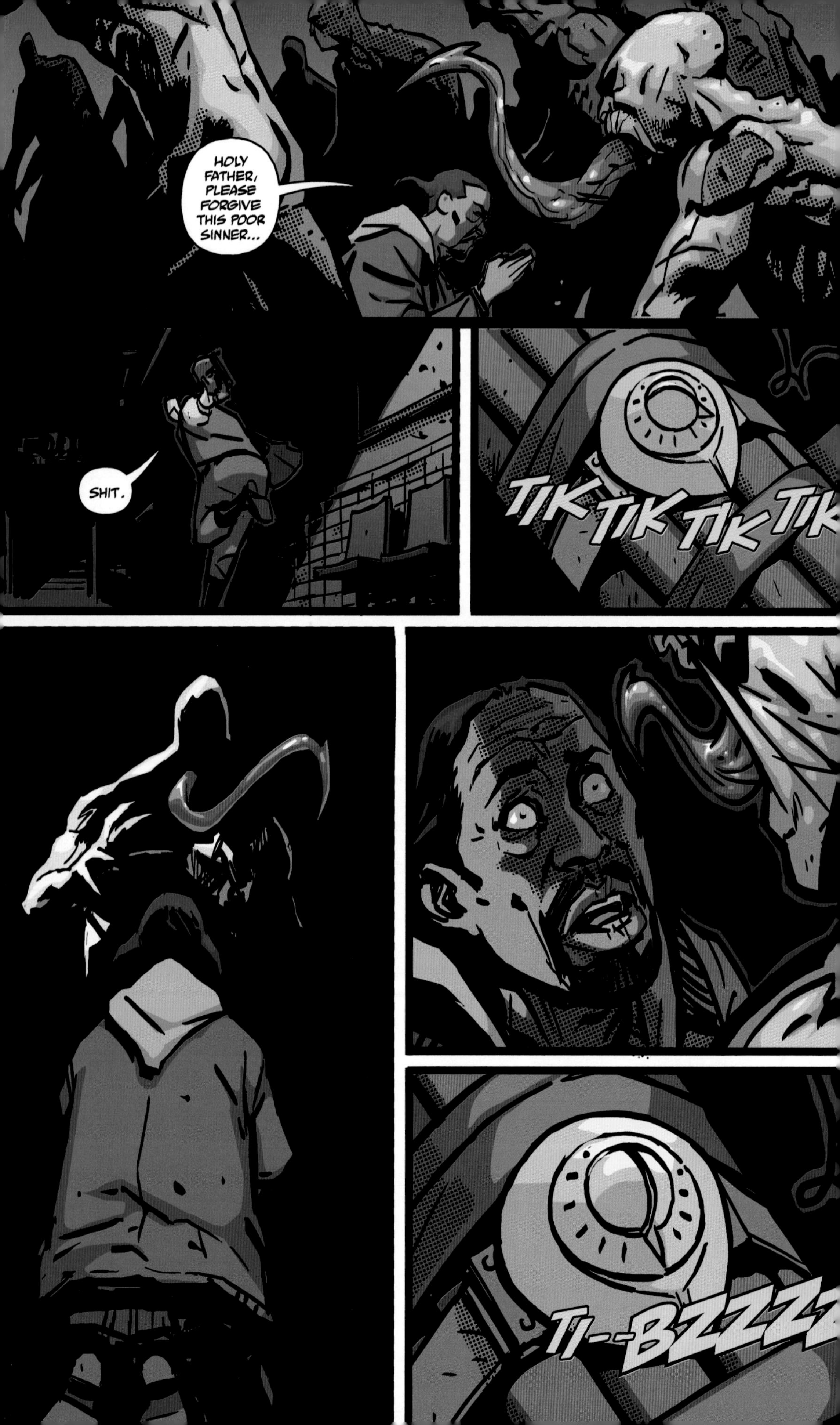
HOLY FATHER, PLEASE FORGIVE THIS POOR SINNER...
SHIT.
TIK TIK TIK TIK
TI--BZZZZ

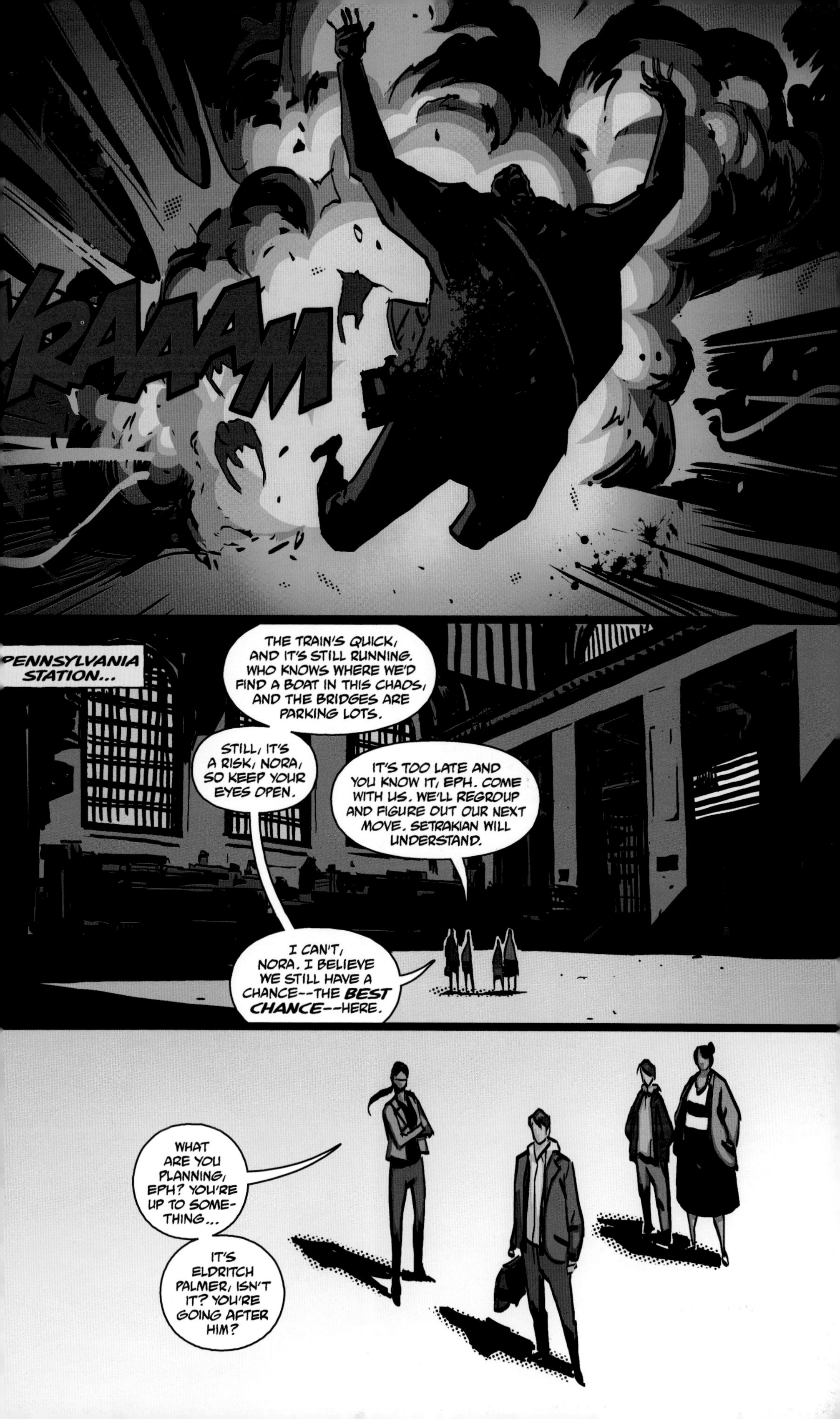
KRAAAM
PENNSYLVANIA STATION...
THE TRAIN'S QUICK, AND IT'S STILL RUNNING. WHO KNOWS WHERE WE'D FIND A BOAT IN THIS CHAOS, AND THE BRIDGES ARE PARKING LOTS.
STILL, IT'S A RISK, NORA, SO KEEP YOUR EYES OPEN.
IT'S TOO LATE AND YOU KNOW IT, EPH. COME WITH US. WE'LL REGROUP AND FIGURE OUT OUR NEXT MOVE. SETRAKIAN WILL UNDERSTAND.
I CAN'T, NORA. I BELIEVE WE STILL HAVE A CHANCE--THE BEST CHANCE--HERE.
WHAT ARE YOU PLANNING, EPH? YOU'RE UP TO SOME-THING...
IT'S ELDRITCH PALMER, ISN'T IT? YOU'RE GOING AFTER HIM?

HE'S THE KEY, NORA. I'M SURE OF IT. WHATEVER THE MASTER'S PLAN IS, HE NEEDS PALMER. HE NEEDS HIS MONEY, HIS POWER.

OTHERWISE HE WOULD HAVE KILLED HIM OR TURNED HIM BY NOW.

BUT PALMER'S STILL ON THE NEWS, PLEDGING TO HELP THE CRISIS...

PROMISE ME YOU'RE NOT DOING ANYTHING ON YOUR OWN.

I'M NOT STUPID, NORA. IT'S OKAY. TAKE THIS. WEAPONS. JUST IN CASE.

YOU HELP NORA WITH MRS. MARTINEZ, OKAY?

PROMISE YOU'LL COME MEET US SOON, DAD?

I.

...PROMISE

C.D.C. CANARY PROJECT HEADQUARTERS, MANHATTAN...

BRRRIINNG

DIRECTOR BARNES...

BRRIING

HURM...

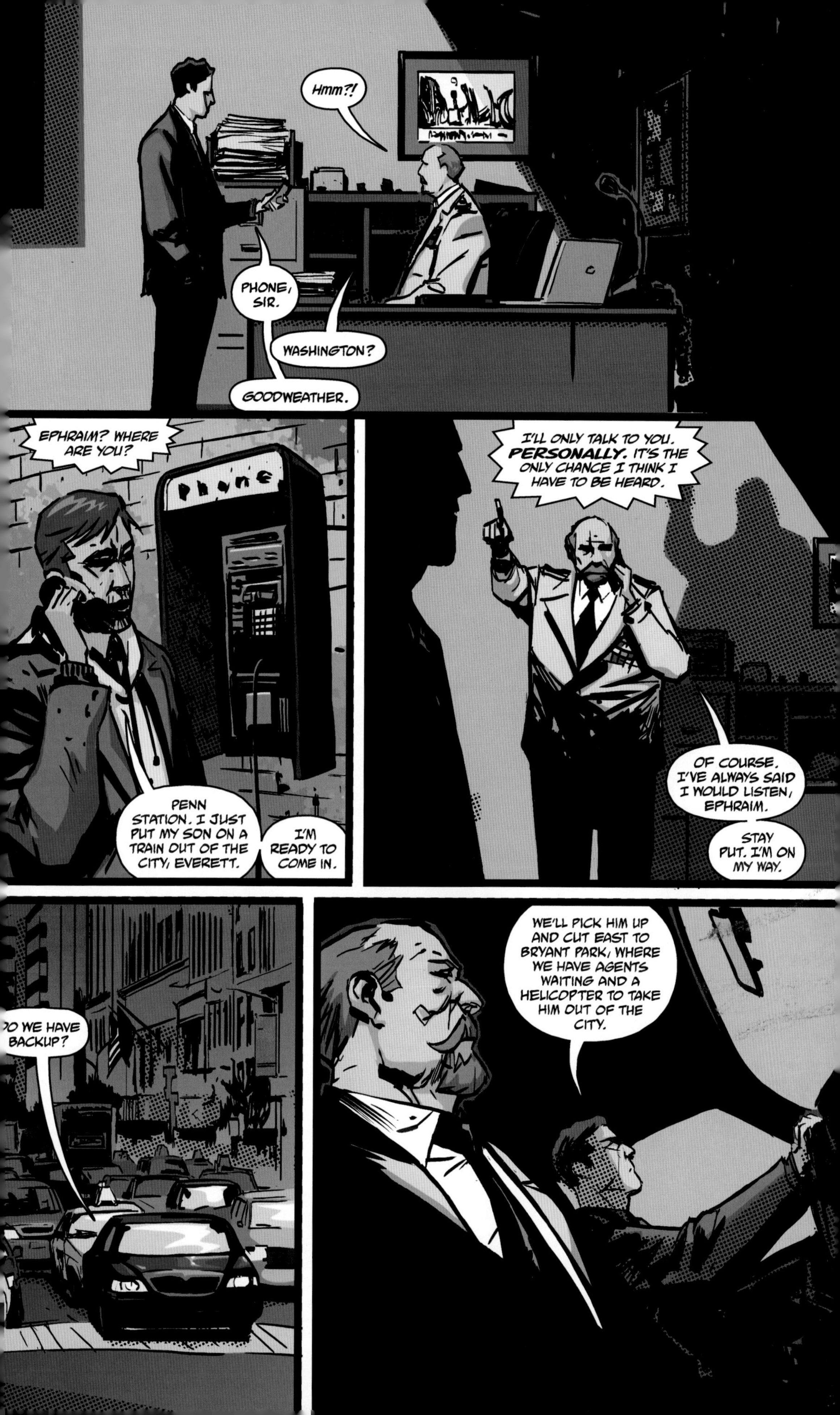
Hmm?!
PHONE, SIR.
WASHINGTON?
GOODWEATHER.
EPHRAIM? WHERE ARE YOU?
Phone
PENN STATION. I JUST PUT MY SON ON A TRAIN OUT OF THE CITY, EVERETT.
I'M READY TO COME IN.
I'LL ONLY TALK TO YOU. PERSONALLY. IT'S THE ONLY CHANCE I THINK I HAVE TO BE HEARD.
OF COURSE. I'VE ALWAYS SAID I WOULD LISTEN, EPHRAIM.
STAY PUT. I'M ON MY WAY.
O WE HAVE BACKUP?
WE'LL PICK HIM UP AND CUT EAST TO BRYANT PARK, WHERE WE HAVE AGENTS WAITING AND A HELICOPTER TO TAKE HIM OUT OF THE CITY.

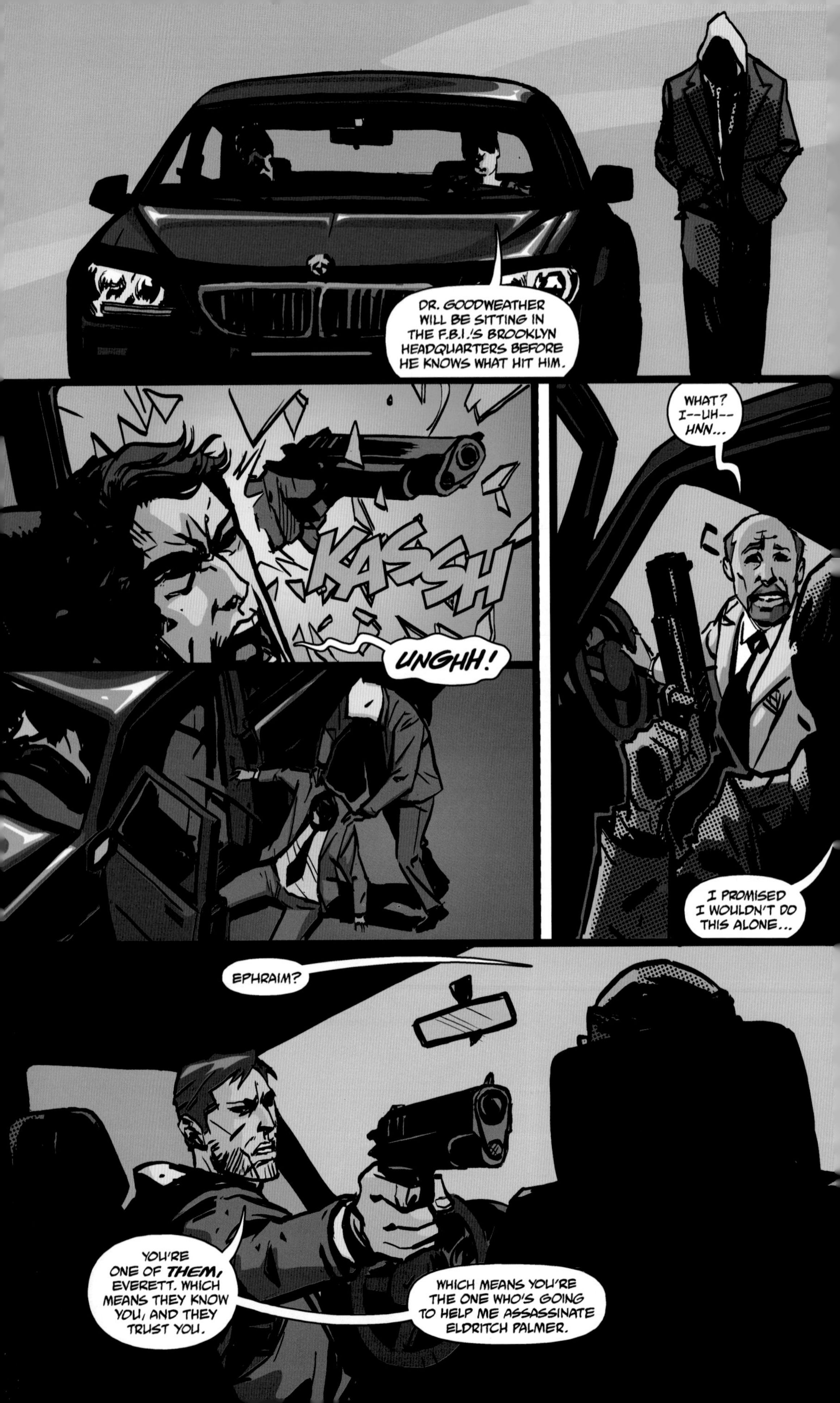

DR. GOODWEATHER WILL BE SITTING IN THE F.B.I.'S BROOKLYN HEADQUARTERS BEFORE HE KNOWS WHAT HIT HIM.
KASSH
UNGHH!
WHAT? I--UH--HNN...
I PROMISED I WOULDN'T DO THIS ALONE...
EPHRAIM?
YOU'RE ONE OF THEM, EVERETT. WHICH MEANS THEY KNOW YOU, AND THEY TRUST YOU.
WHICH MEANS YOU'RE THE ONE WHO'S GOING TO HELP ME ASSASSINATE ELDRITCH PALMER.

ART BY GABRIEL BÁ AND FÁBIO MOON

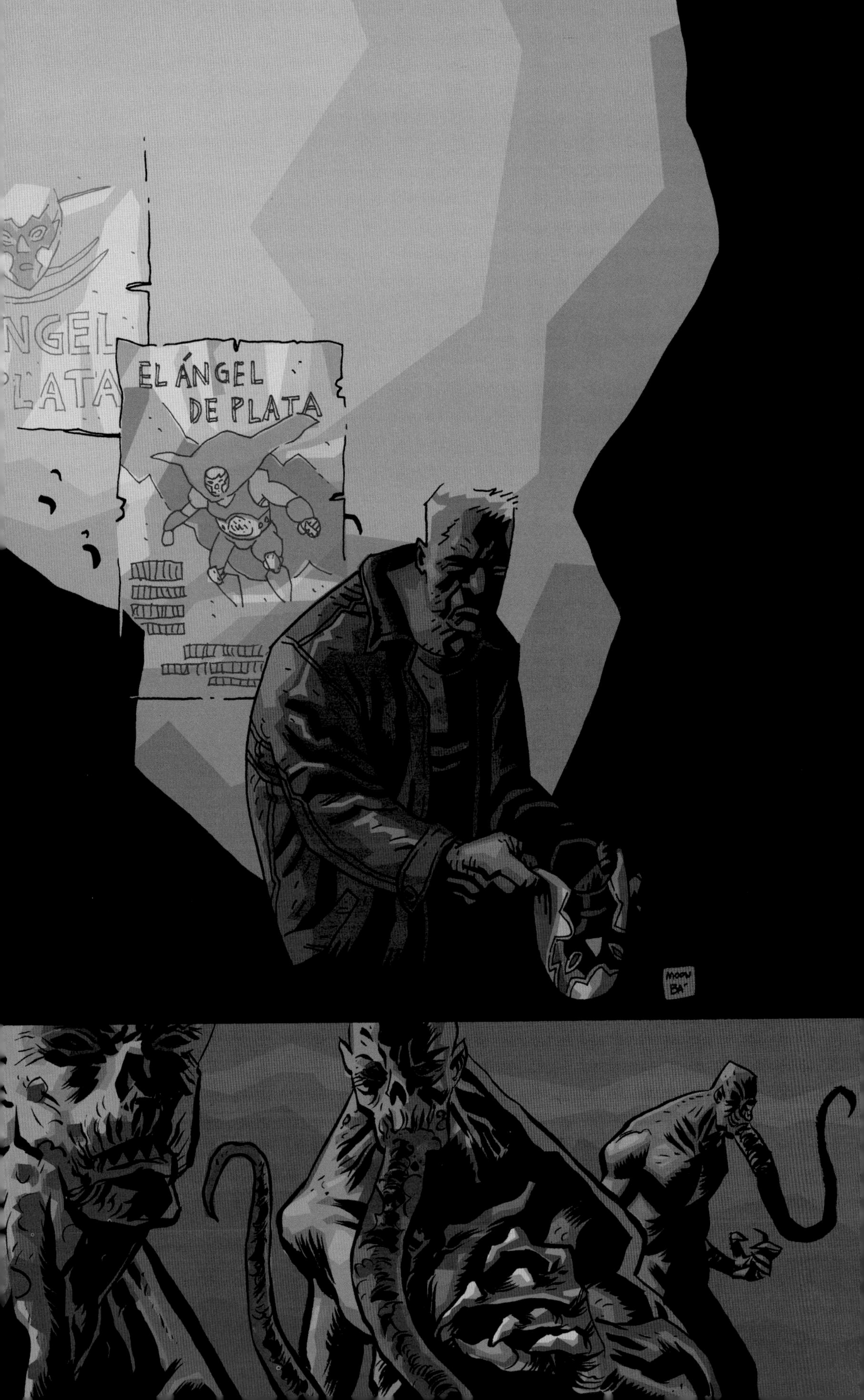
EL ÁNGEL
DE PLATA

In a world being overrun by a plague of vampires, there are many stories and many horrors. This one belongs to a broken old *luchador* named Angel Guzman Hurtado, once known to many as…

THE SILVER ANGEL Part 1 of 3

Written and Drawn by
DAVID LAPHAM

Colors by
LEE LOUGHRIDGE

Letters by
CLEM ROBINS

The Strain created by
GUILLERMO DEL TORO and CHUCK HOGAN

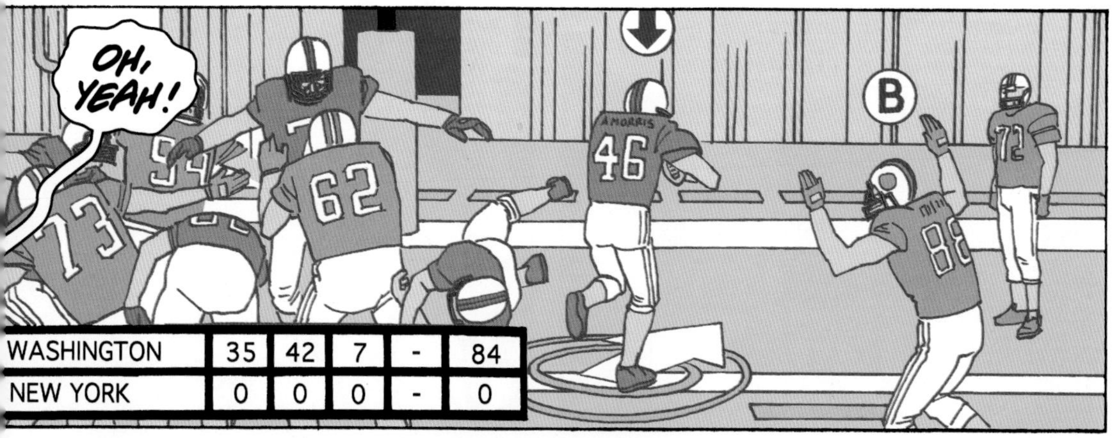

OH, YEAH!
A MORRIS
WASHINGTON 35 42 7 - 84
NEW YORK 0 0 0 - 0

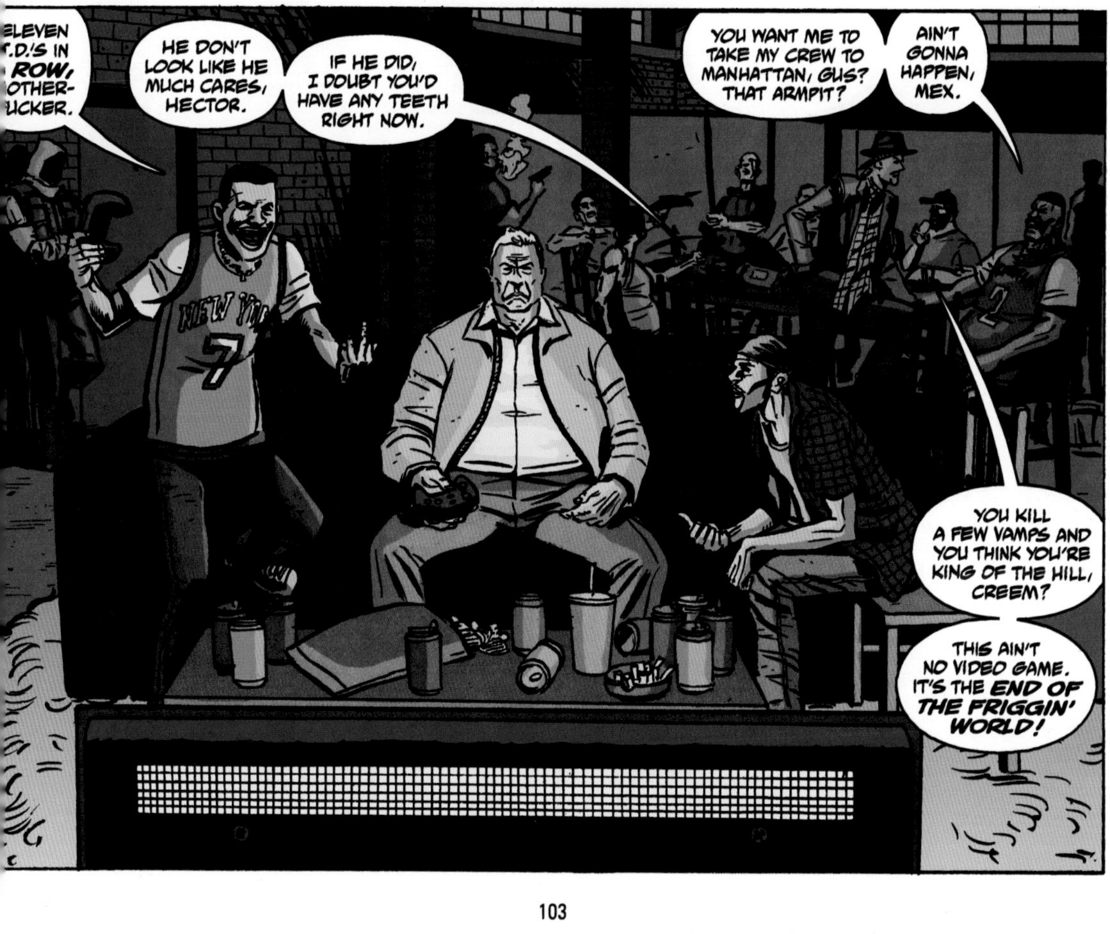

ELEVEN .D.'S IN ROW, OTHER- UCKER.
HE DON'T LOOK LIKE HE MUCH CARES, HECTOR.
IF HE DID, I DOUBT YOU'D HAVE ANY TEETH RIGHT NOW.
YOU WANT ME TO TAKE MY CREW TO MANHATTAN, GUS? THAT ARMPIT?
AIN'T GONNA HAPPEN, MEX.
NEW YORK 7
YOU KILL A FEW VAMPS AND YOU THINK YOU'RE KING OF THE HILL, CREEM?
THIS AIN'T NO VIDEO GAME. IT'S THE *END OF THE FRIGGIN' WORLD!*

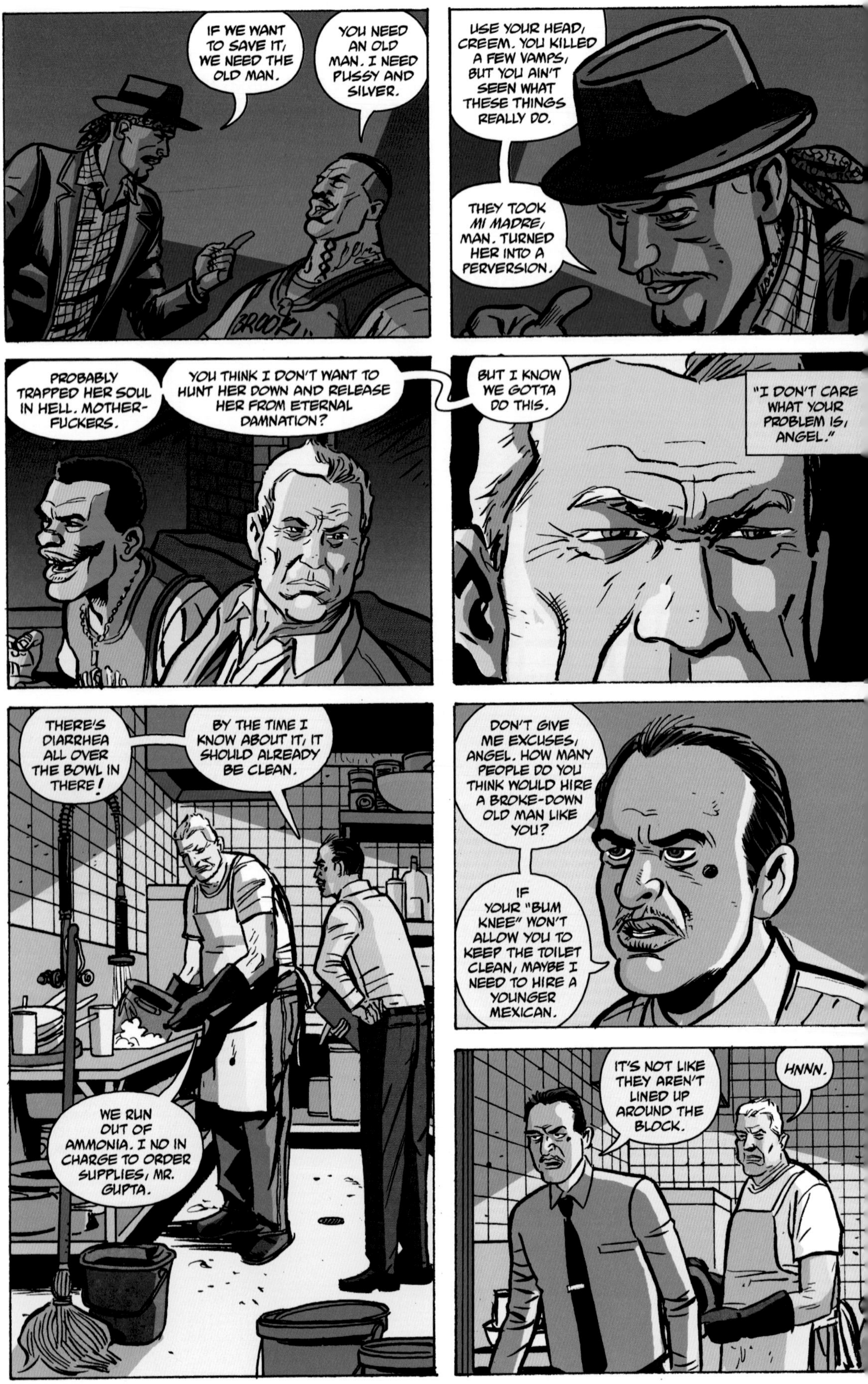
IF WE WANT TO SAVE IT, WE NEED THE OLD MAN.
YOU NEED AN OLD MAN. I NEED PUSSY AND SILVER.
USE YOUR HEAD, CREEM. YOU KILLED A FEW VAMPS, BUT YOU AIN'T SEEN WHAT THESE THINGS REALLY DO.
THEY TOOK MI MADRE, MAN. TURNED HER INTO A PERVERSION.
PROBABLY TRAPPED HER SOUL IN HELL. MOTHER-FUCKERS.
YOU THINK I DON'T WANT TO HUNT HER DOWN AND RELEASE HER FROM ETERNAL DAMNATION?
BUT I KNOW WE GOTTA DO THIS.
"I DON'T CARE WHAT YOUR PROBLEM IS, ANGEL."
THERE'S DIARRHEA ALL OVER THE BOWL IN THERE!
BY THE TIME I KNOW ABOUT IT, IT SHOULD ALREADY BE CLEAN.
WE RUN OUT OF AMMONIA. I NO IN CHARGE TO ORDER SUPPLIES, MR. GUPTA.
DON'T GIVE ME EXCUSES, ANGEL. HOW MANY PEOPLE DO YOU THINK WOULD HIRE A BROKE-DOWN OLD MAN LIKE YOU?
IF YOUR "BUM KNEE" WON'T ALLOW YOU TO KEEP THE TOILET CLEAN, MAYBE I NEED TO HIRE A YOUNGER MEXICAN.
IT'S NOT LIKE THEY AREN'T LINED UP AROUND THE BLOCK.
HNNN.

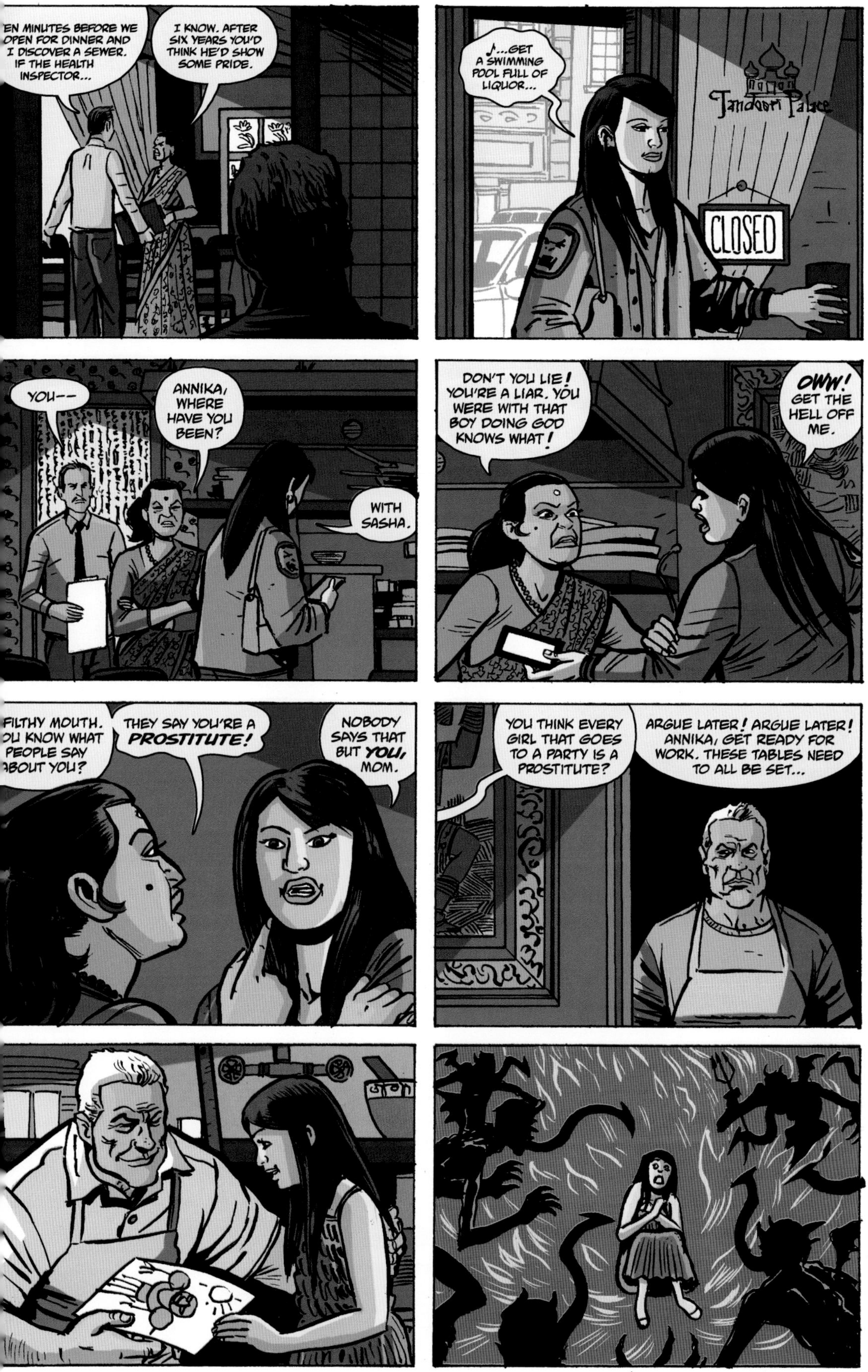
EN MINUTES BEFORE WE OPEN FOR DINNER AND I DISCOVER A SEWER. IF THE HEALTH INSPECTOR...
I KNOW. AFTER SIX YEARS YOU'D THINK HE'D SHOW SOME PRIDE.
♪...GET A SWIMMING POOL FULL OF LIQUOR...
Tandoori Palace
CLOSED
YOU--
ANNIKA, WHERE HAVE YOU BEEN?
WITH SASHA.
DON'T YOU LIE! YOU'RE A LIAR. YOU WERE WITH THAT BOY DOING GOD KNOWS WHAT!
OWW! GET THE HELL OFF ME.
FILTHY MOUTH. OU KNOW WHAT PEOPLE SAY BOUT YOU?
THEY SAY YOU'RE A PROSTITUTE!
NOBODY SAYS THAT BUT YOU, MOM.
YOU THINK EVERY GIRL THAT GOES TO A PARTY IS A PROSTITUTE?
ARGUE LATER! ARGUE LATER! ANNIKA, GET READY FOR WORK. THESE TABLES NEED TO ALL BE SET...

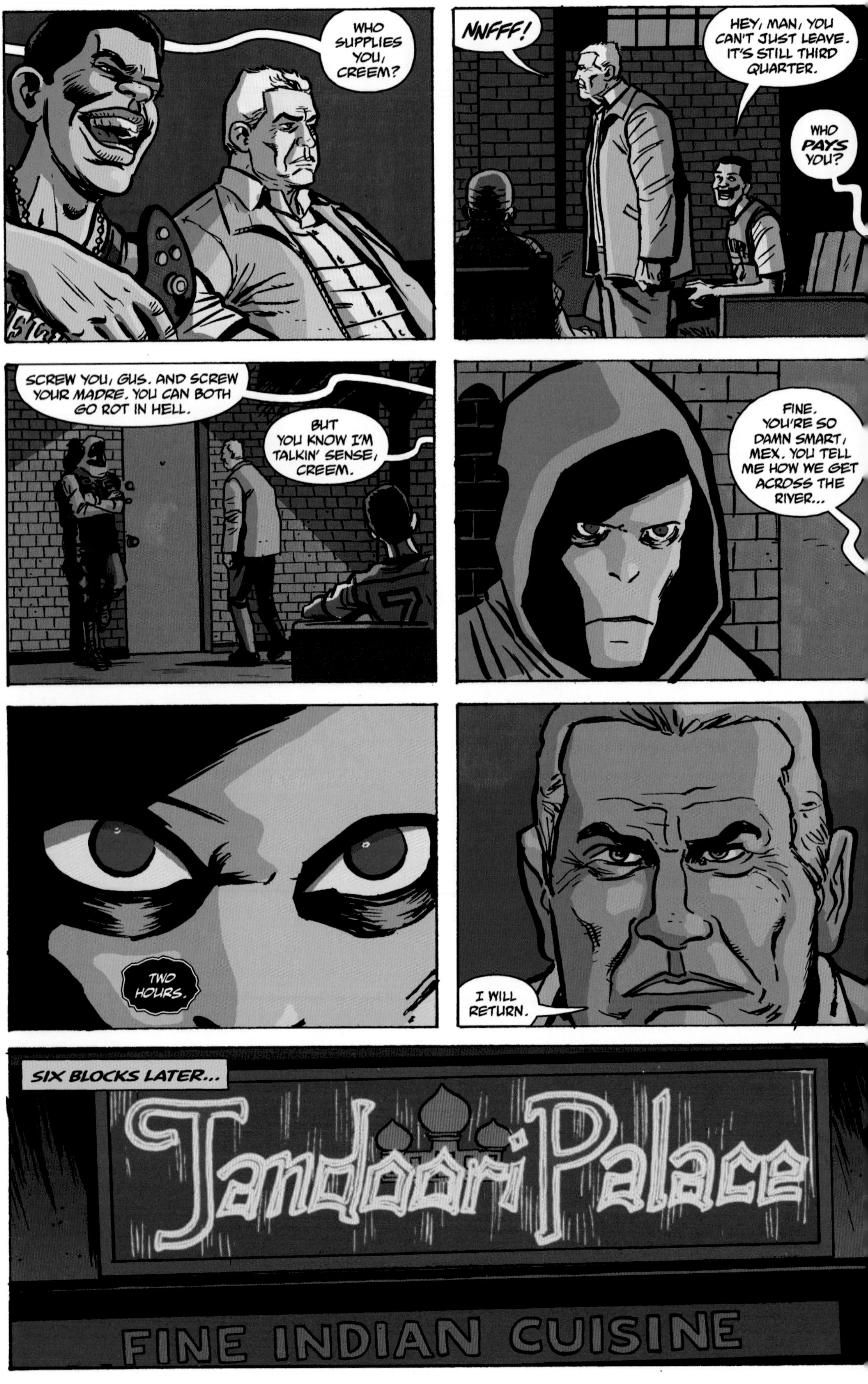
WHO SUPPLIES YOU, CREEM?
NNFFF!
HEY, MAN, YOU CAN'T JUST LEAVE. IT'S STILL THIRD QUARTER.
WHO PAYS YOU?
SCREW YOU, GUS. AND SCREW YOUR MADRE. YOU CAN BOTH GO ROT IN HELL.
BUT YOU KNOW I'M TALKIN' SENSE, CREEM.
FINE. YOU'RE SO DAMN SMART, MEX. YOU TELL ME HOW WE GET ACROSS THE RIVER...
TWO HOURS.
I WILL RETURN.
SIX BLOCKS LATER...
Tandoori Palace
FINE INDIAN CUISINE

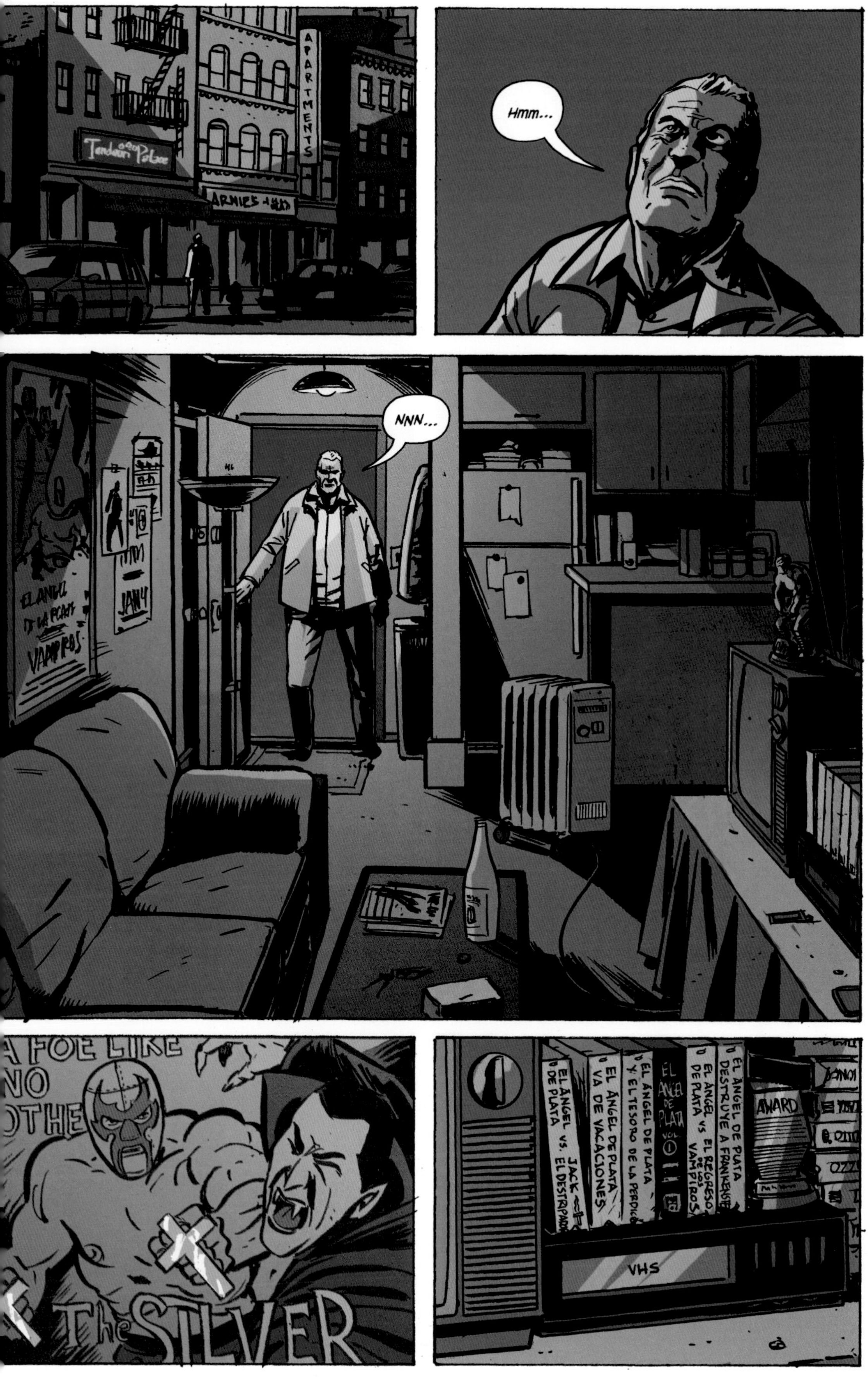
APARTMENTS
Tandoori Palace
ARNIES
Hmm...
NNN...
EL ANGEL DE LA PLATA VAMPIROS
A FOE LIKE NO OTHE
The SILVER
EL ANGEL DE PLATA VS. JACK EL DESTRIPADOR
EL ANGEL DE PLATA VA DE VACACIONES
EL ANGEL DE PLATA Y EL TESORO DE LA
EL ANGEL DE PLATA VOL 1
EL ANGEL DE PLATA VS EL REGRESO DE LOS VAMPIROS
EL ANGEL DE PLATA DESTRUYE A
AWARD
VHS

HRNNN...

⟨WHAT A MOVE BY EL CHUPACABRA OFF THE TOP ROPE. TOOK THE SILVER ANGEL COMPLETELY BY SURPRISE.⟩*

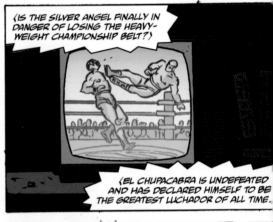

⟨IS THE SILVER ANGEL FINALLY IN DANGER OF LOSING THE HEAVY-WEIGHT CHAMPIONSHIP BELT?⟩

⟨EL CHUPACABRA IS UNDEFEATED AND HAS DECLARED HIMSELF TO BE THE GREATEST LUCHADOR OF ALL TIME.⟩

⟨WHEN ASKED ABOUT THIS BEFORE THE MATCH, THE SILVER ANGEL LAUGHED AND TOLD ME, "THE CHILD BELIEVES HIM-SELF GREAT IN HIS OWN MIND.⟩

⟨"BUT THE MAN GOES OUT AND PROVES IT. HE PROVES HIMSELF CHAMPION IN THE RING."⟩

⟨AND HE'S CERTAINLY DOING THAT HERE TONIGHT.⟩

⟨THE SILVER ANGEL'S SHOWING WHY HE'S THE BIGGEST SUPERSTAR SINCE THE GREAT EL SANTO.⟩

*TRANSLATED FROM SPANIS⟩

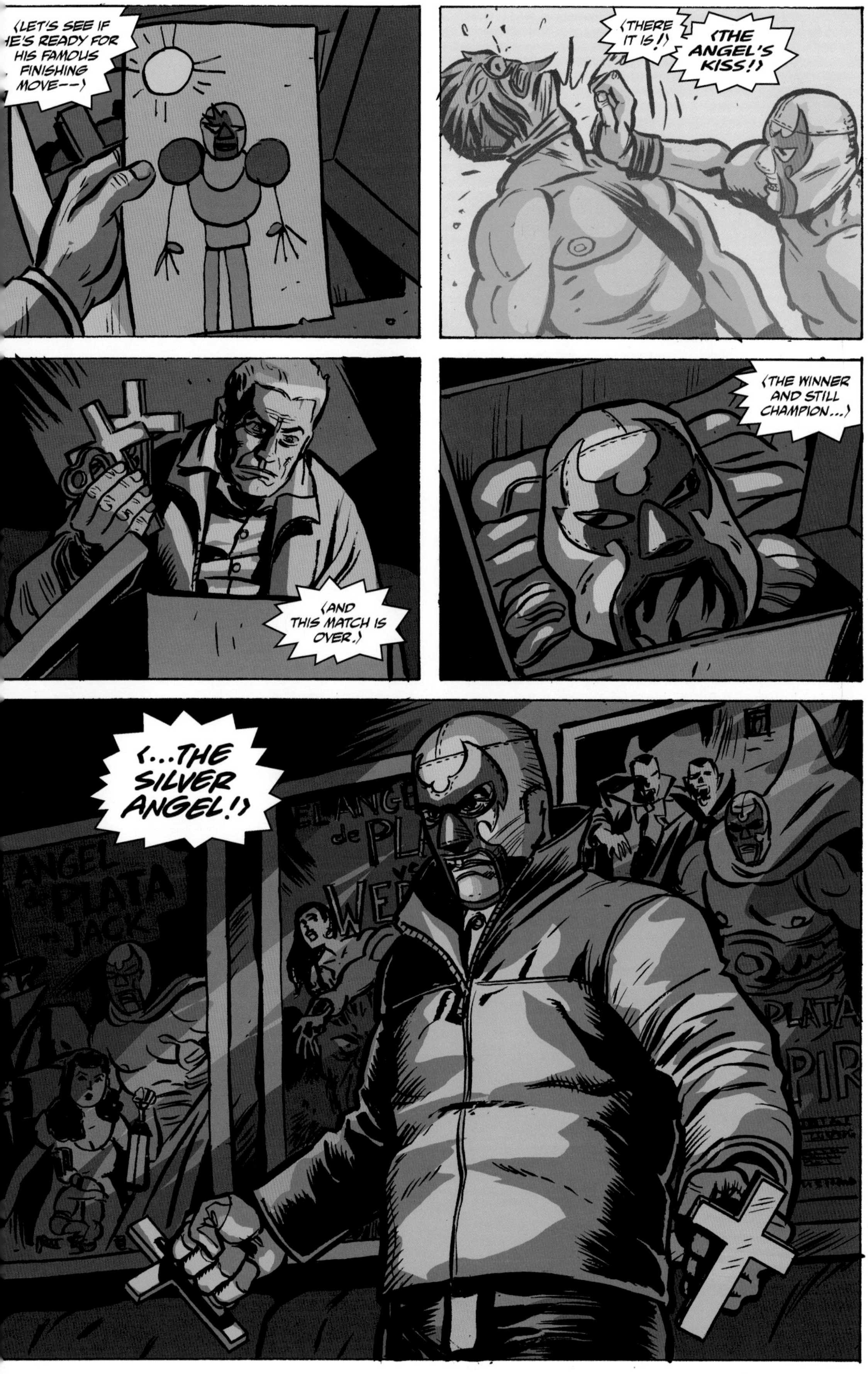
‹LET'S SEE IF E'S READY FOR HIS FAMOUS FINISHING MOVE--›
‹THERE IT IS!›
‹THE ANGEL'S KISS!›
‹AND THIS MATCH IS OVER.›
‹THE WINNER AND STILL CHAMPION...›
‹...THE SILVER ANGEL!›

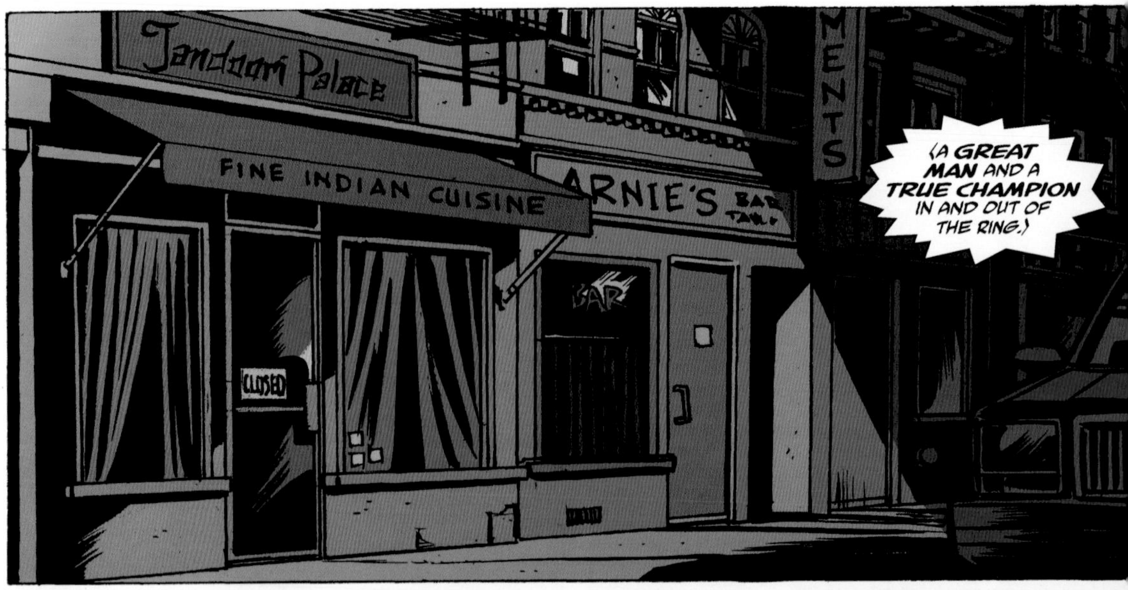
Tandoori Palace
FINE INDIAN CUISINE
ARNIE'S BAR
BAR
CLOSED
MENTS
(A GREAT MAN AND A TRUE CHAMPION IN AND OUT OF THE RING.)

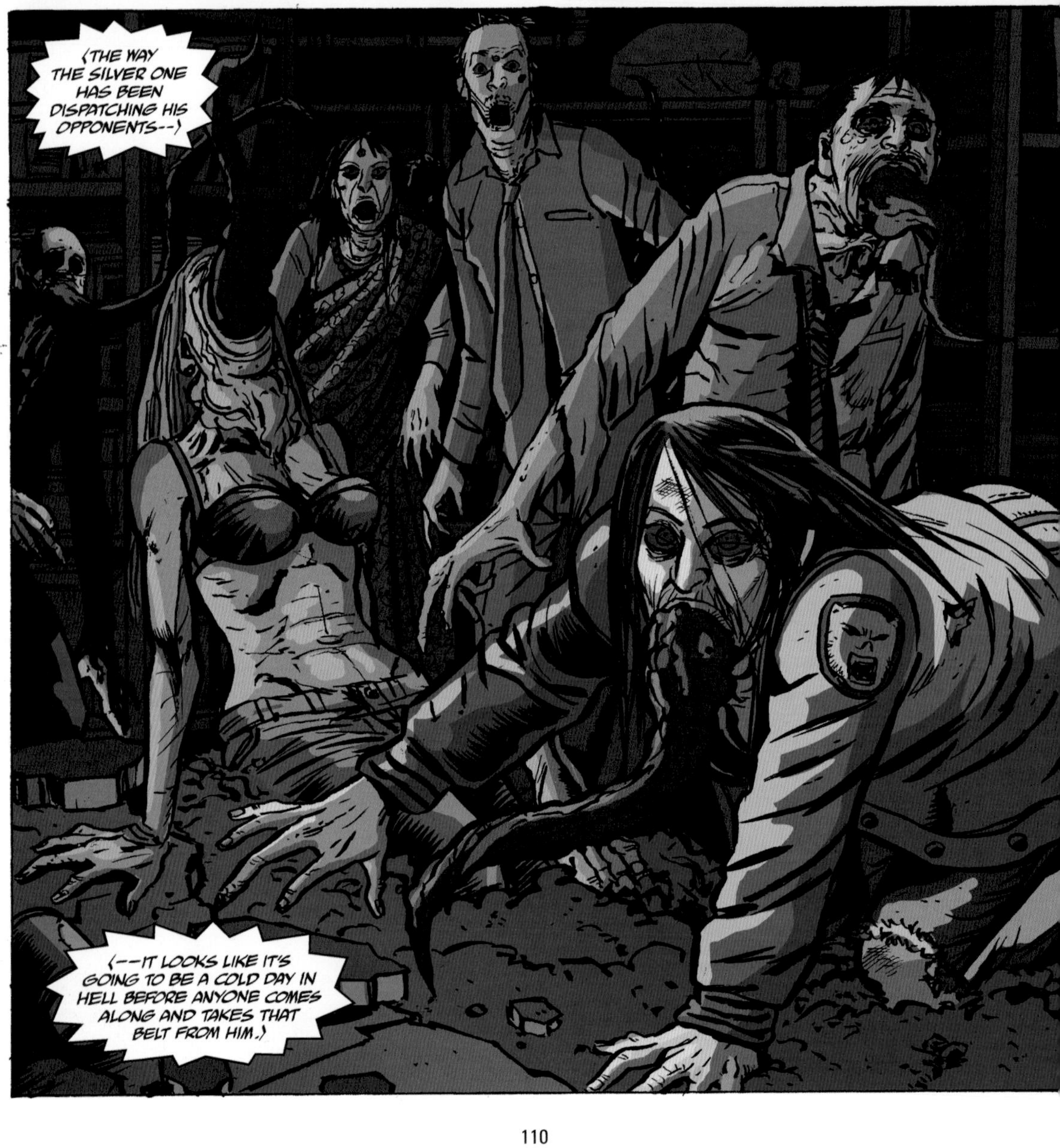
(THE WAY THE SILVER ONE HAS BEEN DISPATCHING HIS OPPONENTS--)
(--IT LOOKS LIKE IT'S GOING TO BE A COLD DAY IN HELL BEFORE ANYONE COMES ALONG AND TAKES THAT BELT FROM HIM.)

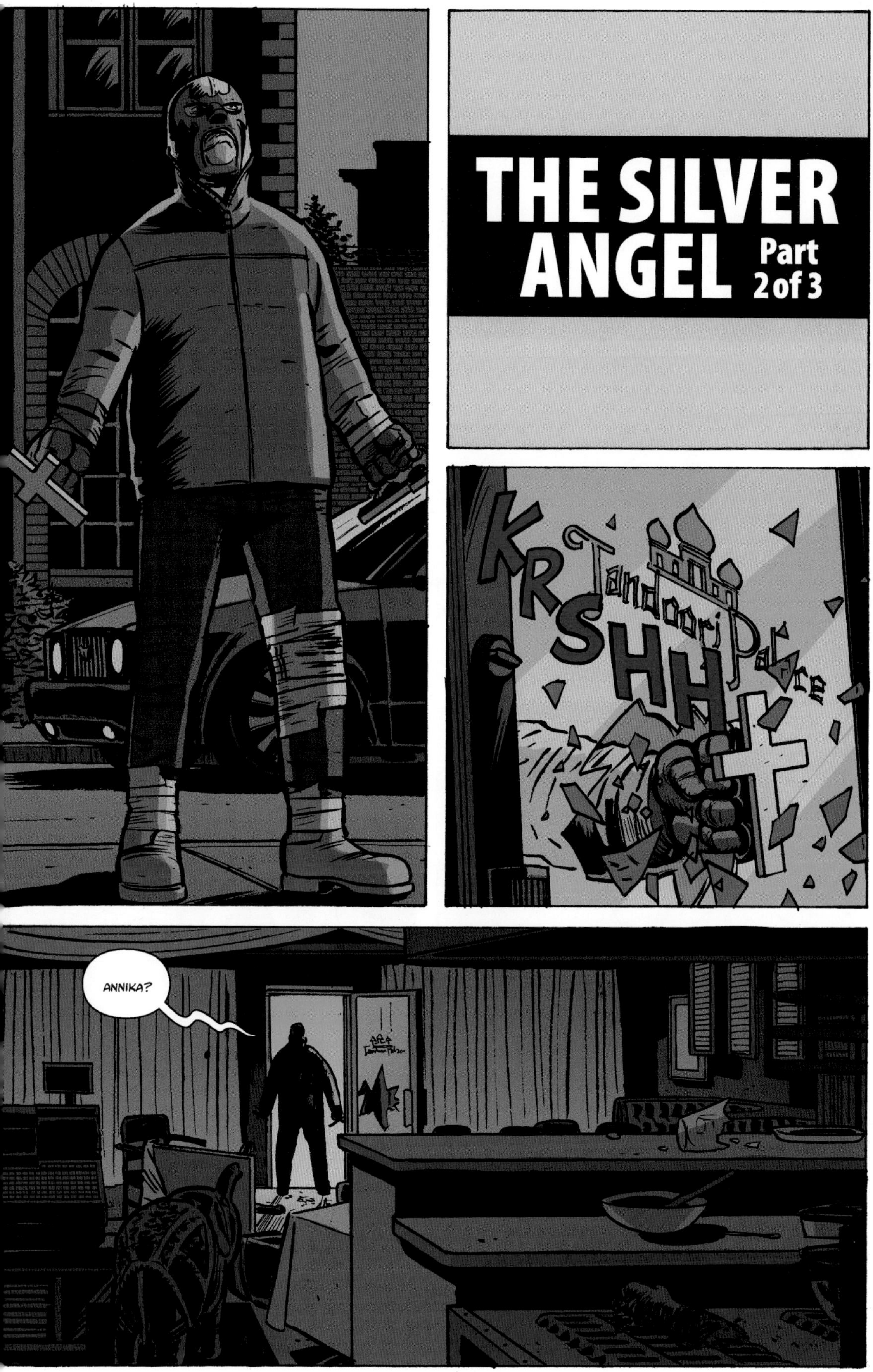
THE SILVER ANGEL Part 2 of 3
KRSHH
Tandoori Palace
ANNIKA?

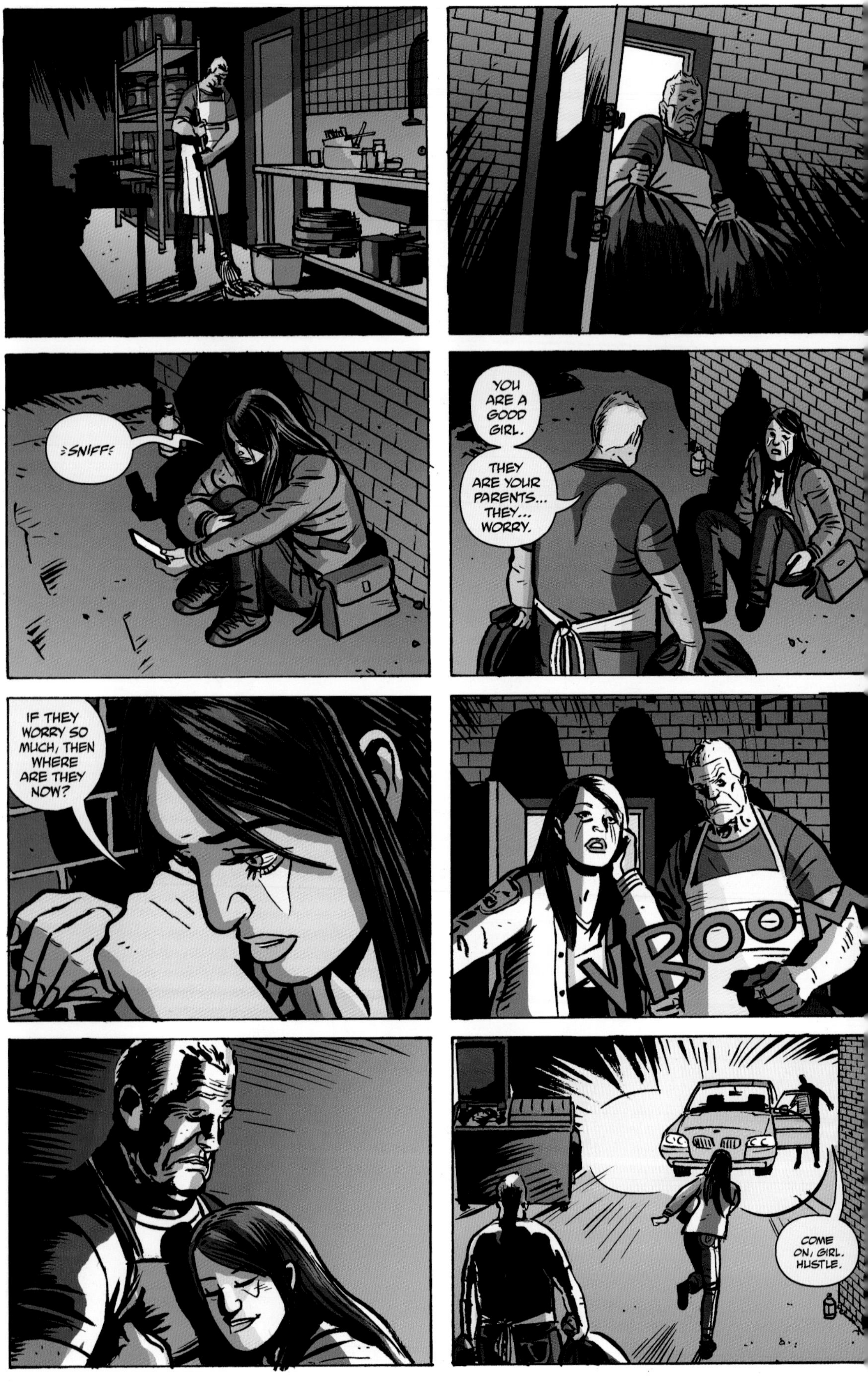

SNIFF
YOU ARE A GOOD GIRL.
THEY ARE YOUR PARENTS... THEY... WORRY.
IF THEY WORRY SO MUCH, THEN WHERE ARE THEY NOW?
VROOM
COME ON, GIRL. HUSTLE.

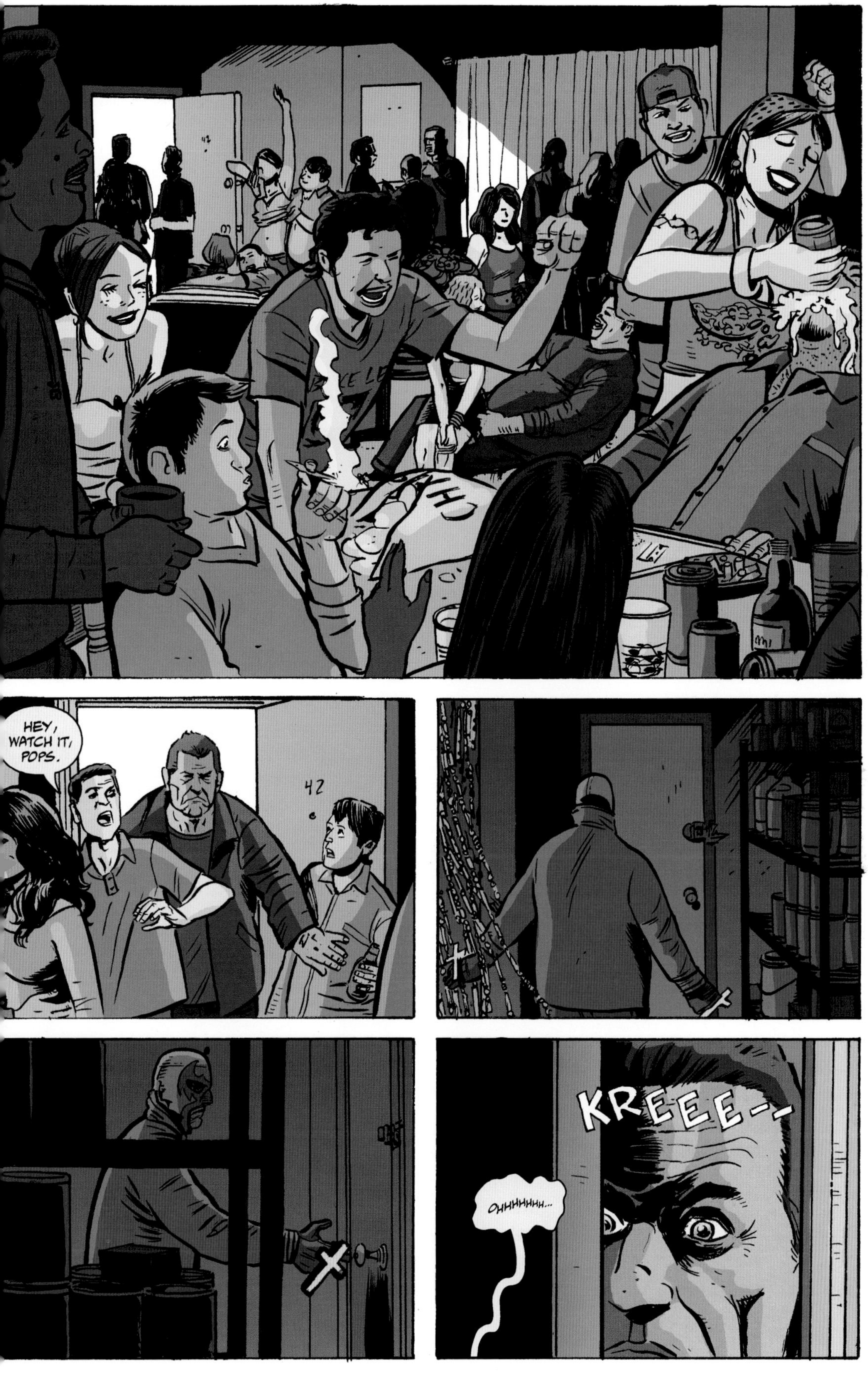
HEY, WATCH IT, POPS.
42
KREEE--
OHHHHHHH...

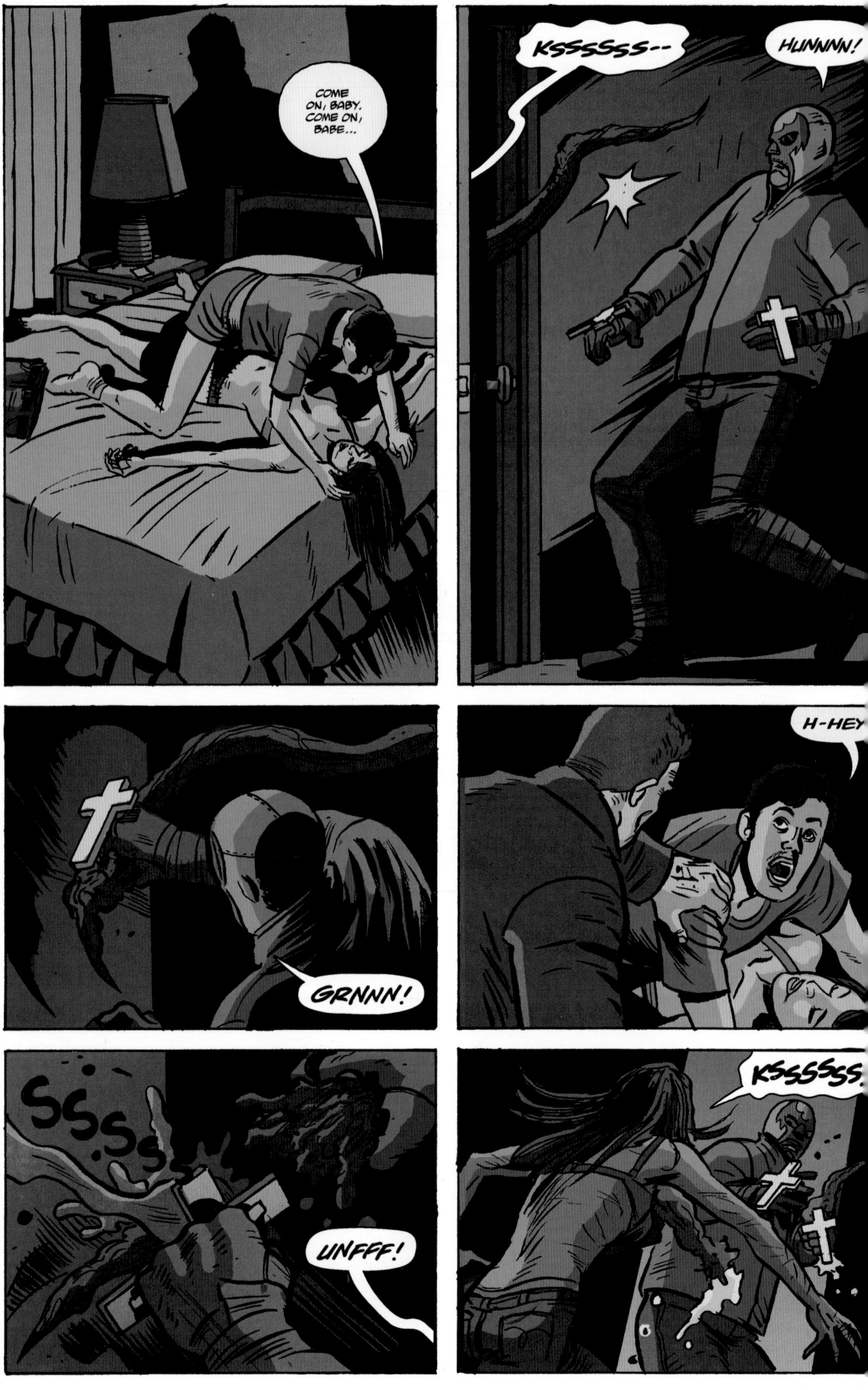
COME ON, BABY. COME ON, BABE...
KSSSSSS--
HUNNNN!
H-HEY
GRNNN!
SSSSS
UNFFF!
KSSSSS

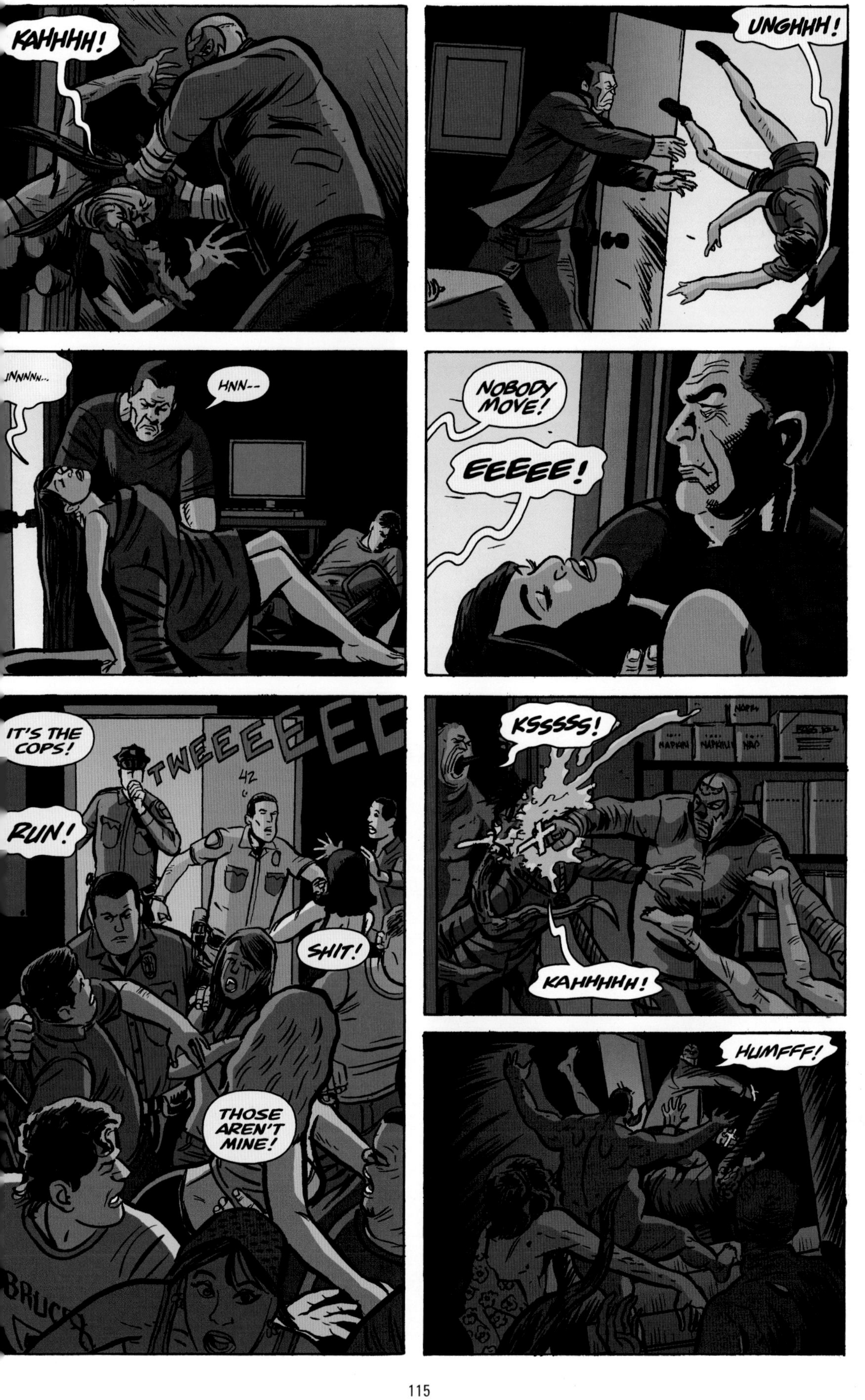
KAHHHH!
UNGHHH!
NNNNN...
HNN--
NOBODY MOVE!
EEEEE!
IT'S THE COPS!
RUN!
TWEEEEEEE
SHIT!
THOSE AREN'T MINE!
KSSSSS!
KAHHHHH!
HUMFFF!

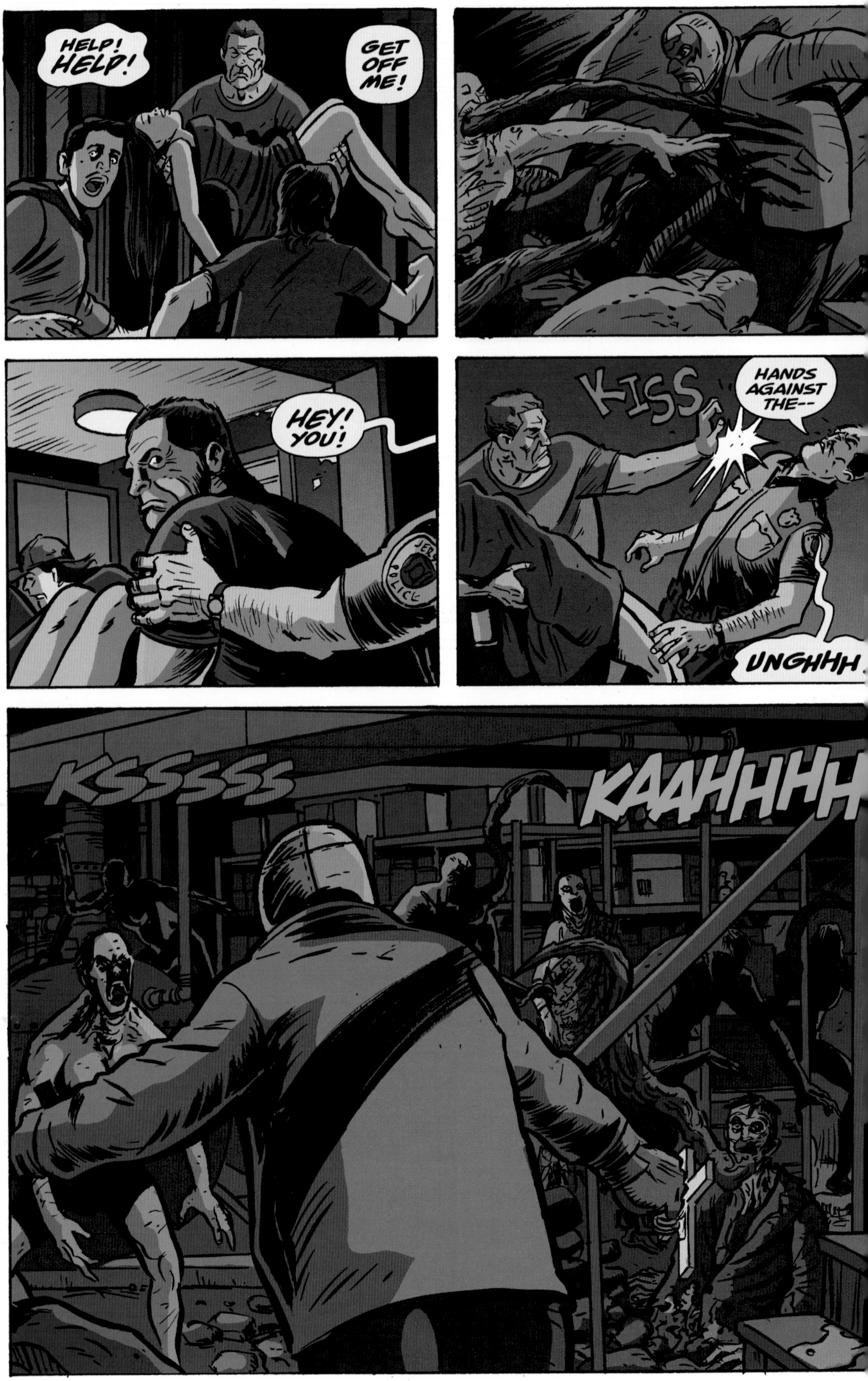
HELP! HELP!
GET OFF ME!
HEY! YOU!
KISS
HANDS AGAINST THE--
UNGHHH
KSSSSS
KAAHHHH

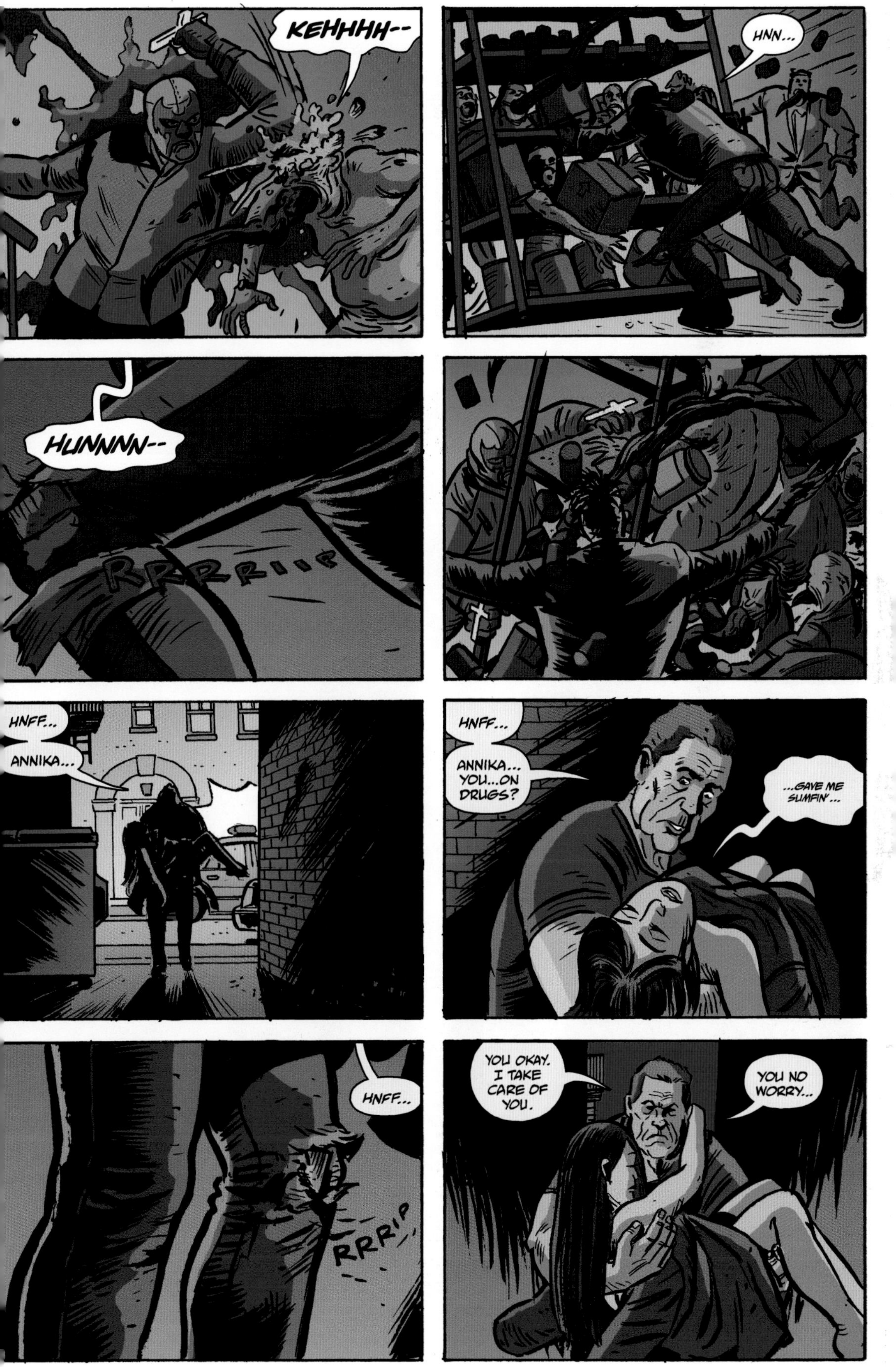
KEHHHH--
HNN...
HUNNNN--
RRRRIIIP
HNFF...
ANNIKA...
HNFF...
ANNIKA... YOU...ON DRUGS?
...GAVE ME SUMFIN'...
HNFF...
RRRIP
YOU OKAY. I TAKE CARE OF YOU.
YOU NO WORRY...

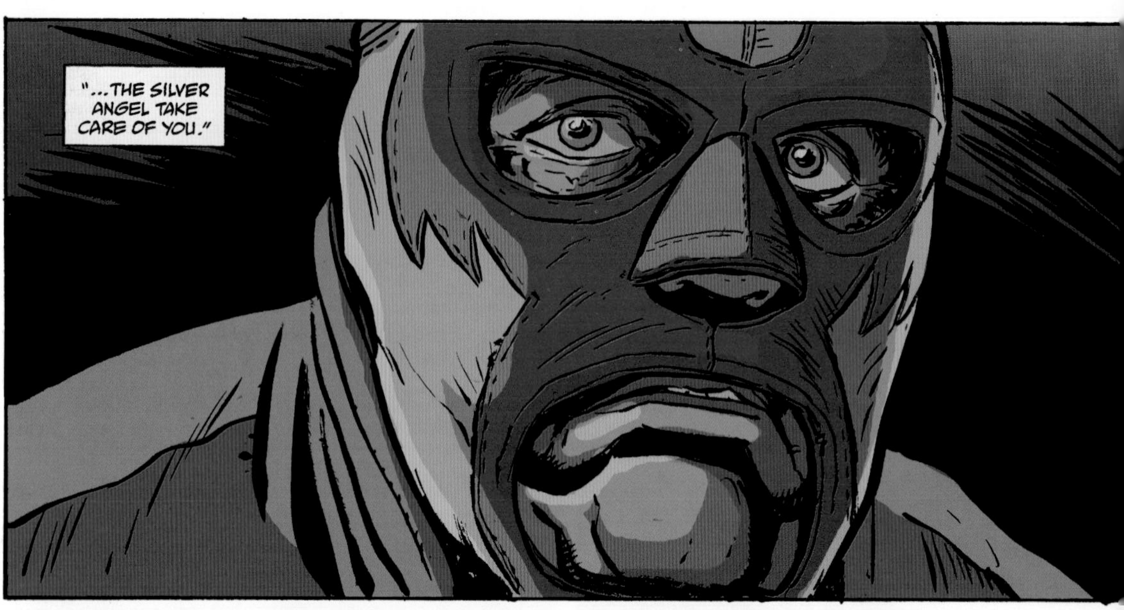
"...THE SILVER ANGEL TAKE CARE OF YOU."

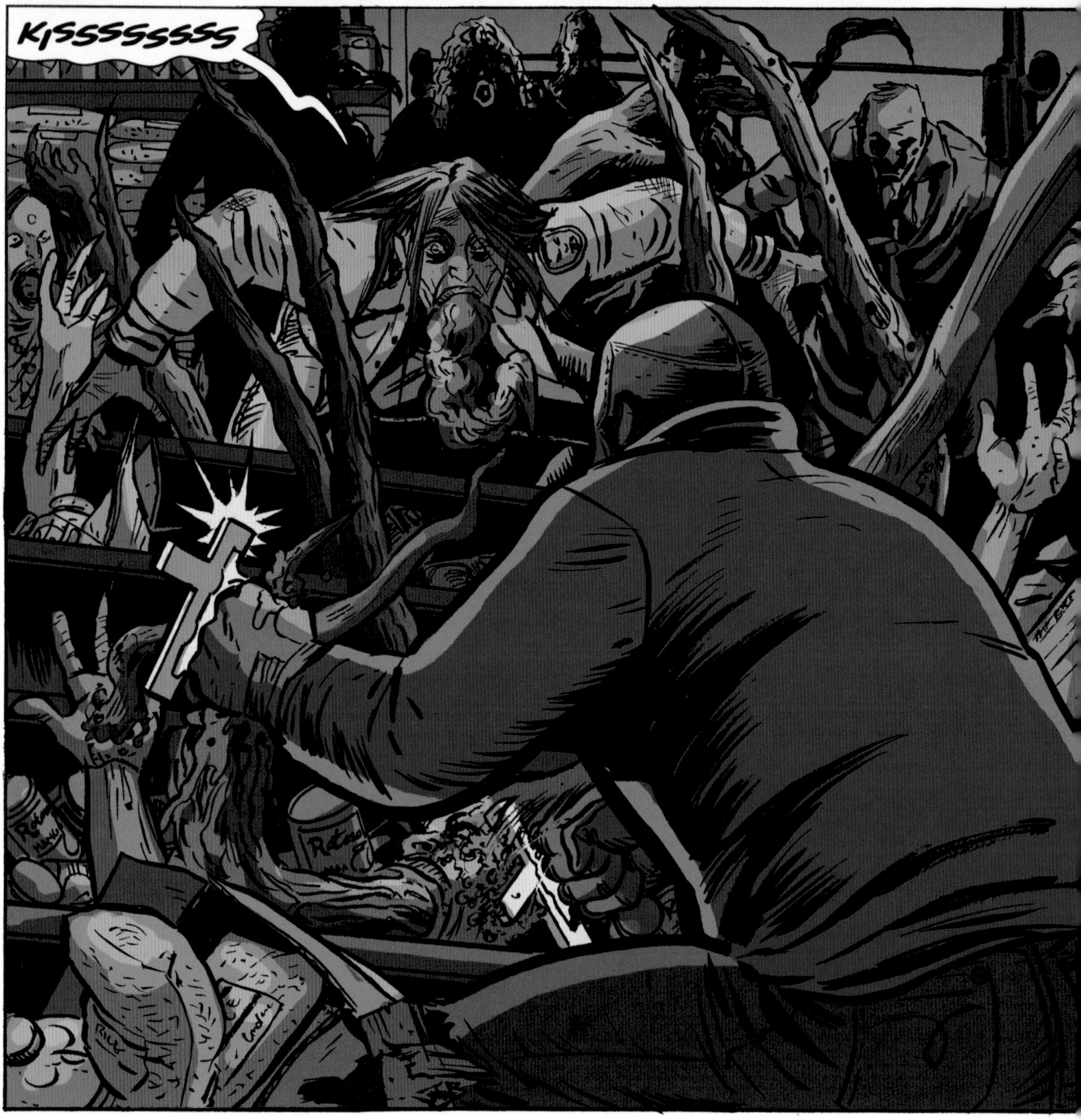
KISSSSSSSS

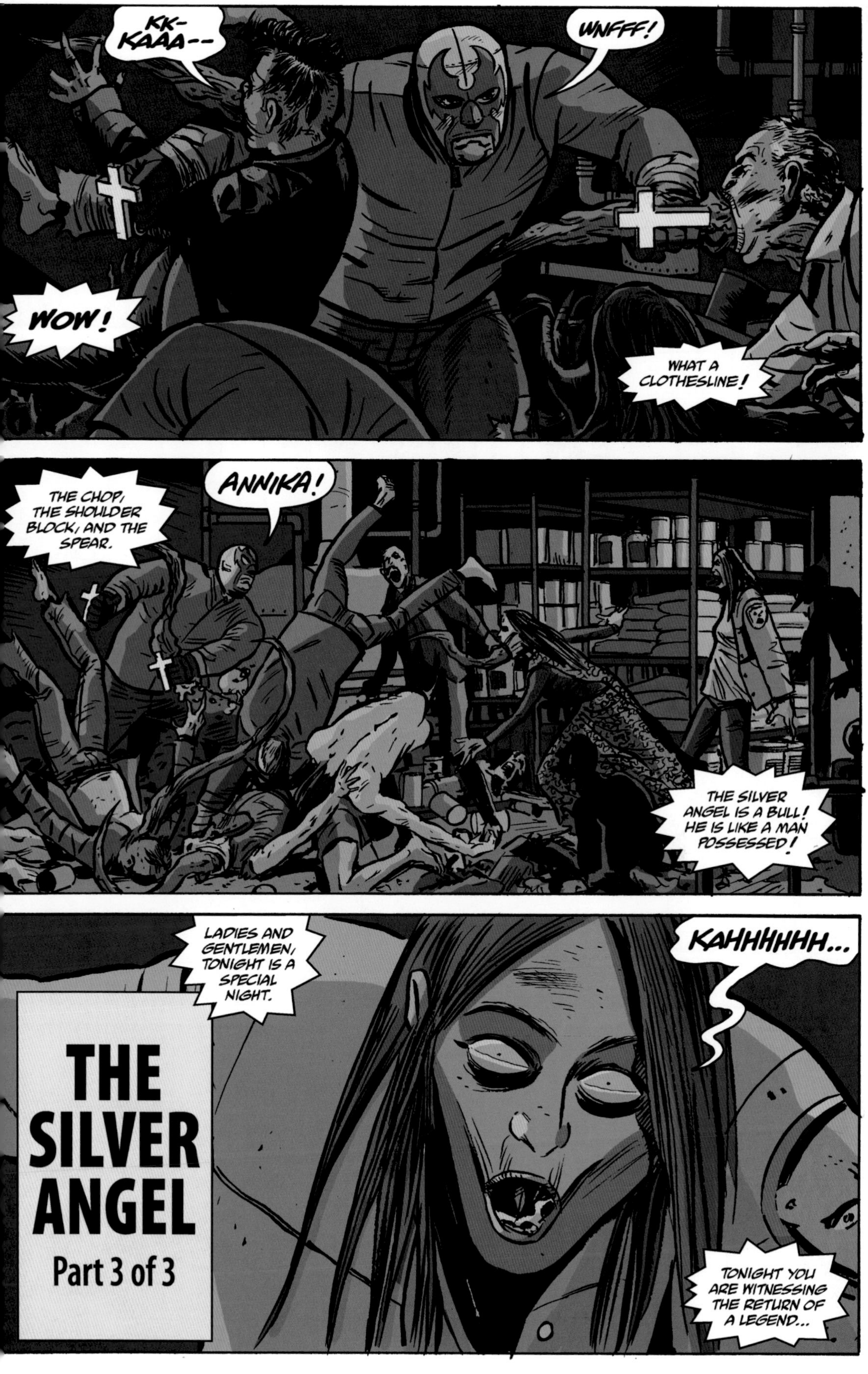
KK-KAAA--
UNFFF!
WOW!
WHAT A CLOTHESLINE!
THE CHOP, THE SHOULDER BLOCK, AND THE SPEAR.
ANNIKA!
THE SILVER ANGEL IS A BULL! HE IS LIKE A MAN POSSESSED!
LADIES AND GENTLEMEN, TONIGHT IS A SPECIAL NIGHT.
KAHHHHHH...
THE SILVER ANGEL
Part 3 of 3
TONIGHT YOU ARE WITNESSING THE RETURN OF A LEGEND...

NNNN...

GOD... MY PARENTS ARE NEVER GOING TO LET ME HEAR THE END OF THIS.

I NO SAY ANYTHING.

HERE... TAKE THESE.

THANKS. I WAS PRETTY STUPID.

WEREWOLF

EL ANGEL & DEATH VAMPIRE

Mmm... YOU ARE YOUNG. I...WAS YOUNG, TOO... ONCE.

THIS ALL YOU? ALL THESE POSTERS?

YOU WERE A WRESTLER? A PRETTY BIG DEAL, HUH?

I WAS CHAMPION.

BUT... THAT WAS... ANOTHER LIFE.

NOW I AM DISHWASHER.

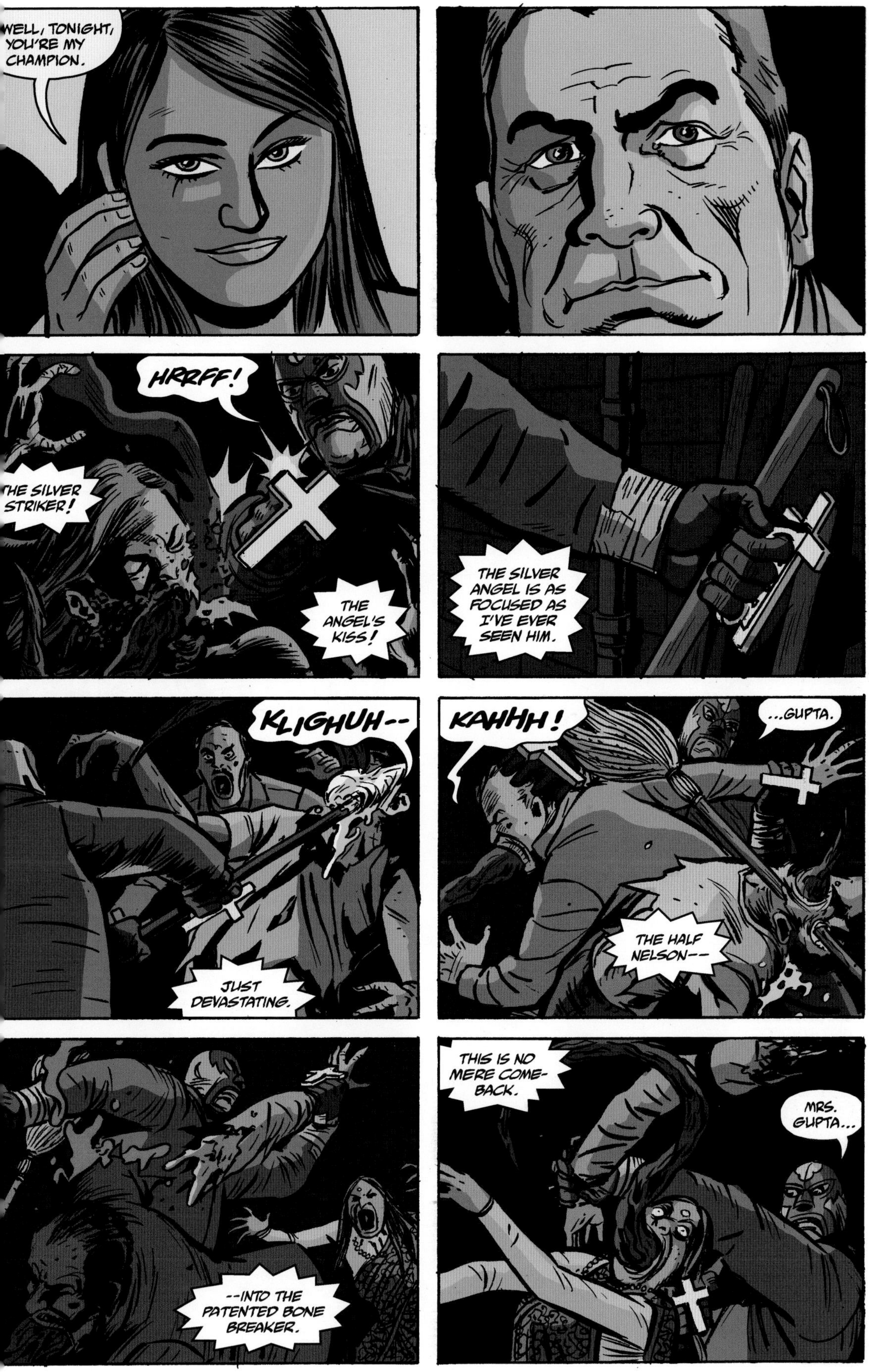
WELL, TONIGHT, YOU'RE MY CHAMPION.
HRRFF!
THE SILVER STRIKER!
THE ANGEL'S KISS!
THE SILVER ANGEL IS AS FOCUSED AS I'VE EVER SEEN HIM.
KLIGHUH--
JUST DEVASTATING.
KAHHH!
...GUPTA.
THE HALF NELSON--
--INTO THE PATENTED BONE BREAKER.
THIS IS NO MERE COME-BACK.
MRS. GUPTA...

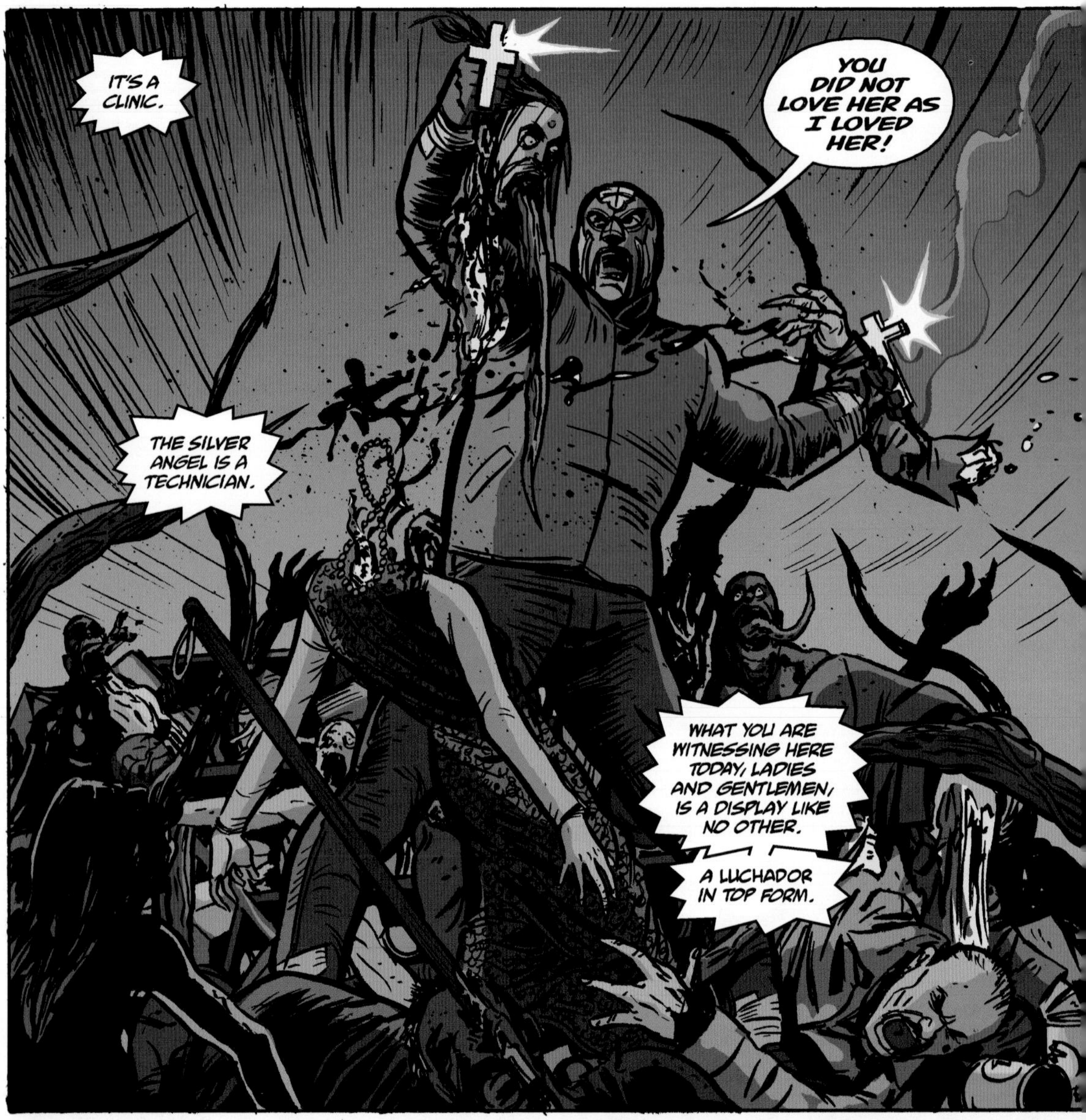
IT'S A CLINIC.
YOU DID NOT LOVE HER AS I LOVED HER!
THE SILVER ANGEL IS A TECHNICIAN.
WHAT YOU ARE WITNESSING HERE TODAY, LADIES AND GENTLEMEN, IS A DISPLAY LIKE NO OTHER.
A LUCHADOR IN TOP FORM.

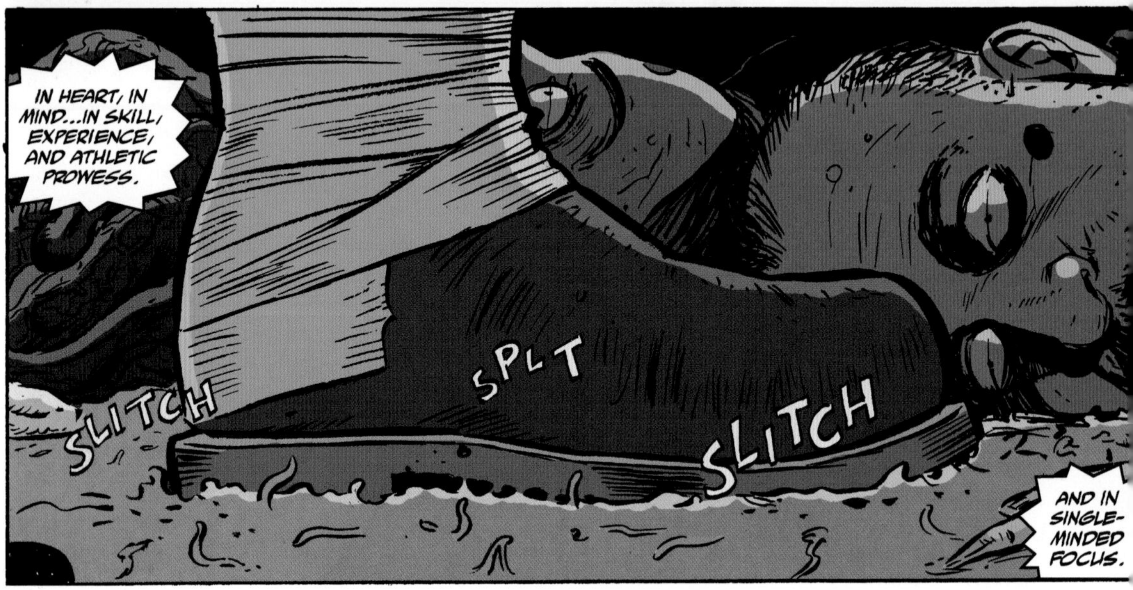
IN HEART, IN MIND...IN SKILL, EXPERIENCE, AND ATHLETIC PROWESS.
SLITCH
SPLT
SLITCH
AND IN SINGLE-MINDED FOCUS.

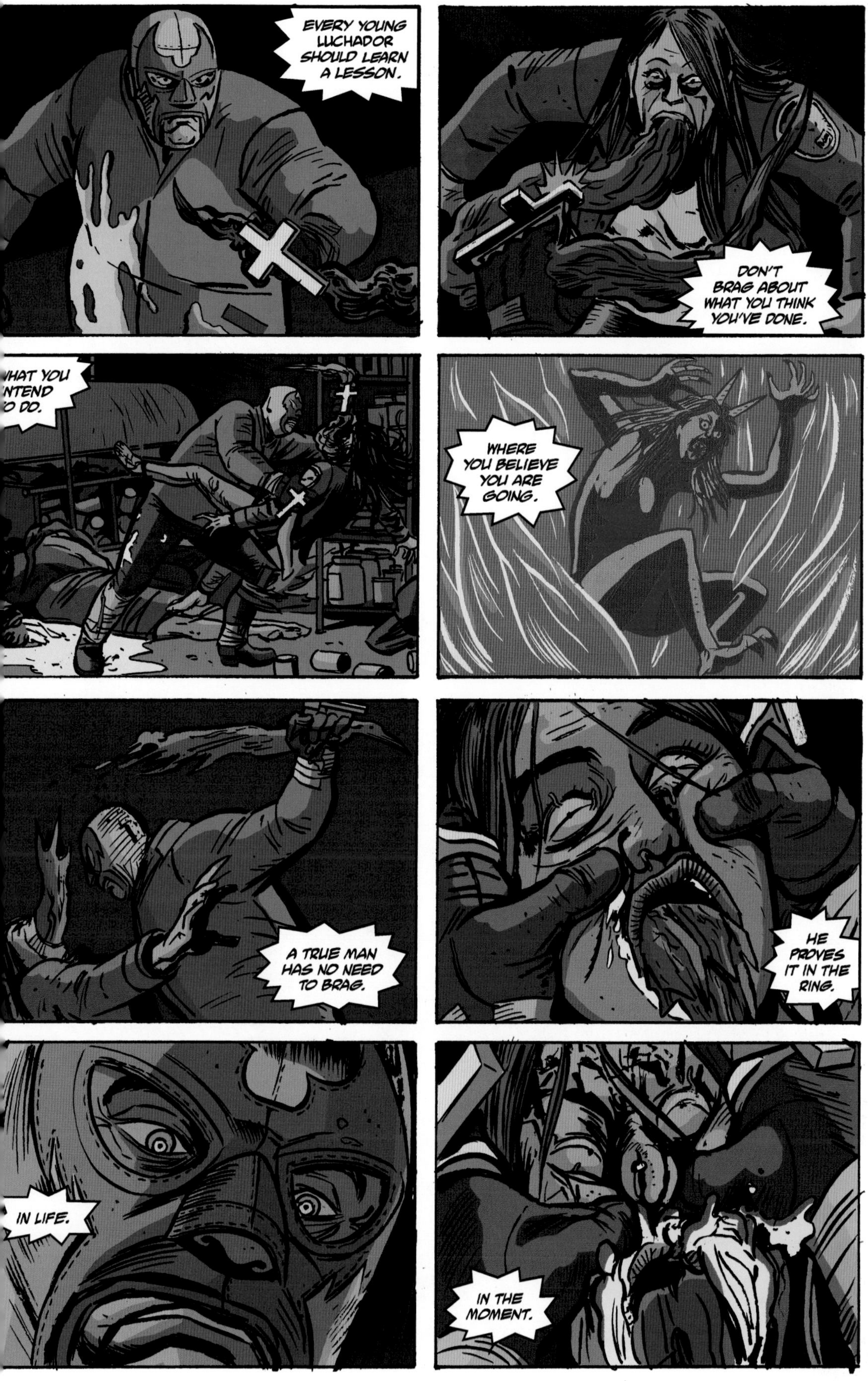
EVERY YOUNG LUCHADOR SHOULD LEARN A LESSON.
DON'T BRAG ABOUT WHAT YOU THINK YOU'VE DONE.
WHAT YOU INTEND TO DO.
WHERE YOU BELIEVE YOU ARE GOING.
A TRUE MAN HAS NO NEED TO BRAG.
HE PROVES IT IN THE RING.
IN LIFE.
IN THE MOMENT.

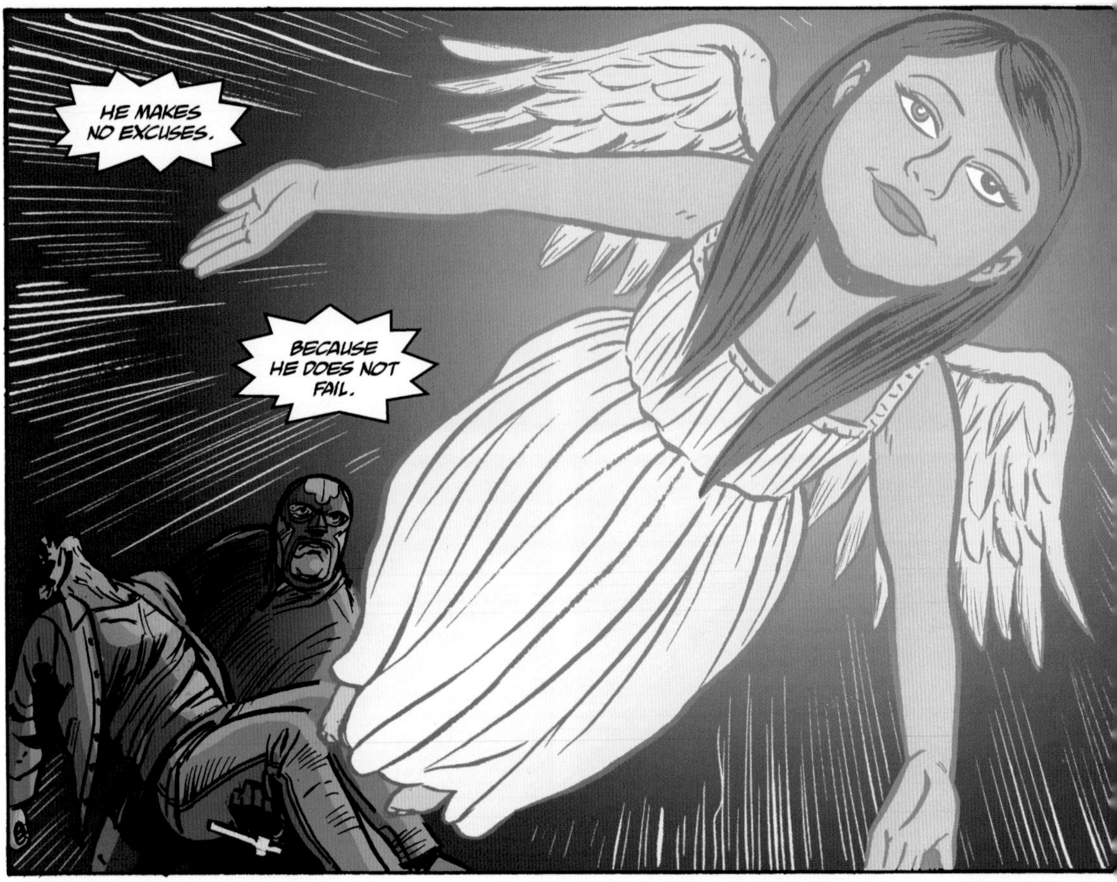
HE MAKES NO EXCUSES.
BECAUSE HE DOES NOT FAIL.

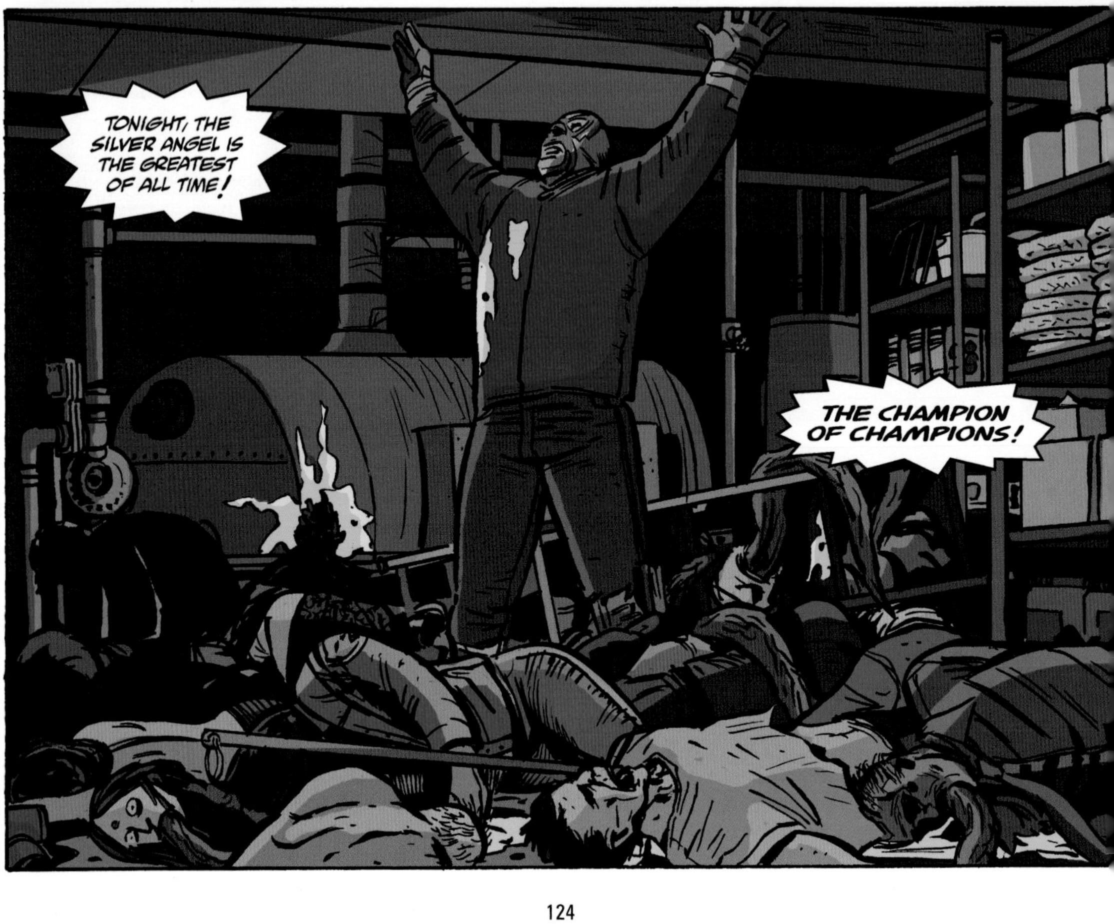
TONIGHT, THE SILVER ANGEL IS THE GREATEST OF ALL TIME!
THE CHAMPION OF CHAMPIONS!

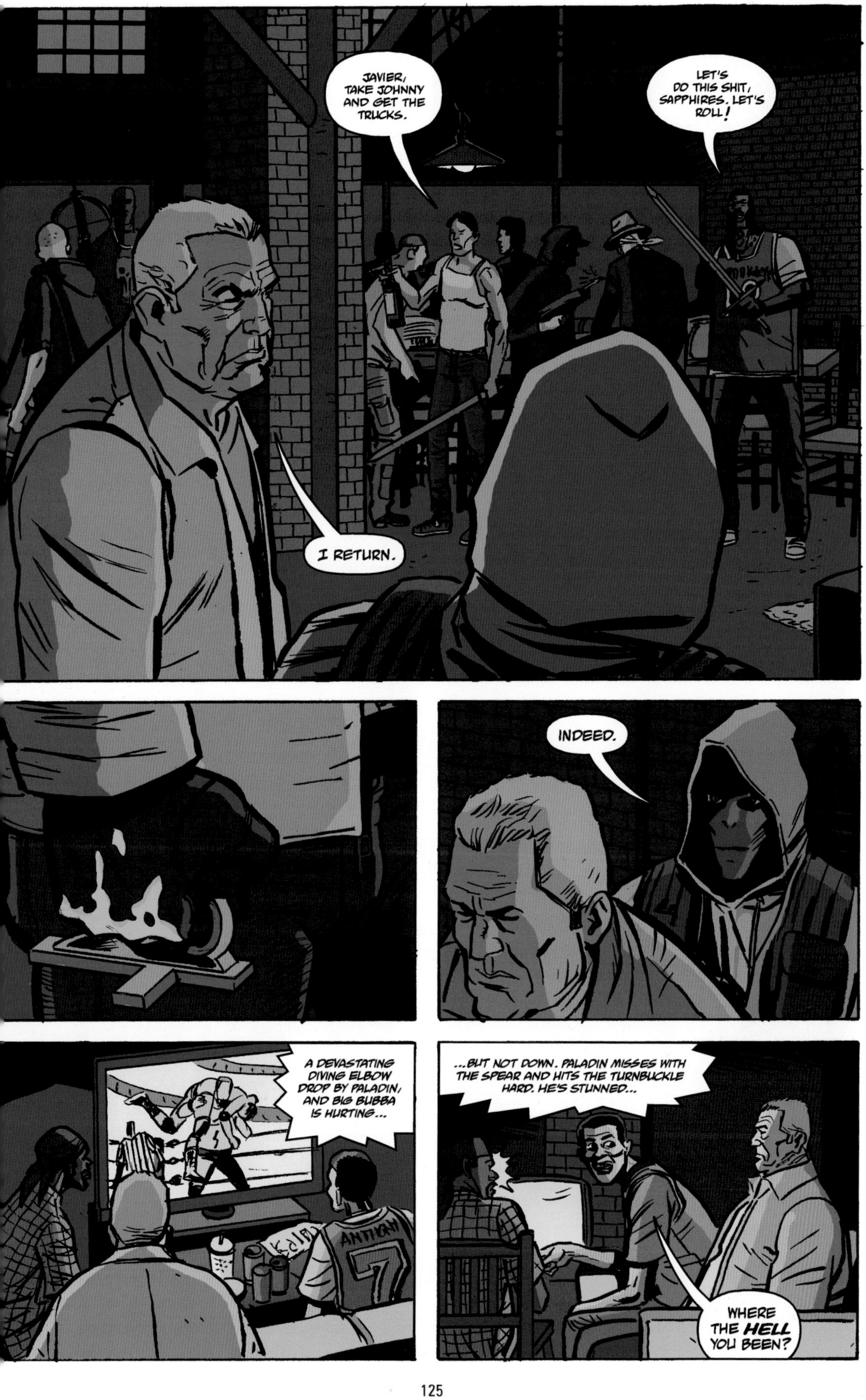
JAVIER, TAKE JOHNNY AND GET THE TRUCKS.
LET'S DO THIS SHIT, SAPPHIRES. LET'S ROLL!
I RETURN.
INDEED.
A DEVASTATING DIVING ELBOW DROP BY PALADIN, AND BIG BUBBA IS HURTING...
...BUT NOT DOWN. PALADIN MISSES WITH THE SPEAR AND HITS THE TURNBUCKLE HARD. HE'S STUNNED...
WHERE THE HELL YOU BEEN?

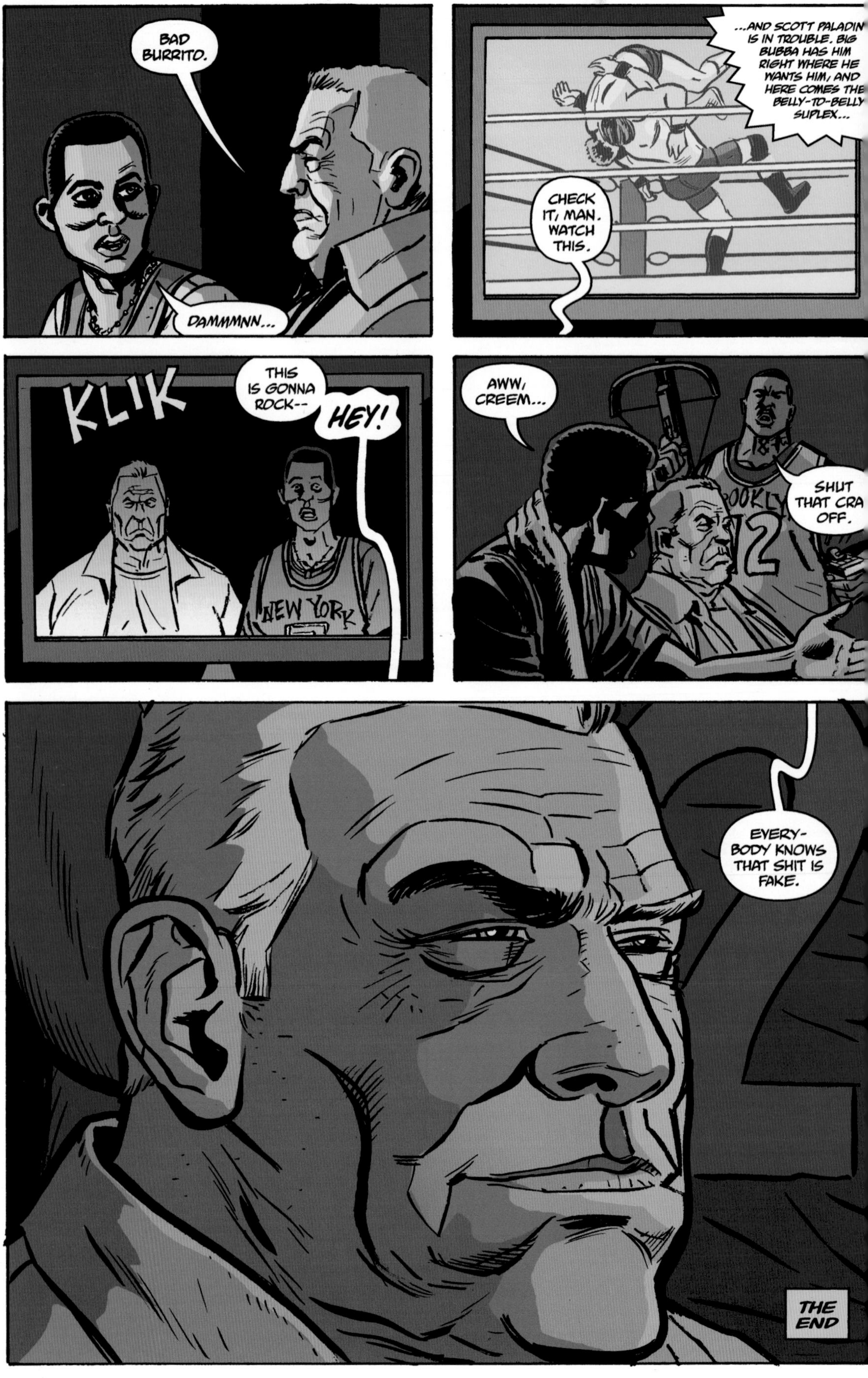
BAD BURRITO.
DAMMMNN...
...AND SCOTT PALADIN IS IN TROUBLE. BIG BUBBA HAS HIM RIGHT WHERE HE WANTS HIM, AND HERE COMES THE BELLY-TO-BELLY SUPLEX...
CHECK IT, MAN. WATCH THIS.
KLIK
THIS IS GONNA ROCK--
HEY!
NEW YORK
AWW, CREEM...
SHUT THAT CRA OFF.
EVERY-BODY KNOWS THAT SHIT IS FAKE.
THE END

NEW YORK TIMES BESTSELLING TRILOGY

"The most credible and frightening of all the vampire books of the past decade." —*San Francisco Chronicle*

AVAILABLE NOW

THE STRAIN

Book One of The Strain Trilogy
Mass Market
ISBN: 978-0-06-155824-5
$9.99 ($11.99 Can.)

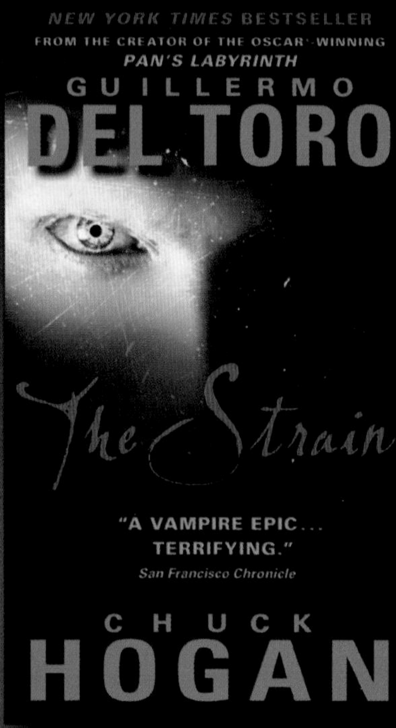

NEW YORK TIMES BESTSELLER
FROM THE CREATOR OF THE OSCAR®-WINNING
PAN'S LABYRINTH
GUILLERMO
DEL TORO
The Strain
"A VAMPIRE EPIC... TERRIFYING."
San Francisco Chronicle
CHUCK
HOGAN

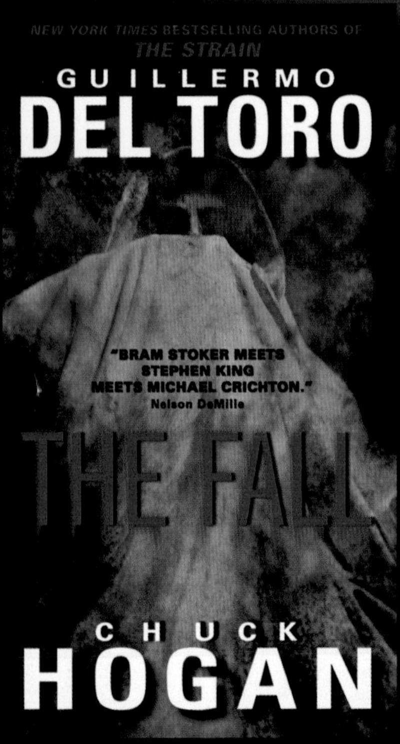

NEW YORK TIMES BESTSELLING AUTHORS OF
THE STRAIN
GUILLERMO
DEL TORO
"BRAM STOKER MEETS STEPHEN KING MEETS MICHAEL CRICHTON."
Nelson DeMille
THE FALL
CHUCK
HOGAN

THE FALL

Book Two of The Strain Trilogy
Mass Market
ISBN: 978-0-06-155825-2
$9.99 ($11.99 Can.)

THE NIGHT ETERNAL

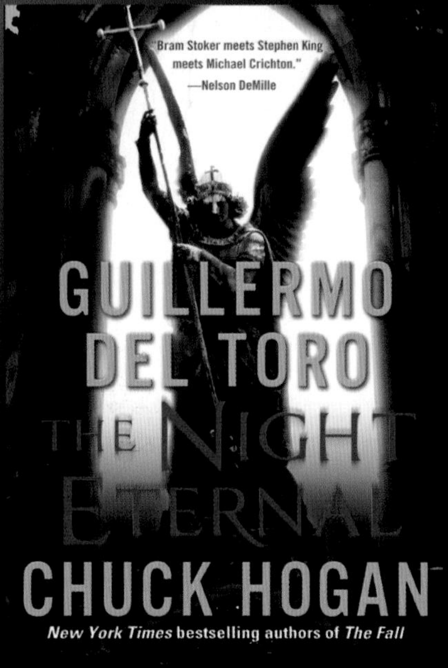

"Bram Stoker meets Stephen King meets Michael Crichton."
—Nelson DeMille
GUILLERMO
DEL TORO
THE NIGHT ETERNAL
CHUCK HOGAN
New York Times bestselling authors of *The Fall*

"Arresting vividly imagined ..." —*Newsweek*